Managing Television News

A Handbook for Ethical and Effective Producing

LEA's COMMUNICATION SERIES
Jennings Bryant / Dolf Zillmann, General Editors

Selected Titles in the Communication Series include:

Butler • Television: Critical Methods and Applications, Second Edition

Eastman • Research in Media Promotion

Keirstead • Computers in Broadcast and Cable Newsrooms: Using Technology in Television News Production

MacFarland • Future Radio Programming Strategies: Cultivating Listenership in the Digital Age, Second Edition

Metallinos • Television Aesthetics: Perceptual, Cognitive, and Compositional Bases

Orlik • Electronic Media Criticism: Applied Perspectives, Second Edition

Plum • Underwriting 101: Selling College Radio

Sterling/Kittross • Stay Tuned: A Concise History of American Broadcasting, Third Edition

Webster/Phalen/Lichty • Ratings Analysis: The Theory and Practice of Audience Research, Third Edition

For a complete list of titles in LEA's Communication Series
please contact Lawrence Erlbaum Associates, Publishers
at www.erlbaum.com

Managing Television News

A Handbook for Ethical and Effective Producing

B. William Silcock

Don Heider

Mary T. Rogus

2007

LAWRENCE ERLBAUM ASSOCIATES, PUBLISHERS

Mahwah, New Jersey

London

Photo Credits

The authors would like to thank the staff and management of WCNC-TV, Charlotte, North Carolina; WCPO-TV, Cincinnati, Ohio; WDTN-TV, Dayton, Ohio; WHIO-TV, Dayton, Ohio for allowing our photographers to capture them in action while they prepared for daily newscasts.

Photos of WCPO-TV, WHIO-TV, WDTN-TV were taken by Sarah E. Burns, freelance photographer. Ms. Burns was assisted by Rachel Durst, a senior broadcast journalism major in the E. W. Scripps School of Journalism.

Photos of WCNC-TV were taken by author Mary T. Rogus, Ohio University.

Photos and graphics of WOUB-TV, Athens, Ohio, are courtesy of the Center for Public Media, Ohio University.

Photos of Edward R. Murrow are courtesy of Casey Murrow and Washington State University Murrow School of Communication.

Photo of Walter Cronkite and producer James Dove, on the back cover, taken by Scott Troyanos.

Lawrence Erlbaum Associates, Inc., Publishers
10 Industrial Avenue
Mahwah, New Jersey 07430
www.erlbaum.com

Cover design by Tomai Maridou

Additional cip information may be obtained by contacting the Library of Congress

Silcock, B. William; Heider, Donald; Rogus, Mary T.
   Managing television news : a handbook for ethical and effective producing.

          p. cm.

   Includes bibliographical references and index.

ISBN 0-8058-5373-1 (pbk. : alk. paper)

Books published by Lawrence Erlbaum Associates are printed on acid-free paper, and their bindings are chosen for strength and durability.

Printed in the United States of America
10   9   8   7   6   5   4   3   2   1

*We dedicate this book to our students, and all students
of the producing craft, in remembrance of those who taught us,
collectively and individually, the great lessons.*

*Bill Silcock expresses gratitude to his teacher-mentors
Tom, Dale, Ken, and Elmer
Missouri colleagues Kent, Stacey, Linda and Sara,
his mother Ruth, a master wordsmith who shares talent with
grandchildren Nick, Jane, and John
and Angela, forever his Executive Producer.*

*Mary T. Rogus thanks her family who, for 20 years, understood
when breaking news trumped holiday gatherings,
and her News Director mentors Dave, John, Tom, and Mark.*

*Don Heider thanks Anna, Ella, Cole, and especially Jeanne,
the one who holds us the rest of us together.*

Contents in Brief

Introduction   xiii

Chapter 1
WHAT MAKES NEWS?   1

Chapter 2
WHO WATCHES AND WHY?   11

Chapter 3
WHAT MAKES A GOOD   29
PRODUCER?

Chapter 4
THE ETHICS OF PRODUCING   45

Chapter 5
DEADLINES, DATELINES,   71
AND DECISION MAKING

Chapter 6

THE ART OF PRODUCING   91

Chapter 7
WRITING WELL   113

Chapter 8
PUT ON YOUR MARKETING CAP   129

Chapter 9
LIFE IN THE BOOTH   145

Chapter 10
MANAGING LIVE   161

Chapter 11
MANAGING PEOPLE   183

Chapter 12
MANAGING SWEEPS: THE GOOD,   207
THE BAD, AND THE UGLY

Chapter 13
MANAGING THE BUSINESS   223

Chapter 14
MANAGING LIFE   239

Index   **251**

Contents

Introduction   xiii

Chapter 1
WHAT MAKES NEWS?   1

Why Are We Here?   *3*
To Serve   *3*
The Public   *4*
The Producer's Role in Making News   *7*

Chapter 2
WHO WATCHES AND WHY?   11

Who Is Out There?   *13*
   Intimate Medium   *13*
   So Just Who Is Watching?   *14*
Why Do They Watch (or Not)?   *15*
   Why People Watch The News   *16*
   Reasons Why People Watch Less Local
     TV News   *18*
What Do They Want?   *18*
Demographics   *20*
   Target Audiences   *22*
   Who Is Available?   *22*
   Who Advertisers Want   *24*
   Diversity   *24*
Conclusion   *26*
Sources   *27*

Chapter 3
WHAT MAKES A GOOD   29
PRODUCER?

Got Influence? By Jill Geisler   *32*

Moving From The Classroom To The
   Newsroom By Tom Dolan   *34*
What Is In A Name?   *39*
Good Producer = Good Relationships   *42*

Chapter 4
THE ETHICS OF PRODUCING   45

RTNDA   *47*
The Murrow Tradition   *48*
SPJ and the Ethical Influence of Print   *49*
Comparing the Codes   *54*
   Creating Your Code   *55*
Getting Beyond the Gut   *56*
Audience-Oriented Ethics   *57*
Ethical Duty and the Myth of
   Objectivity   *59*
When to Warn the Viewers   *61*
Crime Coverage and Family Sensitive
   News   *61*
Coverage Guidelines   *63*
A Higher Calling, A Professional
   Producer   *65*
Get Involved in Ethics   *68*
Sources   *70*

Chapter 5
DEADLINES, DATELINES,   71
AND DECISION MAKING

The Rundown Recipe   *72*
The Clock and the Computer   *73*
Backtiming The Day—Time Management
   of Datelines and Deadlines   *76*

Jump Starting the Day   *77*

Timeliness   *80*

Picking the Freshest Ingredients for Your
Newscast   *81*

Discovering Cupboards of Content   *81*

Determining the Lead   *81*

The Rundown Meeting   *84*

Unbundling the Lead   *87*

Breaking News and Live   *88*

Story Management   *88*

A Most Satisfying Feast   *90*

Sources   *90*

Chapter 6

THE ART OF PRODUCING   91

Formats   *92*

Building Credible News Blocks—No
Stacking and Packing   *94*

Pace and Flow   *98*

Story Format   *99*

Sound   *99*

Graphics/Production Techniques   *99*

Building News Blocks for Visualization   *104*

Anchor Input in the Art of the Lineup   *105*

Anchor Blocking   *105*

Two-Shots   *106*

Weather—Your Best Friend   *108*

Sports—Your Worst Enemy?   *109*

Newscast Mission Statements   *111*

Sources   *112*

Chapter 7

WRITING WELL   113

TV Is Personal   *113*

Short Is Better   *115*

Simple Is Good   *115*

Write Like You Talk   *116*

Phone Mom Theory   *118*

Clichés   *120*

What Goes Where?   *121*

Leads   *122*

The Middle   *122*

Video Referencing   *122*

The End   *124*

Writing For The Anchor   *126*

The Seamless Show   *126*

What Makes Good Writing Good?   *127*

Becoming a Good Writer   *127*

Chapter 8

PUT ON YOUR MARKETING CAP   129

Types of Promotion   *129*

Is It Teasable   *130*

It's the Video, Stupid!   *131*

Get It *Only* Here   *132*

When, Where, and How Often?   *133*

What Are They Watching?   *133*

Emotional Rollercoaster   *133*

What's Next?   *134*

Cross-Show Promotion   *134*

Repetition   *134*

Let's Write   *135*

Context   *136*

Reason to Watch   *137*

Reason to Watch Toolbox   *137*

The Devil's in the Details   *138*

Video Reference   *138*

Sense of Immediacy   *138*

Red Flag Words   *139*

Reporter Teases   *139*

We're in the Communication Business   *139*

News Branding   *139*

Ethics of Promotion and Branding   *142*

Sources   *142*

Chapter 9

LIFE IN THE BOOTH   145

Getting Oriented   *145*

Producer's Role in the Booth   *148*

Arrive Early   *148*

Married to the Director   *149*

During the News   *152*

Eyes Go Where? *152*

Troubleshooting *153*

Time Flies, Really *153*

The Big Finish *154*

Professional Demeanor *155*

Talking To Talent *156*

Dealing With Crises *157*

Post Mortems *159*

Chapter 10
MANAGING LIVE   161

Why Do We Go Live? *161*

Big Money Investment *162*

Audience Response *164*

Producing Live Shots *165*

Breaking News *167*

Preparing for Breaking News *169*

Live Weather Coverage *171*

Disaster Plan *173*

Warning: Don't Be Exploitive *173*

But We Didn't Know *That* Was Going
to Happen! *176*

Know the News *178*

Live Special Event Coverage *178*

Election Night *180*

Conclusion *180*

Sources *181*

Chapter 11
MANAGING PEOPLE   183

Managing the Viewer *185*

News Gathering Team: The Assignment
Editor—Heartbeat of the
Newsroom *188*

News Gathering Team: Reporters *190*

News Gathering Team: The Videojournalist
—The Faces Behind the Camera *191*

The Talent Team: The Fine Art of Ego
Stroking *195*

The Production Team: The Director, the
Artist, and the Rest of the Techies *199*

Graphics *201*

Managing Up: The News Director
and the General Manager *202*

A Style of Your Own *205*

Sources *206*

Chapter 12
MANAGING SWEEPS: THE GOOD,   207
THE BAD, AND THE UGLY

The "R" Word *208*

How Does Nielsen Count Viewers? *210*

National Ratings *210*

Local Ratings *210*

Local People Meters—The End of
Sweeps? *212*

Sweeps Survival 101 *213*

The Sweeps Squeeze *214*

Sweeps Specials: The Good, the Bad,
and the Ugly *216*

The Good *216*

The Bad *218*

The Ugly *219*

Reality Check *222*

Sources *222*

Chapter 13
MANAGING THE BUSINESS   223

Major Trends *223*

Media Consolidation *225*

Local News Quality *228*

Media Convergence *230*

The Ideal? *230*

Reality *230*

Convergence Models *231*

Converged Consumer *232*

How Convergence Impacts Television
News *233*

Newspaper *233*

Radio *234*

Online *235*

What's Next? *237*

Sources *237*

Chapter 14

MANAGING LIFE   239

   Self Check-Up—Physical Health   *241*

   Mapping Your Career—Personal Mission
      Statements   *242*

   Burnout Factor—Why It Happens and How
      to Smother It   *244*

Encore Anxiety   *247*

A Still, Small Voice   *248*

Sources   *249*

Index   251

Introduction

It's the last day of a successful May ratings book. The News Director has her feet propped up on the desk, knowing with tonight's blockbuster season finale leading into the late news, a highly promoted investigative piece inside that 11:00 newscast and a solid enterprise story to lead the show, the all-important late news ratings are clinched. Then the true hero of this story, the 11:00 producer, comes into her office and hands her "the letter." In two weeks that producer will be gone to a larger market, for a lot more money, winning someone else's 11:00 ratings. Her feet fall to the floor with a thud and the "producer panic" sets in.

The authors of this book know all about the producer panic first hand—we've caused it and we've felt it. We were part of the growth and development of producer-driven newsrooms, and we've fought the battles to keep quality journalism in ratings-driven newsrooms. We know what it takes to be a good producer because we were producers, we have the awards and the heartburn to prove it. We've produced thousands of newscasts in every time period and every format as well as a hundred election nights and dozens of specials, documentaries, and live breaking news or special event coverage.

We've learned some of the best ways to approach aspects of news producing the hard way, with a lot of bad newscasts to go along with the award winners. We've also hired, trained, and said good-bye to dozens of good producers. We know how hard it is to find and keep news producers, which is why many stations and station groups have turned to growing their own producers—only hiring assistant producers and writers and then training them to produce and moving them up through their producing ranks. Certainly one goal we all had as we entered the academic world was to interest more students in a producing career track and then train them to be producers we would have hired.

But none of those reasons are why we wrote this book, or why you should read it, and then keep it as a handy reference. All three of us were news managers in a time when competition grew as the audience fell, and television stations stopped being cash machines that seemed to print money faster than the National Treasury. We worked under the constant pressure from top station management to squeeze one more quarter rating point out of that newscast. We saw good broadcast journalists forced to pander to what consultants and promotion people assumed might bring a quick-fix spike in the ratings. We fought against a growing trend away from respecting the audience with enterprise reporting, in-depth stories, and simple good storytelling through compelling video and sound, to "Live, Local, and Late Breaking" and "Sex, Program Tie-ins, and Undercover Videotape."

This book is not another news media bashing session that harkens you back to the "good old days" of Edward R. Murrow and Walter Cronkite who knew how to do it right. They were giants in our industry, in their time. What this book does show you is how to blaze a new trail, while still following in the high standards their footprints left, to produce relevant and responsible news that also brings in ratings. We will give you the practical and realistic "how to's," but at every step in the process, we'll show you "how to" while still serving the basic journalistic goal to inform viewers of the things they need to know to make civic and life decisions. We'll show you how to win their hearts *and* minds and win the ratings in the process. Quality news does bring in ratings—a recent five year, in-depth study of newscasts in markets across the country proved that (see Project for Excellence in Journalism, journalism.org). This book is designed to teach you how to produce quality, community-oriented news that will attract and keep viewers over the long haul.

Combined we have spent more than 50 years working in local television news, doing many different jobs in the newsroom—but in our hearts and souls, we'll always be producers. In this book we will share a bit of what we learned from nearly 20 different newsrooms, dozens of great mentors, and lots of disasters, near disasters, and a good number of lucky accidents. In other words, we want to pass on a bit of what we have learned, often times the hard way.

We approach producing as part art, part technical skill, part natural ability, and a lot of gut instinct and quick reaction. TV news producing is not for the faint of heart—you have to be a journalist, an advertiser, a juggler, and a diplomat—you have to think fast, love stress, and like to be in charge. That's what makes it one of the toughest jobs in television news, but for those with just the right mix of the above qualities, one of the most rewarding and fun!

So, what *is* a producer? On Broadway a producer brokers deals to find the financial backing to put on a play, and then brings together the key people, such as the director, stars, choreographer, set designer, and so forth, to bring the show to life. Ditto for films in Hollywood. In pop music the record producer matches up a singer's vocal style with the right instrumental backing and unique musical arrangements to produce a hit record.

A TV news producer is part Broadway/film producer, juggling the resource of time and integrating the work of reporters, videographers, anchors, graphic artists, and technical crew to bring a newscast to life. A TV news producer is part record producer, composing a newscast by finding a unique but informative way to arrange the stories. Even with the same batch of news stories, no two producers will line them up in exactly the same way.

A TV news producer arranges the various news items into a lineup or rundown of stories. The rundown items might include images viewers are familiar with: anchor on-camera readers breaking news stories beamed down live from a chopper reporter interspersed with more traditional reporter news packages splashed with graphics and delivered in front of a big screen. Then there are the traditional staples of weather and sports.

Another way to think of a news producer is like a master chef, a Wolfgang Puck, Julia Child, or Emeril. The basic ingredients—news, weather, and sports—may all be the same, but how a producer blends those ingredients together results in a spicy banquet of information or bland meal of editorial and visual boredom. TV news producers certainly work in a pressure cooker world. Ratings and the risk of boring the audience can influence the producer's decision making. Walter Cronkite once remarked, "Some stories are like oatmeal—tasting bland but still vital." The balancing act between the oatmeal and the spice, the journalism side of the newscast and the show biz aspects, worries many producers. It should. In an era of eroding journalistic credibility producers play a vital role to not "dumb down a story" but find a creative, compelling way to communicate it.

How much concern should the producer have over the wide menu of choices the viewer has—not just other local newscasts but the counter programming of game shows or *Simpson* reruns? What about traditional journalistic values in this menu of choice? What exactly is news anyway in the 21st century world of WIFI, 500 channels, instant on-line news access from a cell phone, and blogging? These are critical questions we ask and answer in this book. Above all we illustrate the critical importance of finding the right, delicate balance between the art and journalism of producing, *always* keeping the viewer at the center of the camera's focus.

We believe a producer can learn the art of the newscast in order to provide the television news viewer with a creative and informative visual experience. We believe the traditional journalistic craft of news producing need not be compromised in the process. We believe the primary purpose of television news is to inform—not entertain—and that's what most viewers want—information. After all, we aren't producing a Broadway show, a hit record, or a gourmet meal. We are communicating the stories that shape the daily lives of our viewers.

We recognize the audience is the customer. But we do not believe that good newscasts pander to the customer, or do we believe that the customer is always right. We believe the viewer should be respected and it's our responsibility to make sure that the newscasts we produce are relevant to that viewer.

Producing a television newscast is an exciting, foreboding experience but one that is not focused on an individual ego or positioning for power. We believe in the team approach to television news. The best television news producers go about their daily duties in commanding but unassuming ways. The best producers are news junkies, passionate about their newscasts and willing to take a risk. Producers are the center of the action and the fast track in this business. It's not a job for everyone, but those who do it well and love it can write their own ticket in television news.

Chapter One

WHAT MAKES NEWS?

"News is what I say it is."

David Brinkley

Do you remember where you were on September 11th, 2001? How long was it before you found a television? When something big happens, we all understand why news is important. Imagine for a moment that on 9/11 you had to depend on the Cartoon Network for information, what news would you have seen? What about the soap opera channel or Comedy Central? We depend on credible news organizations, and with breaking news especially broadcast news organizations, for crucial information.

But what about the rest of the time, when the country isn't under attack? Do you watch TV news? For several decades, television news has been most people's pick as their primary source for information about what's going on in the world. But that seems to be changing. The Internet is beginning, according to the Pew Research Center, to make serious inroads as a source where people go to get news. In addition, more and more people in America are no longer interested in news, period. This seems like a good time, then, to begin thinking about what news is, why it's important, and whether or not it's pertinent to people's lives.

What news producers do every day, more than anything else, is to decide what news is. They don't do it alone. In most broadcast news operations there are also news directors, assignment editors, reporters, photographers, and many others who participate in these decisions. But ultimately, a producer's job is to put together a news program, which means, one way or another, deciding what is news.

The producer is the person who is in charge of a newscast. The producer decides what stories go into the half-hour or hour and what stories don't. The producer is in charge of what order stories appear, who reads the stories, what graphics appear, how much time each story or segment gets, whether or not a reporter goes live, and much more. There may be guidelines to help and managers who make suggestions or even give directives, but ultimately a newscast is the work of the producer. That means the producer's view of what is and is not news is important.

Afternoon news meeting, WCNC-TV (Charlotte). News managers, producers, anchors, and reporters discuss rundowns for evening newscasts.

So what *is* news? Many journalism textbooks have defined news by citing a list of characteristics that might make a story newsworthy such as is the story *timely*, what's the *proximity* of the story to the station and the audience, what *impact* does the story have on the audience, are the people involved in the story *prominent*?

We asked some producers and managers how they define news. Dawn Aidinian, a producer for KPRC-TV (Houston) says, "News is the events, people, places, and politics your community cares about, needs to know about, or simply would be interested in learning about." Mike Espinoza, who worked as the executive producer for the San Antonio News Channel says, "I'd say almost anything that is of interest to your community. We (journalists) would like to think the more people affected by something the better, but sometimes even little things could be of interest to others. A plant shutdown is a major event ... but elementary school students planting trees at their school could generate interest as well." WKYT News Director Jim Ogle in Lexington, KY uses three questions to help define what news is in his newsroom: (1) Is it hitting viewers lives in the area we serve? (2) Are people talking about it? (3) Is it important information that people want?

The bottom line is this: News is what we say it is. There are no hard and fast rules, no concrete checklist we can give for defining exactly what might be included in a newscast and what should not. In fact, if you watch enough news, you'll be amazed at times what stories get on the air. But there are some basic principles that might help guide us as we think about what stories should go into a newscast on a given night.

Why Are We Here?

If you buy a TV at the store, come home and turn it on, you can see programming because television stations broadcast signals through the air. Those signals are part of what's called the broadcast spectrum, a limited number of frequencies that work to get pictures and sound from a TV or radio station to your home. Early in America's broadcast history, Congress determined that this spectrum, those airwaves, belonged to the public. That means you and your friends and every other citizen own the airwaves. Congress decided to allow private companies to use those airwaves, but there was a trade off. The Radio Act of 1927 said that companies had to act for the "public interest, convenience and necessity." In other words, the first job of broadcasters is to think about how we might serve the public.

The Radio and Television News Director's Association is the largest organized group of broadcast journalists in the United States. Almost at the very beginning of the organizations' code of ethics, it states, "professional electronic journalists should recognize that their first obligation is to the public."

The largest organized group of all journalists in the United States, the Society of Professional Journalists, also has a code of ethics, and almost right off the top it states that "Conscientious journalists from all media and specialties strive to serve the public with thoroughness and honesty."

This idea of serving the public is the cornerstone of broadcast journalism. It is the foundation on which everything else should be built. Commercial TV and radio stations are owned by private companies. As with most companies, a key goal is to turn a profit—to make money. But by any standard or measure, that desire to make money cannot compromise or overstep journalists' obligation to serve people, to serve the public.

To Serve

But exactly what does this phrase mean; serve the public? Dictionaries define serve as "to work for." In other words, it's our job as broadcasters and especially as broadcast journalists, to work for the public or to work on behalf of the public. What does that look like? Well, for one thing, it would mean getting information to the public that it needs. In 1942 the founder of *Time* magazine, Henry Luce, asked his former college roommate, Robert Hutchins, to put together a panel to examine what the press should be doing. The Commission on Freedom of the Press concluded that the news media should provide:

- A truthful, comprehensive, and intelligent account of the day's events in a context that gives them meaning.
- A forum for the exchange of comment and criticism.
- The projection of a representative picture of the constituent groups in society.
- The presentation and clarification of the goals and values of the society.
- Full access to the day's intelligence.

Although these principles set the bar high for what we are to do in news each day, it's an excellent set of goals that could serve as our guide.

The Public

The other important part of this idea of serving the public is trying to get our hands around what the public is. Often stations will do research to learn more about the audience, or a newscast will be aimed at a certain part of the audience or demographic. But is this serving the public?

In the past we in the newsroom often assumed those of us sitting around the table in morning editorial meetings represented the public. After all, we are citizens, we live in the community, we know what stories we think are important, so that's what others will think as well. But of course when you look around most newsrooms you see that the community is often not well represented. For many years there were no women and people of color continue to be underrepresented. Does the small group of people in the newsroom represent each group that lives in the city? The answer is no.

WCPO-TV (Cincinnati) newsroom as staff prepares for noon news.

So in recent years, people in newsrooms have started thinking more about who might be in the audience. In the 1980s the audience was often described as Rosanne's family, or as Joe Six-pack. In other words, average people. Both terms showed a lack of respect for viewers, but indicated that TV news was aiming at any typical person in the audience. As cable television has offered more competition in the last several decades, now news people often see their audience as more specific, more targeted. Sales departments may push the idea of news being aimed toward a certain part of the public. At some stations there's a perception that news should be written and produced for a wealthy audience—viewers with expendable income—or toward women in upper socioeconomic groups because market research shows that, in many cases, women make buying decisions.

The truth is it's very difficult to program television news to any specific audience. How can we predict, on any given night, for instance, what a woman living in the suburbs might or might not find interesting? Often what this has resulted in is news that panders to an audience, and newscasts full of stories about pantyhose and consumer tests of cleaning products. Considering the number of women who work, are engaged in the world, and well educated, this kind of news programming is often demeaning and not very relevant to the very audience it targets. Plus, what does this kind of news decision making say about our obligation to serve the rest of the public?

Another difficulty is most research over the past 30 years has indicated that news is leaving out significant parts of the audience, specifically, for instance, people of color. If you've looked at any census figures then you already know that the United States is becoming more diverse each year. In cities like Miami, the population of Hispanics is more than 60%, so what we used to think of as minorities are now the majority. If we really want to serve the public, we cannot continue ignoring large groups of people in our communities.

WDTN-TV (Dayton) Reporter Jana Katsuyama writes and edits her story for the noon news.

So who is the public? That's an excellent question to ask when you start work in a newsroom. That's really the question producers and reporters and photographers should ask themselves every day. Are we as journalists in touch with our communities? Look at where news workers live. Do most people in the newsroom live in just one or two neighborhoods? What areas of the city do news workers NOT live? How can we cover these areas effectively? When we look around the newsroom, who is missing? What groups that make up our community are not represented? Is it a racial-ethnic group? A socioeconomic group? An age group? What can we do as journalists to make sure these missing groups are part of our news? According to yearly surveys, broadcast newsrooms are still largely populated by white Americans. What can we do to make sure others are not left out of the news we produce each day?

There are some tools for answering that question. First, people in newsrooms can work actively on discovering who lives, works, eats, and sleeps in their community. Often times news workers did not grow up or go to school in the cities where they now work. But as journalists, we have an obligation to learn something about these cities. This process should start by getting plugged into a community. Leslie Garza is a producer for KOAT-TV (Albuquerque). She suggests a number of ways of keeping in touch with the local community: "Volunteer, go to church, get a manicure, eat out and go to happy hour. While you do it all, keep your ears open. The story ideas just pour in." Mike Wortham, an executive producer for KXAS-TV (Dallas), agrees:

> You have to be IN the community to know your community. Find an organization you care about and volunteer. Many journalists are even picked to serve on the boards of these organizations. On the flip side, get outside your comfort zone every now and then. Have no interest in government? Attend a city council meeting. No interest in sports? Go to a minor league ballgame. Sometimes new experiences will teach you invaluable lessons. Don't just read the big "daily" newspaper. Many cities have weekly "alternative" papers that can provide excellent, sometimes more honest, reporting. Some smaller communities sometimes also have their own newsletters and papers. Get on their mailing lists. Be aware. Notice change in your neighborhood, and ask questions.

Here are some tips for learning about the public, about your audience, about the local community:

• **Experience your community.** Go to areas where you've never been, think about where you eat, shop, worship, play, get your hair cut, take your dry cleaning, and so forth. How can you expand this to include many different parts of the city? While there ask questions, observe what's going on, and be curious.

• **Read about your community.** Try to learn about the history of the community, read community newspapers, and newsletters published by community groups. Is there a newspaper published for the African American community? What are the local publications for the gay and lesbian community? Is there a web site or newsletter for Muslims living in the city?

• **Get to know people in your community.** What are popular hangouts for different groups like a restaurant, a grocery store, or barbershop? Are there bulletin boards or other places where meeting notices are posted? Begin building a Rolodex, a phone list with names of people in your community, so that you are not calling on the same people over and over again to speak on issues in the community.

News producers have a lot of influence each day on what goes into a newscast. Yet they spend most of the day inside the newsroom, separated from the community they are covering. This is why it's essential for producers to spend time outside the newsroom, learning more about the city where they live. It's up to us as journalists to figure out who the public is. Polling can help, but nothing will replace the effort you take to get to know your community in a direct, personal way.

Jan Schaffer is a journalist, teacher, and executive director of J-LAB-The Institute for Interactive Journalism who worked on an idea called civic mapping. The idea is for journalists to create a map not of streets and landmarks, but a map made up of people, groups, and contacts.

A good place to start is with "civic mapping," a simple and systematic way of diversifying our Rolodexes. Here's an overview:

1. Start with newsroom conversations. Identify your preconceived notions about a community of interest. Put them up on the wall.

2 Collect the names of known community leaders—the officials and quasi-officials.

3. Ask them this important question: Whom do they seek out to get news and information about the community?

4. Collect names they give you. These will generally fall into a couple of categories: "Cat- alysts," the go-to people who often get things done but may not carry a title. And "connectors," the civic bumblebees who pollinate many different groups—scouts, sports teams, PTAs, health clubs, church groups—imparting information.

5. Find out where people hang out—the diner or donut shop, the barbershop or swim club— the "third place" where people talk informally about their communities.

6. Hit the streets and start interviewing these folks and visiting these places.

Jan Schaffer, J-LAB-The Institute for Interactive Journalism

The Producer's Role in Making News

In some markets and in some newsrooms, producers may work on more than one newscast, though the norm is for a producer to be responsible for one news program. Many producers start the day with a news meeting, which can be a large or small gathering of people. Also attending the meeting are managers and other workers, and together they begin to decide what will be covered that day (or night). As the day continues, producers begin to plan their newscast, figure out how much time they have to fill, talk to reporters about how stories are coming along, and constantly read other news sources to keep up with what's happening in the world, the country, and the local community.

Along the way the producer puts together what's called a rundown, which is a list of what stories will air and in what order, along with other information like story times, graphics, and whether the story will have any videotape accompanying it. As the news show time approaches, producers do a lot of writing and review a number of scripts. Finally, scripts are printed, collated, and distributed, and the producer proceeds to a control room where she oversees the show as it airs.

How do producers decide what does and does not go into a specific news program? Executive producer Mike Wortham explains:

> Use your morning editorial meeting as a good gauge of what needs to be in the newscast. What story/stories got you and your colleagues talking in the meeting? What stories generated the most follow-up ideas? What stories came with the most elements that you can build a newscast around. Sometimes the sexiest stories don't always make a newscast. A fire at an abandoned warehouse may have great pictures, but more people are going to care about the school zone meeting at city council. The challenge for the producer/reporter team is how to make the city council story as appealing as "great flames."

One of the most valuable assets a producer can develop is news judgment. That's the sense of what should or shouldn't be in a newscast. It comes with time and experience. Haley Cihock, a producer for KXAN (Austin) says she has a checklist in her head for evaluating stories. "Why do I care? (Gets to the heart of the

WCPO-TV (Cincinnati) Producer Heather Trainer in the control room during a newscast.

benefit to and interest of the viewer.) Is this visually compelling? (Obviously, the better pictures will hold more eyes ... we're in a visual medium.) What resources can I afford to put toward this story? (Reporter, photographer, time, etc.) Is this story worth expanding beyond the bare facts?" Using Haley's list as a starting point, we developed more questions that could help guide the decision making concerning any news story:

- Do we have the facts straight? Do we have all the information we need, are there sources we are forgetting, have we verified the basic elements of the story? What basic questions will viewers want answered about this story?

- How important is the story? Does it impact our community, do viewers need to know this information? Has something changed in the story?

- How current is the story? Can we go live, is there something that will be going at the time of our newscast, is the story changing as we go to air?

- Do we have pictures? Television is pictures, so what visual elements do we have to help tell the story, are we doing everything we can to visualize a story, could maps and/or graphics help?

- What perspectives or context do we need to make this a better story? Are there other stories that need to be told on this topic, do we need to have other reporters working on different aspects of this story? Who do we never hear from in this kind of story who might offer a valuable insight?

Once a producer commits to a story, then a myriad of other decisions come into play, like which reporter will cover the story, where will it run in the newscast, how much time will be given to the story?

Each of these decisions may seem small but they add up to make a larger whole. Producers, in making small decisions and big decisions, shape the news each day. Throughout the book, we will discuss those many decisions and give some guidance for how to be the best producer you can be. But all of it starts with developing news judgment and making good decisions each day about what news is.

Chapter Two

WHO WATCHES
AND WHY?

Film Is Art
Theatre Is Life
Television Is Furniture

Now you have a viewer's perspective. As the producer of a newscast you will spend eight to ten hours intensely preparing for one hour or half-hour of the day—the time your show is on the air. And during that hour or half-hour your attention will be focused like a laser beam on what's on the air now, and what's coming up next. Compare that experience with what your viewers are doing at the same time. Think about how you watch television, news specifically, when you're at home. Are you sitting up straight, feet together, hands in lap, intently focused on every word and picture coming out of the box? Of course not! And keep in mind you're more interested in the news than most viewers.

Your newscast is competing for viewers' attention with a dozen other things. Most people are doing at least one other task while the television is on, and many people multitask. Often the news is on "in the background" while viewers are fixing a meal, getting ready for work or school, even reading the newspaper or surfing the web.

What we know about how people watch television is that they typically listen, almost subconsciously. They are monitoring the audio for something that peaks their interest. When they hear that trigger, it brings their visual attention to the television. Just knowing that much about the process should clue you in to one important fact—the words that we write and the way we use sound are extremely important in what is perceived primarily as a visual medium! We will talk a lot more about good broadcast writing in a later chapter, but for now, just know that what you say and how you say it are the keys to capturing the viewer's attention.

BIGresearch Inc. conducts a Simultaneous Media Usage Survey (SIMM V) twice each year. The 2004 results from more than 12,000 media consumers show people are definitely multitasking in their media usage, and television appears to be the medium most consumed along with other media.

Joe Pilotta, PhD, VP Research, BIGresearch, said "The old model of the family sitting down to be entertained by the three major networks ceased to exist long ago. Today primetime isn't just for TV. Consumers are just as likely to go online, read a magazine, newspaper or their mail, thumb through a catalogue, play video games or watch TV in various combinations of simultaneity which has resulted in a decline of time spent with TV (−2.5%)."

What Viewers Do While Watching TV

- 66.3% regularly or occasionally read the mail.
- 60.1% regularly or occasionally go online.
- 55.0% regularly or occasionally read the newspaper.
- 51.8% regularly or occasionally read magazines.

And that's just other media consumption—it doesn't take into account nonmedia activities such as eating, watching the kids, doing chores around the house, and so on.

Center for Media Research. (2005). *Multitasking impacts TV viewing* (Research Brief, 1/04/05). Available from www.centerformediaresearch.com

Watching the words—teleprompter operator follows the rundown during a WCPO-TV (Cincinnati) newscast.

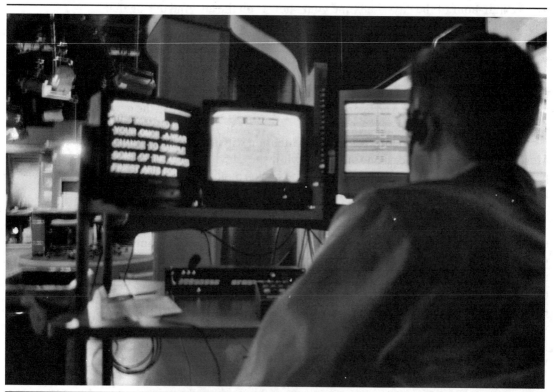

Now here's the good news for you as a producer. We've learned that *visual* attention tends to grow exponentially. In other words, if you can get viewers to *watch* the television for 15 seconds, you have a good chance to keep them watching for 20, and if they continue to watch for 20 seconds, you have a better chance to keep them for 30, and so on. The bad news is, all the while you're working to keep them watching, they're looking for any excuse to stop paying close attention and go back to whatever else they were doing. What sends them away? Anything that's confusing or doesn't make sense, and anything that has no relevance to their lives. Good, clear writing, producing, and use of video and sound will take care of the making sense part, but as we discussed in the previous chapter, making your newscast relevant means knowing your viewers and your market extremely well.

Who Is Out There?

You've probably been told and always thought of television as a mass medium. Before we look at who watches television news, we want you to rethink the idea of producing newscasts for a large audience.

Intimate Medium

While it's true that any newscast you produce will likely be seen by thousands, if not hundreds of thousands of people, that's not who you're producing for. Television is in fact a quite intimate medium. Viewers, one or two at a time, invite us into their homes. Now we hope there are thousands of those homes, but the individual viewer isn't thinking about all the other people watching and they don't want to think about them either.

Think again about how you watch television. If you're watching the morning news, the TV may be on in your bedroom while you shower and dress. You may watch the late news while you're in bed. That's an intimate relationship, and the worst thing you can do as a producer is treat your audience as one massive group—instead think of one or two friends watching. That's why we talk about writing in a conversational style because the best stories are told as if they're a conversation between the anchor or reporter and one viewer. One of the quickest ways to burst that bubble of intimacy is to start a newscast with "Good Evening Everyone."

If you have any doubt that viewers perceive television as an intimate medium, talk to your anchors. Ask them if anyone ever comes up to them and addresses them as Mr. or Ms. Chances are, 99% of the time, people call them by their first names. Anchors and other on-air talent will also tell you people come up to them and expect them to know who they are because they come into the viewers' home every night. One weather anchor in Roanoke, Virginia tells the story of a woman who came up to her in the shower at the gym where she worked out and said, "Aren't you _____ on Channel 10?" The anchor woman was naked and so was the other woman, but that didn't stop her from marching right up and introducing herself! After blushing from her toes to her scalp, the weather anchor politely said, "No, but people say I look like her." So viewers clearly think they know personally the on-air talent at their favorite station and relate closely to them. They perceive a personal relationship with their local news, and you as the producer should always remember that. You are an invited guest in your viewers' homes; don't abuse the privilege or you might not be invited back!

WCPO-TV (Cincinnati) Anchor Tanya O'Rourke during noon news.

So Just Who Is Watching?

There have been many audience studies on the news consumption habits of people, and the results tend to be similar. We'll work from some comprehensive national studies regularly commissioned by the Radio Television News Directors Association and Harris Interactive to give you a brief general profile of who is watching local television news, drawing particularly on the 2003 *Local Television News Study of News Directors and the American Public,* the *1996 Profile of the American News Consumer,* and the *January 2006 Harris Poll.*

First we should look at the demand for news and information in general. In a January 2006 national Harris poll of nearly 3,000 adults more than 75% reported they watch local broadcast news at least several times a week, and only six percent said they never watch local television news. Local television continues to be the most often used source for news, although as you can see below, there are a lot people using multiple sources for their news.

	Daily	Several times a Week	Several times a Month	Several times a Year	Never
Watch local TV news	54%	22%	10%	7%	6%
Watch network/ cable TV news	49%	22%	13%	9%	8%
Read local daily newspaper	41%	22%	13%	12%	9%
Go online for news	40%	24%	15%	11%	11%
Listen to local radio news	32%	21%	13%	13%	20%

January 2006 Harris Poll, Harrisinteractive.com

As you might imagine, there are some pretty dramatic differences in news consumption from all sources when you factor in age. The older someone is, the more likely they are regular news consumers.

Daily/Several times a Week Usage	Echo Boomers (18–27)	Gen X (28–39)	Baby Boomers (40–58)	Matures (59+)
Watch local TV news	52%	69%	83%	88%
Watch network/cable TV news	51%	57%	74%	88%
Read local daily newspaper	43%	49%	66%	80%
Go online for news	53%	68%	70%	57%
Listen to local radio news	26%	49%	64%	58%

January 2006 Harris Poll, Harrisinteractive.com

There are two other interesting differences in choice of primary news source and frequency of viewing. Minorities and women tend to watch television news more frequently than whites or men. Keep those facts in mind as we move through this chapter—we'll come back to them later.

Why Do They Watch (or Not)?

Now that we know a little about who is watching, we want to delve into the question of why viewers watch, or increasingly, don't watch local television news.

Back in the seventies—before TiVO, remote controls, multiple satellite and cable choices, and the Internet—researcher sociologist Mark Levy (1978) watched people watching TV news. Despite technological advances, Levy's main conclusion as to why viewers watched remains relevant today—nobody watches for the same reason.

Why People Watch the News

	6 p.m.	11 p.m.
"Active"		
News quality	12.0	12.4
Program format	18.1	6.0
Newscasters	21.3	29.1
Subtotal	51.4	47.5
"Passive"		
Habit	8.8	4.8
Already on channel	24.3	31.2
Don't know	5.1	5.8
Subtotal	38.2	41.8

Levy, M. R. (1978). *The audience experience with television news.* Lexington, KY: Association for Education in Journalism and Mass Communication.

Why people watch the news is really no different than why people go out to eat. Some come to a restaurant starved and hungry, others because they want the social experience, and a few because they want to check out the master chef's reputation. You'll never really know whether you're producing for the gourmand or fast food customer because the audience is not only diverse but it watches your news for a diversity of reasons.

Levy's research also found people watch a particular newscast for both active and passive reasons. Although the largest single category of active viewers chooses a newscast based on the anchor, when you combine those who watch for news quality and program format, more people decide based on newscast characteristics than talent. So don't believe the myth that your producing will have little impact because people only watch a particular newscast for the personalities of the anchors.

The biggest difference between the time when Levy did his research and now is not so much the reasons people watch, but the many reasons they've stopped watching. Back in the late 1970s before cable offered up hundreds of viewing options, at 6:00 p.m. on any given night upwards of 90% of viewers would be tuned into one of typically three local newscasts, and at 6:30 p.m. those same viewers would settle in to watch the network evening news on ABC, CBS, or NBC. Today at 5:00 or 6:00 p.m. less than 40% of those watching TV are watching local news, and that 40% is often divided among four to seven or more local newscasts. An even smaller percentage is watching network news at 6:30 p.m.

WDTN-TV (Dayton) anchors prepare for the start of newscast.

So how did we manage to lose so many viewers over the years? There are many reasons that have nothing to do with the quality or content of newscasts. Obviously, there are many more choices for programming and news. Viewers don't have to wait until 5:00 or 6:00 p.m. to get their national or local news. People are busier than ever before and simply have less time to devote to watching the news or are not available at news times. But our newscasts also have something to do with the reason viewers are watching less than ever before.

In the 2003 *Local Television News Study* nearly 70% of the public said the overall quality of their local TV news was good (50.4%) or excellent (16.8%), less than a third rated it fair or poor. But there was some troubling information when more specific questions were asked. For example just over half of those surveyed said local television stations did a good or excellent job of providing information needed to make decisions about viewers' community or lives, but 40% said their stations did just a fair or poor job. And more than 55% agreed with the statement, "Lately, I've become more skeptical about the accuracy of anything I hear on the news." In addition nearly as many viewers think local TV news is mainly interested in making a profit (43%), as think it's mainly interested in serving the public interest (45%) (Papper, 2003, pp. 18–20, 41).

Another disturbing fact is that many viewers strongly believe local television news is improperly influenced by outside sources. As many as 40% of those

surveyed in 2003 said that the local news was *often* influenced by elected officials, big business, advertisers, the federal government, interest groups, or TV
station owners (Papper, 2003, pp. 54–55).

When viewers are asked open-ended questions about their complaints
against local television news, a few common responses top the list. These were
the most common complaints of people who said they watched less local TV
news, according to a national phone survey in 2001 by Insite Media Research:

Reasons Why People Watch Less Local TV News

Too much repetition	37%
Sensationalism	34%
Balance of positive/negative news	33%
Irrelevant crime coverage	32%
Irritating/misleading promotion/teases	25%
Limited coverage of real issues	22%
Want more than spot news	21%
Limited regional coverage	20%
Not getting enough respect	20%

Tallal, S. (2003). *Highlights from American voice poll III: Local TV news "paradigm
shift."* Insite Media Research, BEA Convention, 2003.

What Do They Want?

As you look at the above list, items such as "irrelevant crime coverage," "limited
coverage of real issues," "want more than spot news," and "limited regional coverage" can be summarized in one way—viewers seem to want news that's relevant to their lives. There is an age-old debate in journalism over what we should
give the public—do we give them what they want or what they need? The basic
assumption in that debate may be flawed. It assumes that people don't know
what they need. The classic example of this is blaming viewers for the ever-de-
creasing coverage of world news, especially prior to 9/11.

The argument went that audience research showed interest in national and
especially international news dropping steadily during the late 1980s and 90s.
One study of news items devoted to international news on the three broadcast
networks found that while a third or more of the stories were world news in
1970, by 2000 that level had dropped to 20% or less (Riffe & Budianto, 2001).
Local stations weren't any better, often by the late 1980s relegating all world
and national news to a preproduced 90 second spin around the globe (many literally used spinning globe graphics) where each story got less than 15 seconds,
and if there was no good video, it didn't get that.

What replaced our coverage of news abroad? Health and consumer "news
you can use," because the research said that's what viewers wanted.

The problem with the research that lead to these decisions is much of it was
flawed. We asked the wrong questions. It was always, "How important is inter-

national news as a reason to watch your local news station?" Well, surprise, surprise, people reported it ranked somewhere down with sports and environmental news at most stations. If researchers asked the question in a different way, we bet there'd be a different answer. Ask viewers in Pittsburgh how important are stories about Russian steel imports or ask people in Dayton, Ohio how important are stories about foreign car parts flooding U.S. markets and you'll get a different answer. But in order to know the right question, you need to know your market. You'd need to know that steel production was a major industry in Pittsburgh but many steel mills shut down because of foreign steel dumping, and you'd need to know that Dayton was second only to Detroit in the assembly of vehicles and manufacture of auto parts.

How international news impacts viewers locally

WCNC-TV (Charlotte) Health Reporter Kara Linnstrom is live with a "Medical Check-Up" report on the 5 p.m. news.

So when you see research such as presented in the following graphs, showing viewer interest by news topic, be skeptical. Realize that while they may provide some general guidelines of the types of news stories your viewers consider relevant, the questions in many cases are too broad to really get at the stories important to your market. The interest inventories come from the 1996 *Profile of the American News Consumer* (RTNDF, 1996).

These interest inventories deal with news content preferences overall, from all media. When you ask viewers what they want specifically from local television news, inevitably weather moves up to the top as the number one reason people watch. Despite their very general nature, you still can see from these charts that again, people want news most relevant to their lives—the number one and number two choices for most people is news from their own communities and their own state. Those interest inventories will vary from

News Content Preference by Gender. Radio-Television News Directors Foundation. (1996). Profile of the American news consumer. *News in the Next Century Project.* Washington, DC. Figure 5, p. 31.

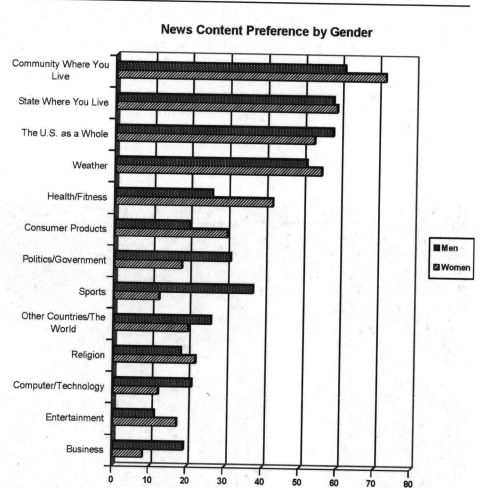

News Content Preference by Gender

market to market depending on the main employers and life style choices of viewers in that market.

Demographics

It is vital then if you are going to be a good producer that you have a thorough community demographic profile to help you decide which stories are most important for your viewers. This includes knowing the make-up of your potential audience, as well as several important things about the market.

News Content Preference by Age. Radio-Television News Directors Foundation. (1996). Profile of the American news consumer. *News in the Next Century Project.* Washington, DC. Figure 6, p. 32.

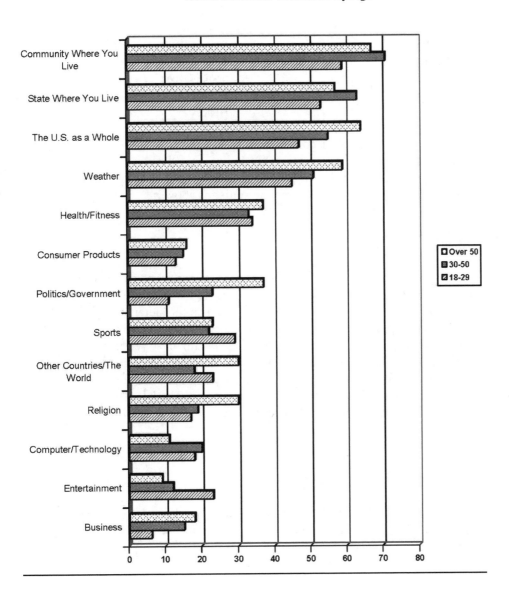

News Content Preference by Age

Population Demographics	Community Profile
Gender	Major employers
Age	Geography
Race	Local government/politics
Education	Public schools/higher education
Income	Unemployment level
Religion	Arts and entertainment
Family status	Sports
Leisure time activities	Social issues
	Transience of residents
	History

The local chamber of commerce and the U.S. Census Bureau are great sources of much of this information, but don't forget to talk to people in the community, as suggested in chapter 1. The civic mapping discussed in that chapter is a great way to put a human face on the statistics above.

Target Audiences

Getting a solid sense of who your potential viewers are and what's important to them is the positive side of demographics; audience targeting can be the negative side. As a producer you will hear a lot about target audience, and it will have a substantial impact on your decision making. If you look back at the charts on news content preference, you can see that even with those very general topic areas there are differences in preference depending on age and gender. Race, political leaning, and family status are other demographic factors that also can strongly influence interest in various news topics. The key is not to get so focused on a target audience that you are excluding other viewers and sending them to other stations.

Who Is Available?

Part of audience targeting is who is available to watch a newscast at a particular time and what information is most important to them at that time. This type of targeting simply makes good sense. Here are some general examples of how this type of audience targeting works:

Morning News (5–7 a.m.)

Available Audience—people getting ready for work, parents getting kids ready for school

Targeted Content—frequent weather and traffic reports, short news updates

Noon News

Available Audience—stay at home parents (usually women), senior citizens

Targeted Content—health reports, gardening and cooking segments, long interview segment (slower pace to the show), often no sports

5 p.m. News

Available Audience—mostly women 25–54, stay-at-home parents

Targeted Content—education and community news, health and consumer reports, entertainment news, human interest features, rarely any sports

6 p.m. News

Available Audience—adults 25–54

Targeted Content—more political news, business and economic stories, sports

10/11 p.m. News

Available Audience—adults 25–40 wanting a wrap of the day's events before bed

Targeted Content—more shorter stories including world and national news, weather (often a quick forecast in the first block), special longer form segments, sports

While it makes sense to think about who is available to watch when you choose your stories and decide how to allocate resources, it's very easy to get too caught up in target audience. That usually happens when the sales department enters the picture.

Don't Assume

Even though you think you may have a good idea who is available to watch and a likely target audience for your newscast, don't assume you know what that group is really like. For example, the 5 p.m. producer at a Pittsburgh station forgot her market demographics when she targeted women as her audience. Yes, the primary viewers for the newscast that followed *Oprah* were women, but because Pittsburgh skews toward an older demographic, they were women at the upper end of 25–54 instead of the lower end. So, all the stories about child safety seat recalls and parenting, primary education and fitness, weren't grabbing viewers. When she looked at who her women viewers really were, she realized that most either had grown children or no children. When she replaced those discretionary parenting stories with health and medical, consumer and financial planning stories, ratings improved.

Who Advertisers Want

Most television sales people will tell you that a prime demographic for advertisers is women 25–54 because they control so much of the buying power. More recently advertisers have been hot after the youth market, 18–29 year olds. Fox News Channel and many Fox affiliates have been somewhat successful attracting younger viewers with fast paced newscasts that include bold graphics, lots of music, and multiple images on the screen at the same time. The problem comes when a target demographic becomes tunnel vision and the goal of producing a newscast is to win that demographic or the demos, as they're called.

In the early 1980s, when many stations expanded their early news and started 5:00 p.m. newscasts designed to capture more women, this tunnel vision lead to failure. Using interest inventories such as those presented earlier, the newscasts were often formatted with lots of soft news and features but no real hard news. The stereotype that women were only interested in soft news was wrong. By the mid-1980s to early 90s the 5:00 Feature Show had gone the way of the Edsel, to be replaced by hard news and information for at least the first couple of blocks of the newscast.

Producer, director and technical director at WCNC-TV (Charlotte) during 5:30 p.m. newscast.

Diversity

The other problem with the tunnel vision of target demographics is that the diversity of our communities gets lost, and our resulting newscasts look very white and suburban. This again takes us back to the importance of knowing the true demographic make-up of your market. As mentioned in the previous chapter, more and more of our communities are predominantly minority. Minorities are becoming the majority, but we're still covering them the same way, if at all.

In his book, *White News*, Don Heider (2000) looked at coverage of people of color in local news. He found that basically coverage was limited to cultural celebrations such as Kwanza, heritage festivals, and pow wows and crime news. Subsequent studies have found similar results. In a content analysis of local news from 26 stations in 12 cities over the years of 1987 and 1989 through1998, researchers found "Latinos, Asian Americans and Native Americans were virtually invisible as anchors, reporters and subjects in the news." African Americans had more of a presence as news talent but tended to be given certain types of stories to report and were often only secondary news sources (Poindexter, Smith, & Heider, 2003, p. 524).

Now you may be wondering how a target audience mindset contributes to this problem. Well, senior broadcast journalism students at Ohio University found a connection in their 2004 and 2005 senior seminar research project. The students were required to research the Columbus market and create a complete demographic profile of the market and potential news audience. Then they interviewed news personnel at three of the four stations about their perceptions of the market demographics and how well they thought their station covered and represented the entire market. Finally the students did content analysis of the early and late newscasts for those two stations.

First what they found: The Columbus market is about 25% minority, with a growing Latino population. However the content analysis of more than 36 hours of news found only one minority reporter on the air at each station, one African American anchor, and NO minority experts interviewed for any story. The only place where minority faces on the air matched their percentage of the population was among criminals and crime victims or victims families.

These results were not surprising given the many other studies of minority representation in the news. What were surprising were the comments of news managers and personnel. Nearly everyone interviewed, which included news managers, anchors, and producers, said their station was more concerned with their target demographic—usually women—than matching the demographics of the market as a whole. They all said they thought they did a pretty good job of covering the diversity of their community, but no one knew the correct proportion of the market which was minority. They all underestimated it. Then came the most telling comment from a news manager, who said, "We don't pay conscious attention to diversity—we're color blind in our coverage. We just focus on our target audience." Obviously it's time all the Columbus stations, and stations across the country, took their blinders off and became more conscious of the diversity in their markets.

That example brings us back to where we started—who is watching? Remember we showed you that the groups relying most on local television news as their primary source of news and information are women and minorities. It makes sense that women would be attracted to local television news because so much of it is specifically targeted at them. But our minority audiences are being highly underserved by local television news, yet they *want* to use local television as their primary news source. This growing audience is leaving the traditional network affiliate stations in droves and flocking to stations that specifically cater to them. The fastest growing news audiences are for Spanish speaking networks and local stations.

Conclusion

It's vital for you as a producer to find out who lives in your community and what goes on in their daily lives, so you can produce newscasts that are relevant to them and angle the important stories in such a way that they want to watch your station. People are busier than ever and have access to news 24/7. That means you've got to make it worth their while to watch your newscast during its appointed time. The best way to do that is to focus on relevance.

One of the scariest trends uncovered by audience research is the fact that not only are fewer people watching local news, but those who do watch care less about which station they watch. In the early 1990s upwards of 70% of those surveyed said they did have a favorite station and cared which local news they watched. By 2001 that percentage dropped to less than half (Tallal, 2003). But about 60% of those same people said they would switch to a particular station or go back to watching local news if the local news addressed their complaints of too much sensationalism, crime news, and spot news and not enough relevant local, regional, and in-depth stories (Papper, 2003; Tallal, 2003).

The bottom line is don't be satisfied with audience research and a sales department designated target audience. If you really want to serve your viewers and produce a newscast that will bring the largest number of them back to watch again and again—do your own research:

- Create your own community demographic profile and viewer demographic profile for your entire market.
- Know who among your viewers is available during your newscast and target all of them, not just those that advertisers want.
- Remember there's diversity in any target audience group, and know the range of that diversity for your market. A 30 year old Hispanic stay-at-home mom in the suburbs is very different from a 30 year old African American single woman living and working in the city, and both are substantially different from a 30 year old white single mom surviving on welfare. But all of them are part of the 25–54 women target demographic.
- With every story you select for your newscast, ask yourself what about this story impacts my viewers and make sure that is the primary angle of the story.
- Be wary of audience research that doesn't ask the right questions, yet purports to tell you what kinds of stories your viewers want.

Ultimately, all the research you and the station do only goes so far. To really produce relevant newscasts, as we told you in the previous chapter, get out of the newsroom and become part of the community you produce for. No amount of research can replace personal experience and face to face contact with the viewers you serve. As you progress through the following chapters and get into the real "how to" of newscast producing, always keep the viewer at the center of your focus.

Sources

Center for Media Research. (2005). *Multitasking Impacts TV Viewing* (Research Brief, 1/04/05). Available from www.centerformediaresearch.com.

Heider, D. (2000). *White News: Why Local News Programs Don't Cover People of Color.* Mahwah, NJ: Lawrence Erlbaum Associates, Inc.

Levy, M. R. (1978). *The audience Experience With Television News.* Lexington, KY: Association for Education in Journalism and Mass Communication.

Papper, R. (2003). *Local Television News Study of News Directors and the General Public.* Washington, DC: Radio-Television News Directors Foundation.

Poindexter, P., Smith, L., & Heider, D. (2003). Race and Ethnicity in Local News: Framing, Story Assignments, and Source Selections. *Journal of Broadcasting and Electronic Media, 47,* 524–536.

Riffe, D., & Budianto, A. (2001, August). *The Shrinking World of Network News.* Paper presented to AEJMC National Conference, Washington, DC.

Radio-Television News Directors Foundation. (1996). Profile of the American News Consumer. *News in the Next Century Project.* Washington, DC.

Tallal, S. (2003). *Highlights from American voice poll III: Local TV News "Paradigm Shift."* Insite Media Research, BEA Convention, 2003.

Chapter Three

WHAT MAKES
A GOOD PRODUCER?

"Success usually comes to those who are too busy to be looking for it."
                                             Henry David Thoreau

T his chapter is about what it takes to be a good producer and a successful producer. Good producers *are* busy. But even though there's a lot to accomplish each day for a newscast producer, most often there's no indication of the amount of work to be done when you look at or talk to a good producer. "The best producers are the ones who can keep their calm during the craziest breaking news situations," says Dawn Aidinian, a producer with KPRC (Houston). Good producers are calm, organized, and at least give out the illusion of being in control.

Becoming a good producer means mastering a number of different skills. Good producers are a combination of **journalist, drill sergeant, cheerleader, peacemaker, maestro, strategic planner, contortionist, poet, huckster,** and **nitpicker.** What do all these titles entail? Keep reading and you'll see.

Journalist is always first on the list, because that's our primary job description. As journalists it is our job to serve the public by sifting through lots of information each day, making good choices in regard to stories that are important to people's lives, and then presenting those stories in as clear and concise a way as is possible. All other roles are important, but journalist always takes precedence. The principles of excellent journalism should always be our final measure, the way we know ultimately whether we are successful or not. Mike Wortham, an executive producer for KXAS-TV, puts it this way:

> You're in charge of a very valuable commodity … 30 minutes to an hour to two hours of television airtime. The responsibility that comes with that needs to be at the forefront of every decision you make. You're not producing the newscast for you, your anchors or your news director. Your responsibility is to the viewers. The airwaves you're "borrowing" belong to them.

Maestro, et al. One of the biggest challenges of being a producer, however, is that although you are in charge of the newscast, there's no way you alone could produce enough material to fill that newscast. Even if you could, you could not get it on the air without anchors, directors, and a number of other technicians. In other words, producing by its very nature is collaborative. If you don't like working with people, if you can't get along with people, if you want a job where you work in isolation, then producing is not the job for you. On the other hand, if you like interacting with people and, perhaps even more important, if you have a take-charge personality, than you may feel very comfortable being a newscast producer.

Producers are often the people in the newsroom left to manage the day, to make sure things get accomplished and reporters and photographers complete assignments, so management skills are essential. Being a manager means you must be able to deal with lots of different kinds of people, often under deadline pressure. Phil Hendrix is the News Director for WLNS-TV 6 (Lansing). He says one of the biggest things he's learned along the way about producing is:

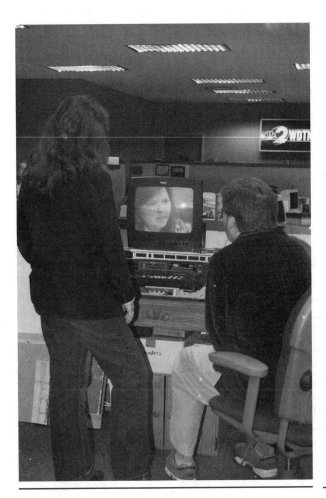

WDTN-TV (Dayton) producers review video for newscasts.

How to rely on others. While a producer has a lot of responsibility, news is really a team effort. A good producer can set a vision, but has to work closely with a lot of people if they are to succeed. Young producers typically try to do too much and, in the end, miss something important because they don't see the big picture. Good producers are hands-on enough to know everything that is going on in their show and set high standards … yet know the strengths of their reporters, anchors, photographers, and technical crew and allow them to shine in their jobs.

delegate

One thing you will learn as you deal with people is that different people will respond differently to you as a manager and coworker. Some people need a **drill sergeant,** they will look to you to give instructions and keep them on task. Some people work best when someone is checking up on them. Others may need to see you more as a **cheerleader,** not someone to bark out orders. These people need someone to encourage them, to be their advocate and to root for them each day. For these folks, an encouraging word or recognition of their contributions goes a long way. Still others feel conflicted about their work, the story they're working on, their relationship with the boss or other workers, and they will lean on you as **peacemaker,** someone to listen to their problems and help them resolve issues. As a producer you'll have to address people's varied personalities and moods, and learn to deal with each accordingly. KPRC producer Dawn Aidinian puts it this way:

The roles to different people

> A newsroom is filled with many different personalities. You need to understand and recognize these personalities and then deal with each person accordingly. When you have a different opinion on how something should be done, decide how important getting your way is. I usually consider who I am dealing with (i.e., seniority, expertise), whether it will truly affect the quality of my show, and if there may be a battle more worth fighting in the near future.

WCNC-TV (Charlotte) Producer Erin Grider and Crime Reporter Glenn Counts discuss a story for the 6 p.m. news.

No matter which style you prefer, from drill sergeant to peacekeeper, as a newscast producer you definitely will have to learn to be the **maestro**, the person in charge of orchestrating the newscast. You must be willing to lead, to take charge, and to make decisions. Some people love the leadership role and relish the attention, others are more quiet leaders who lead through example. You may not think of yourself right now as a leader, but you can develop these skills, and even now, you may have more influence than you know. Jill Geisler is a former news director who now teaches at the Poynter Institute, a nonprofit organization that works on making journalism better. She developed a test to see whether you have influence or not. If you work in a newsroom already take the test as is. If you don't, you might take the test with a student news organization in mind or any group that you are currently part of.

Got Influence?

Jill Geisler
The Poynter Institute
Grade Yourself on the Influence Inventory
Jill Geisler, Poynter Institute

It's easy to spot the managers in an organization; they have titles and formal power. But *leaders* emerge at all levels. Leaders may or may not have formal power, but they always have *influence*. Influence, like trust, grows from a person's expertise, integrity, and empathy.

Using a scale of 1 to 5, with 5 being the most positive, how would you grade yourself on each question?

1. How do colleagues assess my work performance? Am I seen as a top performer? ___4___
2. Am I a "go-to" person? Do people turn to me when the task has a high degree of difficulty? ____
3. Do people view me as ethical? Am I known for honesty and openness? ____
4. Do people know what I stand for? If they know, do they believe I walk my talk? ____
5. Do people see me as empathetic? Do they think I have their best interests at heart? ____
6. Am I known as a good listener, one who doesn't jump to conclusions before hearing people out? ____
7. Am I cool under pressure? Am I effective and professional when passions are high and/or deadlines are tight? ____
8. Am I known as generous with my time and ideas, even in areas outside my immediate work duties? ____
9. Do people feel comfortable confiding in me or asking me to coach or mentor them? ____

10. Do people feel better about the work when I'm on the team?

____

Scoring: If you gave yourself an overall score of 40–50, *and your colleagues would give you a similar score,* then you are very likely seen as a leader, a person of influence in your organization. Key to this, however, is a "balanced scorecard": a high grade for every question. If an individual is seen as lacking in any one area—expertise, integrity, or empathy—that person's influence and leadership is significantly diminished. Those qualities in combination grow and sustain a leader's influence.

In addition to having some people skills, most producers like being in charge. A very big part of the job is being a **strategic planner**. Producers need to know the overall news philosophy of the newsroom where they work. What are your organization's goals for each newscast and how will your newscast fit in with those goals? Once that's established, there are a number of big decisions that need to be made each day. What stories should you cover? Who should cover each story? What resources should you commit to a story?

One of the biggest decisions producers make each day is deciding on a lead story. The lead story is usually considered the most important story of the day. In newspaper terms, your lead is what would be on the front page. There's a lot of attention paid to a lead story, because it is the first impression the viewers will have about the news of the day. It's a strategic decision because that lead story sets into motion a series of other decisions about the order the other stories in the newscast will follow. Picking a lead story is often no easy task. Should you lead with the most important story of the day? How do you know what *most important* is? Should the lead story be the most current story? Should the lead be the story that will impact the viewers the most? Should you lead with the story that

Video Journalist Gar Brown edits the lead story for WHIO-TV (Dayton).

has the best pictures? All of these questions must be taken into account, weighed, and balanced, often with the advice of news managers.

But there are other strategic decisions made every day as well. How much time will each story get? Should you go live, should you commit more than one reporter to a story? There are hundreds of decisions each day, and all of them eventually work together toward the finished product. We'll go into more detail about how to make some of those decisions in later chapters, but strategic planning is a big part of the job.

What Makes a Good Producer: Moving From the Classroom to the Newsroom

Tom Dolan, Dolan Media Management

Tom Dolan is a former news director and newscast producer who now has a business that tries to help television news managers find jobs and improve what they do. He offers some suggestions for succeeding in your first producing job:

Overview/Expectation.   Get agreement from key managers on what is a good working newscast format. But understand formats are meant to evolve in at least two ways: First, they need to reflect changing viewer tastes and life styles; second, they must respond and be flexible to the breaking news of the day.

Key Elements to a Good Newscast.   Producers should also have a good sense of *key* elements to a good newscast. These include:

- **Lead story** treatment that will immediately engage the viewer.

- An **"A" Block** that must be a complete summary of the day's important local news.

- An "A" Block **closing story** that may be more of an emotional "connector" for balance in the segment. It should be followed by a three-element tease that serves as a menu for the rest of the newscast and keeps the viewer watching.

- A strong **"B" Block** beginning story that becomes a "second lead." The B Block should contain a unique, teaseable/promotable story or a clear, differentiated sidebar to one of the day's high interest stories to flow viewers.

Tom Dolan, Dolan Media Management (http://smartrecruit.com/)

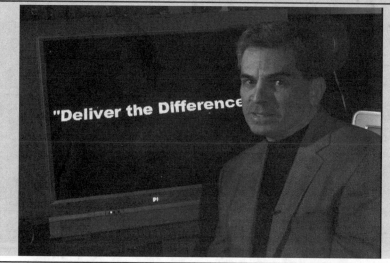

- A highly produced **weather segment** that is also presented with the feel of "This is today/tonight's weather story." The segment should be forecast-driven. All the graphics should be built to support and *explain* the weather story. The weather anchor should devote time to the upcoming weekend forecast since viewers look at that right after the next day's forecast.

- Produce **sports as news**. Look for "storylines" in sports stories versus just a re-hash of highlights.

- Save a good human-interest story for the newscast **kicker**. It is also important how you say goodbye or good night to your viewers.

Understand News Is a Lifestyle.   To succeed, you need to know your viewers. You live in a city and a community not a "market." You have to study and try to understand the core values of the people who live there. Education, for example, is newsworthy for everyone. Aside from the obvious stories of what children are being taught, education is financed by property taxes that all homeowners pay. Debates over tax hikes can be made interesting and do not have to be covered as dull "meeting" stories.

The First Search.   Treat your job search like a news story. Figure out what type of company, company "culture," management style, and newscast content appeal to you. You are in demand as a producer. As a producer, you can quickly become unhappy if you land a position at a station with a very different news philosophy.

Growing in the Job.   Part of being a successful producer means you have to produce coverage that is heavy on content as well as compelling television. You need to be knowledgeable on diverse content issues as well as stay current on production issues to "make good TV." With so many choices in the crowded broadcast and cable environment, it has become more important to learn how to differentiate newscasts to break through.

It will not be good enough for the producers of the future to simply produce a solid newscast. Growing in the job means becoming good at producing distinctive LIVE coverage, which really demonstrates something versus the predictable standup in front of a dark building. It means partnering with reporters to shape their storytelling and explain issues that go beyond the simple who, what, where of an event and get to the "why."

Ever seen a **contortionist?** Those are the people who are so flexible, they can put their bodies in almost any position. Flexibility is a key trait for becoming a good news show producer. Why? One example says it all. You've finished planning the news, all the stories are written, all the teases are finished, the scripts are printed, and all is well. It's 4:40 p.m. and your newscast starts at 5:00. Suddenly the scanners screech to life. Phones start ringing in the newsroom. You get word of a fire at a major downtown building. Everything in your newscast must now change. You have to dispatch a live crew and begin rethinking what stories will stay and go, and where the fire will play in the newscast. In fact that reshuffling to deal with breaking news or other issues is becoming more the norm for today's producers than the exception. Because of the recent trend toward more live real time television and the easy flexibility of news producing software, there aren't too many days when the newscast on the computer at 4:40 p.m. is the newscast that gets on the air at 5 p.m.

Newscast rundown on the computer.

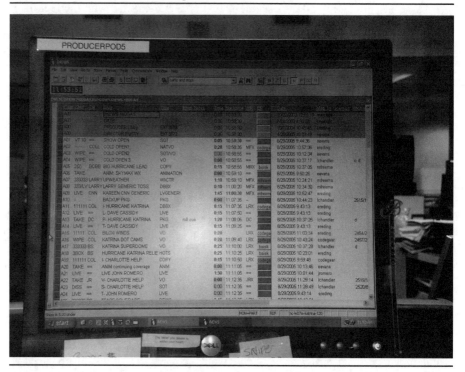

If you don't like change, you won't like news. If you love adrenaline and rising to the occasion when the unexpected occurs, then television news is just the place for you. Leslie Garza, a producer at KOAT-TV, says flexibility is the key to success in her job.

> You have to be willing to work even when you're not scheduled. Your attitude has to be flexible. You have to emotionally give and take. This includes taking and accepting criticism. You have to be flexible when it comes to story ideas. Sometimes you have to go the extra mile to make stories relevant to your audience. And you have to push the envelope a little. Pick stories that matter, not only those that are great TV. Flexibility in your producing skills is also a must. It's okay to keep things crisp and clean. But sometimes, it's better to experiment. Put in that extra V.O. Try adding that animated map. Make a wish list. If others can't get it done, then scale back. But don't short change the newscast and your audience without trying.

If you are flexible and can handle change and the unpredictable nature of news, you can become an excellent show producer.

You might think writing news and writing poetry don't have much in common, but they do. Producers are **poets** in a sense, because they should care deeply about language. They are always striving to be concise and choose their words very carefully. Some of the best poems are relatively short, and the poet has taken care to convey much in few words.

Chapter 3

The Fish

by William Butler Yeats

Although you hide in the ebb and flow
Of the pale tide when the moon has set,
The people of coming days will know
About the casting out of my net,
And how you have leaped times out of mind
Over the little silver cords,
And think that you were hard and unkind,
And blame you with many bitter words.

Poets speak volumes in just a few words. Broadcast news writers must do the same. Producers must write short copy stories that sing, introductions to stories that compel viewers to continue watching, and teases that grab and hold people's attention. Yet also, like poets, producers are constantly trying their best to convey truth. It's a challenge to be concise and not lose meaning. It's also a challenge to grab someone's attention without exaggerating or distorting. So in these ways, producers must be journalistic poets.

Good writing in news attracts viewers, gets their attention, and makes the news seem important and pertinent. Part of this art of writing has to do with writing what we call teases, which are the short bits that anchors read to tell us what is ahead. Think about headlines in a newspaper or a Web site. They are markers that tell you what other content you can find by reading an article or by clicking on a link. Broadcasters write these kinds of headlines, too, but they are complete sentences. These are teases. So producers are put in the position of selling a story, and this way they are, at times, **hucksters,** trying to convince viewers to continue to watch the program. We'll have more on tease writing, and writing in general, later in the book, but the key is to grab attention and still tell the truth.

Finally, news producers are **nitpickers**. That means they must pay careful attention to details. If you work at a station now or you visit a TV station, take one page of the script and take a look. There are many details that must be correct for everything to go smoothly in a newscast. The story must have the correct title or slug. If the slug varies between the script and, say, the videotape that's supposed to air along with the story, the tape may not air. There are director's instructions on the script, usually along the left side of the page, under the slug. These tell the director who's reading the story, if it's just an anchor or whether there's a live shot or any videotape, if there's tape how long it runs, and so on. If any of these directions are missing or incorrect, there's a good chance something will go wrong on the air.

Then there's the part of the script the anchor reads. Is the script written in the proper format? Different stations have different rules for writing scripts. Some use all capital letters, some use upper and lower case. Many indent for every new sentence. There are very particular rules for writing numbers and using phonetic spelling for names. All of this must be correct or the anchor may not read something correctly on the air. Are all the facts contained in the story accurate and true? In just one page of script, there are dozens of details that must be correct. The producer is the one that checks each script, ensuring everything is correct so the newscast can go on air without a hitch. Good newscast producers pay careful attention to these and other details. It may seem like nitpicking, but that attention to detail can be very, very important to how a newscast comes across on the air.

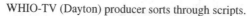
WHIO-TV (Dayton) producer sorts through scripts.

In this book, when we use the word *producer,* we are talking about people in television newsrooms who produce newscasts. But there are other people in the newsroom with the title of producer, to read more about them check out the box "What's in a Name?"

So what exactly does a producer do all day? Here's a partial list of a newscast producer's responsibilities:

- They come to work on time, with a good knowledge of what's going on, having read local papers and monitored other news organizations.
- They figure how much time they need to fill in a given show.
- They assess what stories might be covered during the day.
- They help determine who will cover what stories.
- They decide what stories will go where in a newscast.
- They decide how much time will be dedicated to a story.
- They decide whether a story should be a reader/VO/VO-SOT/Package/ live shot, and so on.
- They communicate with crews during the day to see how stories are developing.
- They look for additional elements (maps, video, graphics, etc.) to enhance stories in their newscast.
- They monitor wires (and scanners) to see what other news is taking place as the day continues.
- They check with bureaus to see what news may be available for the day.

What's in a Name?

In Hollywood, the people who find scripts, set up financing, and hire people to direct and act in movies are called producers. The person who has the most creative control over a motion picture is the director. But in the world of TV news, the person who has the most creative control over the newscast is called a producer. The newscast producer is also called the line producer, or a show producer, or in some shops may have the time of the newscast in their title, like 6:00 p.m. Producer or Morning Show Producer. A director is usually the person responsible for the technical aspects of a news show: They often decide which cameras get which shots, they direct the framing of camera shots, and usually they are the ones giving technical commands in the control room during a newscast. The producer is in charge of the content of the program. Job titles do vary from station to station, but these descriptions generally hold true. There are also some other TV news people with the word producer in their job titles:

- **Executive Producer:** A newsroom manager, often second only to a news director, who oversees all the newscasts and sometimes the entire newsroom day to day.

- **Field Producer:** This person functions like a reporter. They come up with story ideas, set up stories, go into the field, and supervise the shooting of a story. They may do the interviews, they often write the script, but they most often do not appear on the air. Their stories are often narrated by reporters or anchors. Some field producers might work for special units in a newsroom, like an investigative unit, a consumer unit, or they might help produce health stories.

Other titles you should be familiar with:

- **News Director:** The person in charge of a news room, they often oversee the budget, hiring, and firing of employees and set the overall news philosophy for the newsroom. In short, they are the boss in the newsroom.

- **General Manager:** The person in charge of the entire television station. He or she is the News Director's boss.

- **Station Manager:** Often the #2 person at a station, works under the General Manager.

- **Assignment Manager:** One of the managers in the newsroom, oversees the assignment desk and staff. The assignment desk coordinates daily activities, keeps track of news releases, court dates, and monitors where news crews are during the day.

- They communicate with sports and weather to let them know how much time they have and if they will be needed in any special role.
- They decide on graphic elements in the newscast, such as maps, full screen graphics, lower third supers, over-the-shoulder graphics, and so on.
- They write teases.
- They write stories.
- They review all copy that is filed for the newscast.
- They fact-check stories, as needed.

- They ensure that scripts are formatted correctly and have the proper directions for the technical crew.
- They assign stories to be written to anchors and other writers.
- They decide which anchor will read what.
- They book satellite time if needed and communicate transponder information to appropriate personnel.
- They print scripts.
- As news changes during the day, they make appropriate changes and adjustments and notify people involved about those changes.
- If a news story involves an advertiser, they might check the program log to see what commercials run in the show and notify the sales department of potential conflicts.
- They back time the newscast to make sure the newscast will fill the allotted time, but not run over (more about this later).
- They sit in the control room, monitor time and content of the show, and make adjustments accordingly.
- They communicate from the booth with live crews, letting them know when their live shot is coming.
- They communicate with live interview subjects, letting them know who will be talking with them and when they will be on the air.
- They keep the anchors appraised of timing and content issues.
- They make appropriate on-air corrections, if needed.
- They help the director and talent get the show off the air on time.
- They participate in a postshow critique.
- They file scripts in an electronic archive.
- They take some stories and reformat them for the Web site.
- They write news updates.

Managing all these tasks and keeping on deadline is a lot of work. That's why producers are busy. Most producers don't leave the building for lunch or dinner. Many come in early and leave late. The great producers are passionate about their newscasts.

Most producers have some kind of internal schedule they follow for each day. For a 5:00 p.m. producer it might look something like this:

8:30 a.m.—Arrive at work, check local paper and wire services.

9:00 a.m.—Attend morning meeting—this is where management and staff begin discussing and making plans for the day ahead.

10:00 a.m.—Check your on and off time, the time when the newscast begins and ends. Calculate your news hole—this is figuring out exactly how many commercials are in your show and exactly how much time you have for news that day.

10:30 a.m.—Draft a preliminary rundown.

11:00 a.m.—Check with crews and see what progress is being made on stories. Do another comprehensive sweep of wires for news, check with lineups for daily feeds from news sources like CNN, and see what stories they will be sending along.

11:30 a.m.—Begin writing any stories you can for the show, like kickers (light stories to end the show) or teases.

Noon—grab a quick bite at your desk, watch competitor's noon newscasts to see what stories they are featuring.

1:00 p.m.—Attend afternoon meeting. Plans are "finalized" for your show and now the people who work the late shift are on hand to discuss later newscast(s).

2:00 p.m.—Make sure anchors know what stories they are writing, you continue writing, and begin assigning stories to videotape editors to be edited.

3:00 p.m.—Review package scripts with reporters. Check writing others have done for the show and rewrite as needed. Write transitions between stories. Try to finish all teases.

4:30 p.m.—All scripts should be completed and printed. You, an assistant producer, or an intern needs to put together the paper copies of the script and distribute them.

4:30 p.m.—Check with video editing and see how stories are progressing. Check with anchors and make sure they have no questions.

4:40 p.m.—Go to control room, check on status of live shots, see if the technical crew has questions.

5:00 p.m.—Show time.

5:35 p.m.—Attend postmortem meeting with managers, anchors, and director to analyze how the show went and how things might have been better.

5:45 p.m.—Archive your show scripts in the computer, check with late producer(s) to see if they have questions, and perhaps even hit the door and head home.

There is a lot of detail left out here, but it gives you a general idea of what a typical day looks like for a television news producer. Most producers set little deadlines for themselves throughout the day so they don't run behind and end up frantic the last 30 or 40 minutes before the show airs. What any schedule like this can not account for is when things happen—there's a late breaking spot news story that may lead the newscast, or a reporter calls in and their story has fallen through, or the computer freezes and loses scripts that have already been written. It's all part of a normal day for most producers.

Good Producer = Good Relationships

One of the most important relationships producers have is the relationship with their anchors. The anchors are the most recognized members of the news staff. They are the people that viewers depend on for credible information. There's no one an anchor depends on more than the show producer. We asked Karen Foss, an outstanding anchor from KSDK-TV (St. Louis), to explain a bit about the relationships between anchors and producers:

Producers and Anchors

The relationship between producer and anchor is very much like a marriage; an arranged marriage to be sure, but nonetheless a very intense and collaborative partnership. In the earlier years of television the producer was likely to be the crusty veteran newsman with younger reporters and anchors reporting to him. Today the table is often turned: producers are frequently women and they're often the junior members of the news team. But the best producer/anchor relationships are still based on mutual respect and clear communication.

When anchors and producers share a high regard for journalistic best practices; a commitment to presenting the best product possible to the news viewer; and a sense of camaraderie; the news product will be superior, both of their careers will flourish and their job satisfaction will be at its highest.

The best producers I've known exhibit a contagious enthusiasm for television news and establish a sense of accountability for all participants in the newscast. They expect anchors to be available for input and discussions for planning the newscast. They also hold brief post-mortems with all the staff invited (director, writers, reporters, assignment manager, anchors, editors and photo journalists) after the newscast to review problems and note outstanding work. Interestingly,

I've never known any producer to insist on such meetings but in a business notoriously short on feedback everyone seems attracted to them.

The best producers also master headset etiquette. They speak in a calm voice—even when everything is going haywire—and they clearly and briefly convey only what the anchor needs to know at the moment. For instance, "Set aside page 36; bump is next." Not, "Caroline—you won't believe this!! Maxwell is late editing his package—once again—and he'll never

Karen Foss, KSDK-TV

---

make slot, so when Davis finishes, read the tease to the next segment and we'll regroup during commercials—if I don't slit my wrists first!" See the difference?

I would urge young producers who occasionally feel "in over their heads" to simply ask questions. Perhaps you're uncertain about a courtroom procedure or the correct location or which city hall positions are appointed and which are elected. We've all been there; most people are glad to help and share their knowledge. The worst thing you can do is fake it. There's too much at stake. One of my early mentors advised me the best way to look wise in your work is to be willing to acknowledge your ignorance during your preparation.

One last thing: Criticize in private and praise in public. Respect the relationship with your anchors like you would any important relationship in your life. Producers have a great deal of responsibility and few people outside the newsroom know how critical they are to the success of a newscast. One person who does know how dedicated and effective you are is your anchor. He and/or she can be your best advocate as well as your daily partner.

Chapter 3

What makes a good producer? No one thing. To be a good producer, or even better, to be a great producer, you have to take on a number of different roles, deal with lots of different kinds of people and personalities, and enjoy completing a lot of different tasks on time under deadline pressure. In many of the following chapters, we're going to give you tools, tips, and examples of how to do all of that. Do them and success is yours.

THE ETHICS
OF PRODUCING

"We cannot make good news out of bad practice"
Edward R. Murrow

"Give light and people will find their own way"
Corporate motto of Scripps-Howard Broadcasting

"Wise shall be the bearers of light"
Etched in the stone entrance to the Missouri School of Journalism

Y ou can bet that when a Cleveland television news anchor strips off her clothes in a naked ploy for ratings ethics questions begin to fly ("Cleveland TV Anchor," 2004)! Or, when a network anchor leaves his position in the wake of a scandal over the use of sources in a story about the president's military record, ethical issues are front and center. When network cameraman ("Announcing the 2005 Payne Awards," 2005) captures a U.S. marine shooting a supposedly unarmed Iraqi insurgent, news producers debating how much of the video to show on their local newscasts find themselves in a tough ethical dilemma. Local and global ethical issues seem to ignite and explode today on a more frequent basis pushing newscast producers into gut wrenching decisions.

It's odd, but in the middle of these ethics firestorms the job of producer sometimes takes on a solitary character. How so? In a space crowded with assignments editors, desk assistants, anchors/reporters, tape editors/shooters, the noisy newsroom bustles like a shopping mall. Yet many times it's in the quiet moments driving home after the newscast has aired that a loneliness sets in as you reexamine your day's toughest challenges as a producer—the ethical ones.

Editorial choices—like determining a lead or the logistical steps needed to "get the live shot"—often involve group decision making, and staff members frequently feed back opinions. However, the tough, ethical decisions too frequently must be made when the producer flies solo. If you're the late news (10 or 11 p.m.) producer, the news director and executive producer have gone home long ago. Yes, your anchors can copilot. After all, they're often the most experienced journalists on duty with you at night. Yet their own deadlines and demands, such as doing on-air promotions, often prevent them from helping you. Much of the time the rest of the staff is also too busy to help. Certainly there is no time for them to join you in a philosophical debate about whether to use a juvenile's name in a story. Nevertheless, the decision has to be made.

You answer for your critical judgment calls after the newscast, as viewers demand answers to questions like "Why did you air that bloody video?" or "Where was the fairness and balance of that story?" And, it's not just the nighttime viewer calls—the external pressures—you have to answer to. The next morning, when your boss, the news director, or even the television station general manager—internal forces—invites you into the office, you have to be ready to justify your ethical position.

Forward thinking stations have well thought out newsroom ethics policies that lend guidance and have a chain of command that you can go to for advice on the tough calls. But the truth is many don't. As we will see in this chapter, the best ethical decisions come when broadcast journalists engage in a robust discussion to identify stakeholders—all those impacted and connected to the story—and look for alternatives. However, time often cheats this vital vetting process and the deadline clock demands a decision now. Ultimately, many ethical questions and how they are treated rest squarely on the producer's shoulders, which sometimes can make it a difficult and lonely job. However, if you follow a sound process of ethical decision making, which we will lay out in this chapter, the burdens you face as a producer can become much lighter.

WCNC-TV (Charlotte) producers, reporters, and news managers discuss story ideas in the morning meeting.

To make these ethical burdens as light as possible, this chapter illuminates ways for you to face these tough calls. It teaches you the patterns and pathways that will help you acquire the wisdom needed for good ethical decision making. Most important, it will teach that in reality you are not alone in the trenches of tough ethical decision making. Managers want and need to be part of the tough ethical decisions, and many professional organizations are there to help.

RTNDA

R- T- N- D- A—may be five of the most important letters in your career. Learn these letters and become part of the professional organization they stand for—Radio-Television News Directors Association (see www.RTNDA.org). RTNDA puts you in touch with broadcast journalists like yourself who endorse ethical journalism. The association represents local, national, and international broadcast journalists across multiple media platforms from radio to television, over-the air, satellite and cable, to the Web.

RTNDA's annual convention provides comprehensive guidance through a variety of training workshops—many of them focused on ethics—while in the monthly magazine, *Communicator,* the organization publishes articles not only on ethical and legal issues, but on broadcast writing and career planning.

Chapter 4

RTNDA—Radio-Television News Director's Association

Fast Facts

Who? RTNDA represents more than 3,000 news directors, news associates, educators, and students.

What? A professional organization in broadcasting, cable, and other electronic media in more than 30 countries. Publishes the monthly magazine *Communicator.*

Where? www.RTNDA.Org, national headquarters in Washington, DC.

When? Founded as a grassroots organization in 1946, holds an annual international convention each spring, and awards the prestigious annual Edward R. Murrow awards each autumn.

Why? Purpose is to set standards of broadcast news gathering and reporting.

RTNDF, an educational foundation to promote research on electronic journalism and sponsor student scholarships and professional fellowships, is a sister organization of RTNDA.

The first broadcast news ethics code was actually created for radio by the National Association of Radio News Directors, the forerunner of RTNDA. This earlier code called for news departments to be separate and autonomous from the radio announcers (who usually read the news by "ripping and reading" it from the news wires) and pushed for the hiring of journalists who gathered their own news. Why did RTNDA create an ethics code? How did it come about? Dr. Vernon Stone, RTNDA's contracted researcher for many years, traced the evolution of the 2000 edition of the RTNDA code back to 1946! Stone labeled the major evolutions in the RTNDA ethics code this way:

- 1947: Basic standards.
- 1950: Expanded standards.
- 1966: Journalistic practices.
- 1973: Social consciousness added.
- 1987: Corporate consciousness.
- 2000: Guidelines for changing times.

Coming up in this chapter we'll focus in depth on the current RTNDA code, but first we'll introduce you to an important journalist in broadcast news history whose career came to symbolize high ethical standards.

The Murrow Tradition

Each year RTNDA presents some of the top awards in broadcast journalism—named after CBS legend Edward R. Murrow, the pioneer World War II radio broadcaster who set the benchmark in television journalism in the 1950s and 1960s. Murrow's name has become synonymous with the highest ideals of ethical broadcast journalism. RTNDA once defined broadcast journalism in part as "a duty, a calling."

Edward R. Murrow works with producer Fred Friendly.

Edward R. Murrow

Fast Facts

Who? The pioneer journalist of CBS News.

What? His legacy as an ethical journalist resulted in naming broadcast journalism's most prestigious award after him—the RTNDA Edward R. Murrow Awards.

Where? Radio broadcasts from London during World War II followed by TV news programs in the 1950s and early 1960s.

When? 1908–1965.

Why? Sometimes seen as controversial, Murrow remains an ethical role model of broadcast journalism.

Murrow died of lung cancer in 1965.

When it comes to ethical decision making we believe our first duty is to recognize our prejudices and determine how they might impact our choices. Murrow spoke about personal prejudice during a December 31, 1955, television broadcast stating, "Everyone is a prisoner of his own experiences. No one can eliminate prejudices—just recognize them" (www.quotationspage.com/quotes/Edward_R_Murrow). Sometimes it's tough to uphold this duty and be self-reflective enough to recognize personal bias.

SPJ and the Ethical Influence of Print

Let's face it—television news is just a little more than 50 years old. For a couple hundred years newspapers have rolled out the news—a lot longer than we broadcasters. So when it comes to ethics it seems logical to take tips from what the print folks have learned. Indeed, much of the RTNDA code is based on earlier ethics codes from print, and some changes to the current code came about from newspaper and magazine articles critical of the standards of broadcast journalists.

One of the oldest American journalism organizations in this country is the Society of Professional Journalists or SPJ. Sometimes SPJ is viewed as a print organization. This isn't true; many broadcast journalists volunteer to serve in the organization's state and national leadership offices. It's ethical tradition dates back to 1909 when it began as a college journalism fraternity, Sigma Delta Chi. SPJ's mission is to improve and protect journalism, and it remains "dedicated to encouraging the free practice of journalism and stimulating high standards of ethical behavior."

We hope on the wall of your newsroom or classroom, but no doubt needing a dusting, is a poster of RTNDA's code of ethics or a similar one from SPJ. But RTNDA and SPJ are not the only professional organizations with journalism ethics codes.

SPJ—Society of Professional Journalists

<u>Fast Facts</u>

Who? About 9,000 members nationwide, both print and broadcast journalists.

What? America's oldest professional journalism organization.

Where? Founded as the Sigma Delta Chi fraternity in 1909. Headquarters address: Eugene S. Pulliam National Journalism Center, 3909 N. Meridian St., Indianapolis, IN 46208. Phone: 317–927–8000. Fax: 317–920–4789.

When? Monthly national magazine *Quill* frequently covers ethical issues as does their annual convention. See their web site: Spj.org

Why? To improve and protect journalism.

NPPA, the National Press Photographer Association (www.NPPA.org), was founded in 1946 and represented not just print photographers but those who shot newsreels, the forerunners of today's television news videographers. NPPA has served as a critical voice to get cameras into the courtroom and improve media relations with governmental agencies. NPPA's code of ethics contains many of the same do's and don'ts found in other journalism ethics codes, but it also includes seven journalistic ideals related directly to photography and videography. For the complete code see this link, www.nppa.org/professional_development/business_practices/ethics.

Other national professional organizations, such as ASNE, the American Society of Newspaper Editors (www.asne.org), have statements of ethical principles, too. Wire services have their own ethics codes including the Associated Press (www.apme.com/ethics/). The individual news networks frequently update their own news guidelines. Unfortunately, on the local level very few individual stations have taken the time to spell out in writing a code of ethics for their own newsroom as many individual newspapers do, although one owner of a group of broadcast stations, Gannett, has a corporate code of ethics that seems more applicable to their newspapers than broadcast stations (http://www.gannett.com/go/press/pr061499.htm).

But who has time to look up all of these, find the answers to ethical dilemmas, debate them with your news director and other staff, and make a decision all within five minutes? The goal is to think about ethics a lot when you are not facing a deadline and make a lifelong commitment to struggle with the hard questions. But in the meantime it's easy to feel overwhelmed.

Fear not! Two simple steps will help. First compare, and then connect. Yes, this will take some time, but once you've digested the differences through comparisons of the codes you will find the connection that is meaningful for you. Ultimately ethics is an individual decision. During down time away from work or as a class exercise make a simple comparison of the two most relevant codes, RTNDA and SPJ. You'll see many recurring ideas, just expressed differently. Review the individual major codes of RTNDA and SPJ that follow. Then see how the codes compare lined up side by side.

WCNC-TV
(Charlotte) posts
a "Viewer Bill
of Rights"
prominently in
the newsroom.

Code of Ethics and Professional Conduct
Radio-Television News Directors Association

PREAMBLE

Professional electronic journalists should operate as trustees of the public, seek the truth, report it fairly and with integrity and independence, and stand accountable for their actions.

PUBLIC TRUST: Professional electronic journalists should recognize that their first obligation is to the public.

Professional electronic journalists should:
- Understand that any commitment other than service to the public undermines trust and credibility.
- Recognize that service in the public interest creates an obligation to reflect the diversity of the community and guard against oversimplification of issues or events.
- Provide a full range of information to enable the public to make enlightened decisions.
- Fight to ensure that the public's business is conducted in public.

TRUTH: Professional electronic journalists should pursue truth aggressively and present the news accurately, in context, and as completely as possible.

Professional electronic journalists should:
- Continuously seek the truth.
- Resist distortions that obscure the importance of events.
- Clearly disclose the origin of information and label all material provided by outsiders.

Professional electronic journalists should not:
- Report anything known to be false.
- Manipulate images or sounds in any way that is misleading.
- Plagiarize.
- Present images or sounds that are reenacted without informing the public.

FAIRNESS: Professional electronic journalists should present the news fairly and impartially, placing primary value on significance and relevance.

Professional electronic journalists should:
- Treat all subjects of news coverage with respect and dignity, showing particular compassion to victims of crime or tragedy.
- Exercise special care when children are involved in a story and give children greater privacy protection than adults.
- Seek to understand the diversity of their community and inform the public without bias or stereotype.
- Present a diversity of expressions, opinions, and ideas in context.
- Present analytical reporting based on professional perspective, not personal bias.
- Respect the right to a fair trial.

INTEGRITY: Professional electronic journalists should present the news with integrity and decency, avoiding real or perceived conflicts of interest, and respect the dignity and intelligence of the audience as well as the subjects of news.

Professional electronic journalists should:
- Identify sources whenever possible. Confidential sources should be used only when it is clearly in the public interest to gather or convey important information or when a person providing information might be harmed. Journalists should keep all commitments to protect a confidential source.
- Clearly label opinion and commentary.
- Guard against extended coverage of events or individuals that fails to significantly advance a story, place the event in context, or add to the public knowledge.
- Refrain from contacting participants in violent situations while the situation is in progress.
- Use technological tools with skill and thoughtfulness, avoiding techniques that skew facts, distort reality, or sensationalize events.
- Use surreptitious newsgathering techniques, including hidden cameras or microphones, only if there is no other way to obtain stories of significant public importance and only if the technique is explained to the audience.
- Disseminate the private transmissions of other news organizations only with permission.

Professional electronic journalists should not:
- Pay news sources who have a vested interest in a story.
- Accept gifts, favors, or compensation from those who might seek to influence coverage.
- Engage in activities that may compromise their integrity or independence.

INDEPENDENCE: Professional electronic journalists should defend the independence of all journalists from those seeking influence or control over news content.

Professional electronic journalists should:
- Gather and report news without fear or favor, and vigorously resist undue influence from any outside forces, including advertisers, sources, story subjects, powerful individuals, and special interest groups.
- Resist those who would seek to buy or politically influence news content or who would seek to intimidate those who gather and disseminate the news.
- Determine news content solely through editorial judgment and not as the result of outside influence.
- Resist any self-interest or peer pressure that might erode journalistic duty and service to the public.
- Recognize that sponsorship of the news will not be used in any way to determine, restrict, or manipulate content.
- Refuse to allow the interests of ownership or management to influence news judgment and content inappropriately.
- Defend the rights of the free press for all journalists, recognizing that any professional or government licensing of journalists is a violation of that freedom.

ACCOUNTABILITY: Professional electronic journalists should recognize that they are accountable for their actions to the public, the profession, and themselves.

Professional electronic journalists should:
- Actively encourage adherence to these standards by all journalists and their employers.

- Respond to public concerns. Investigate complaints and correct errors promptly and with as much prominence as the original report.
- Explain journalistic processes to the public, especially when practices spark questions or controversy.
- Recognize that professional electronic journalists are duty-bound to conduct themselves ethically.
- Refrain from ordering or encouraging courses of action that would force employees to commit an unethical act.
- Carefully listen to employees who raise ethical objections and create environments in which such objections and discussions are encouraged.
- Seek support for and provide opportunities to train employees in ethical decision-making.

In meeting its responsibility to the profession of electronic journalism, RTNDA has created this code to identify important issues, to serve as a guide for its members, to facilitate self-scrutiny, and to shape future debate.

Adopted at RTNDA2000 in Minneapolis September 14, 2000.

Society of Professional Journalists Code of Ethics

Preamble

Members of the Society of Professional Journalists believe that public enlightenment is the forerunner of justice and the foundation of democracy. The duty of the journalist is to further those ends by seeking truth and providing a fair and comprehensive account of events and issues. Conscientious journalists from all media and specialties strive to serve the public with thoroughness and honesty. Professional integrity is the cornerstone of a journalist's credibility. Members of the Society share a dedication to ethical behavior and adopt this code to declare the Society's principles and standards of practice.

Seek Truth and Report It

Journalists should be honest, fair and courageous in gathering, reporting and interpreting information.

Journalists should:

- Test the accuracy of information from all sources and exercise care to avoid inadvertent error. Deliberate distortion is never permissible.
- Diligently seek out subjects of news stories to give them the opportunity to respond to allegations of wrongdoing.
- Identify sources whenever feasible. The public is entitled to as much information as possible on sources' reliability.
- Always question sources' motives before promising anonymity. Clarify conditions attached to any promise made in exchange for information. Keep promises.
- Make certain that headlines, news teases and promotional material, photos, video, audio, graphics, sound bites and quotations do not misrepresent. They should not oversimplify or highlight incidents out of context.
- Never distort the content of news photos or video. Image enhancement for technical clarity is always permissible. Label montages and photo illustrations.
- Avoid misleading re-enactments or staged news events. If re-enactment is necessary to tell a story, label it.
- Avoid undercover or other surreptitious methods of gathering information except when traditional open methods will not yield information vital to the public. Use of such methods should be explained as part of the story
- Never plagiarize.
- Tell the story of the diversity and magnitude of the human experience boldly, even when it is unpopular to do so.
- Examine their own cultural values and avoid imposing those values on others.
- Avoid stereotyping by race, gender, age, religion, ethnicity, geography, sexual orientation, disability, physical appearance or social status.
- Support the open exchange of views, even views they find repugnant.
- Give voice to the voiceless; official and unofficial sources of information can be equally valid.

- Distinguish between advocacy and news reporting. Analysis and commentary should be labeled and not misrepresent fact or context.
- Distinguish news from advertising and shun hybrids that blur the lines between the two.
- Recognize a special obligation to ensure that the public's business is conducted in the open and that government records are open to inspection.

Minimize Harm

Ethical journalists treat sources, subjects and colleagues as human beings deserving of respect.

Journalists should:

- Show compassion for those who may be affected adversely by news coverage. Use special sensitivity when dealing with children and inexperienced sources or subjects.
- Be sensitive when seeking or using interviews or photographs of those affected by tragedy or grief.
- Recognize that gathering and reporting information may cause harm or discomfort. Pursuit of the news is not a license for arrogance.
- Recognize that private people have a greater right to control information about themselves than do public officials and others who seek power, influence or attention. Only an over- riding public need can justify intrusion into anyone's privacy.
- Show good taste. Avoid pandering to lurid curiosity.
- Be cautious about identifying juvenile suspects or victims of sex crimes.
- Be judicious about naming criminal suspects before the formal filing of charges.
- Balance a criminal suspect's fair trial rights with the public's right to be informed.

Act Independently

Journalists should be free of obligation to any interest other than the public's right to know.

Journalists should:

Avoid conflicts of interest, real or perceived.

- Remain free of associations and activities that may compromise integrity or damage credibility.
- Refuse gifts, favors, fees, free travel and special treatment, and shun secondary employment, political involvement, public office and service in community organizations if they compromise journalistic integrity.
- Disclose unavoidable conflicts.
- Be vigilant and courageous about holding those with power accountable.

- Deny favored treatment to advertisers and special interests and resist their pressure to influence news coverage.

- Be wary of sources offering information for favors or money; avoid bidding for news.

Be Accountable

Journalists are accountable to their readers, listeners, viewers and each other.

Journalists should:

- Clarify and explain news coverage and invite dialogue with the public over journalistic conduct.
- Encourage the public to voice grievances against the news media.
- Admit mistakes and correct them promptly.
- Expose unethical practices of journalists and the news media.
- Abide by the same high standards to which they hold others.

Comparing the Codes

When you compare the RTNDA and SPJ codes of ethics, patterns emerge. Some pretty noble words appear as the core values of the codes. RTNDA selected six core values, while SPJ narrowed them down to four. If you examine the details you'll notice differences, but you'll also begin to realize that common themes emerge, especially toward the end of the codes. Ironically, independence and accountability stand out as *identical* last items in both codes. You can see that in the following figure.

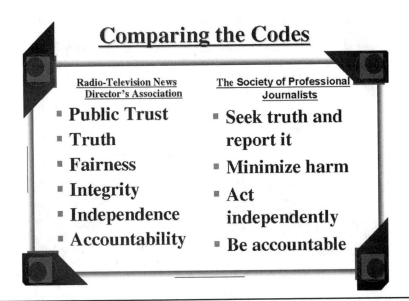

Comparing the Codes

Radio-Television News Director's Association	The Society of Professional Journalists
▪ **Public Trust**	▪ **Seek truth and report it**
▪ **Truth**	
▪ **Fairness**	▪ **Minimize harm**
▪ **Integrity**	▪ **Act independently**
▪ **Independence**	
▪ **Accountability**	▪ **Be accountable**

Creating Your Code

Boiling down the details of the two codes into core values identified by topic headlines helps you identify key areas that should become part of a producer's ethical toolbox. The final and most important step is personally connecting these professional codes to your own actions and attitudes as a producer. Back to the light metaphor espoused by Scripps-Howard Broadcasting and taught at many journalism schools. If you do not internalize these ideas then the deadline pressures will ultimately cloud the rays of your own ethics. Take it from us, you don't want to be someone who responds haphazardly as each ethical dilemma confronts you.

You need a personal code of ethics. It sets you apart as a producer. And it isn't that hard to create. No doubt the RTNDA ethics code and the other codes work well as guides. But this personal code is something more. In fact the elements of the code probably already exist in your mind, but likely you have never taken the time to write them down in a formal way.

Inside each of us is not only a genetic code but also a complex moral system. On the next page, Roots of Your Personal Code, shows the types of influences that have already forged many of the elements of your personal ethics code. For example, as a child you learned various rules of right and wrong in the house you grew up in, the elementary school you attended, and in a church, temple, or mosque if regular worship was a part of your family's belief system. All of these inward influences made impressions on your heart.

As you grew older higher education offered you alternatives to what those earlier environments may have taught. Now you're in the workplace and you realize that, just like on the playground, not everybody plays fair. As you select journalism for a profession you learn it has standards of conduct.

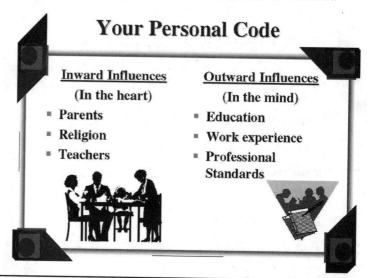

To create your own personal producer's code of ethics do this. First, spend some time thinking about the inward and outward influences that form your own belief system. Write down some memories that can give you clues to the development of your own belief system.

Next, become familiar with the professional codes, especially those of RTNDA and SPJ, so that you can refer back to them for a specific guideline such as the use of hidden cameras, whether to pay sources, or how to handle coverage of a funeral.

Finally, find a way to "anchor" your own code so that it becomes practical and usable. This might be a symbol or picture you place near your word processor. In the Disney movie *Pinocchio,* the character Jiminy Cricket symbolizes decisions guided by a conscience. Your symbol might be a private item you hang from your car mirror. Glancing at it as you get in and out of your car is a way to check in with yourself to see if your decisions in the newsroom that day held up to your own personal standards. Your code might be more public, posted near your desktop. The important thing is that you are reminded about your own ethical commitments so that under ratings pressures or the crunch of deadlines you do not compromise.

Getting Beyond the Gut

Too many journalists rely on what they call "gut feel" in making ethical decisions. But a personal ethics code is not just another name for "going with your gut." You're not reacting but taking action with a series of deliberate steps. A personal code is a holistic expression of your personal value system that is put

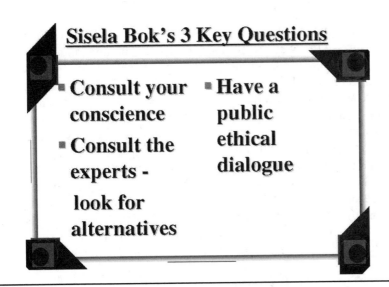

Sisela Bok's 3 Key Questions

- **Consult your conscience**
- **Consult the experts - look for alternatives**
- **Have a public ethical dialogue**

on paper as a code of beliefs. If the word "code" bothers you substitute "creed" or "mission" or "value system."

Your code does not have to be complex. A simple, easy to remember ethical framework created by Harvard sociologist Sisela Bok (1978) has three steps. First, like Pinocchio, consult your conscience. This is akin to the influence of the heart that developed your personal value system.

Next, explore alternatives. Find people—experts—smarter than you, who know about the subject matter. In their book *Media Ethics*, Phillip Patterson and Lee Wilkins (2004) point out that these "experts, by the way, can be those both living or dead—a producer or copywriter you trust or a philosopher you admire" (p. 3). Your news managers should be on the top of the list of these experts to consult.

Finally, no matter what decision you make, tell your audience why. Give the viewer a way to respond. Bok (1978) calls this a "public ethical dialogue." A public dialogue begins right in your own newsroom with the staff and in some instances others at the station so all understand why a particular decision was made. The ethics codes of RTNDA and SPJ admonish journalists to be accountable for their decisions.

Audience-Oriented Ethics

Accountability in ethical decision making establishes a relationship of trust with your audience that brings up the important notion of audience-oriented ethics. As a producer you create newscasts for your audience. For instance, one key demographic in your audience might be a female, age 32, with two children and a full-time job. Not only do you select stories and determine lineups based on the dimensions of this key viewer—who we'll call Mabel—but you consider her in making ethical choices. Will this video offend Mabel? Will this copy interfere with the parenting of her children if she is not ready to explain what oral sex is?

Just make sure you find the balance so that you're not making a decision for one "target demo" to the exclusion of the rest of your potential audience.

Audience-oriented ethics is not pandering to the base desires of viewers in order to win ratings—like when in November 2004 Cleveland television station WOIO-TV aired a story that had female anchor Sharon Reed stripping for an artist's nude group photo shot ("Cleveland TV Anchor," 2004). The station claimed the story had merit because it explored the experience of posing nude in a group photo for a famous artist. If that was true, why did the station shoot the story during the summer, but wait to put it on air until November ratings?

Instead, audience-oriented ethics places the viewer at the center of a triangle. Three sides push on this equilateral triangle to keep news coverage for the viewer in ethical balance. On one side are professional codes such as those of RTNDA. Your own personal code makes up the second side of the triangle, while the third side of the triangle represents your station's policies.

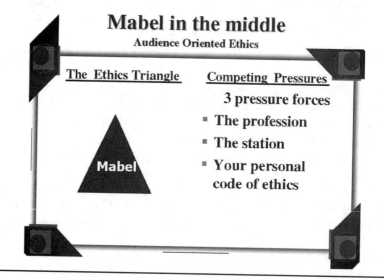

Mabel in the middle
Audience Oriented Ethics

The Ethics Triangle

Mabel

Competing Pressures

3 pressure forces

- **The profession**
- **The station**
- **Your personal code of ethics**

Sometimes a station's actions might conflict with the professional codes or your own personal guidelines. Many staff members in the Cleveland newsroom, for example, objected to the anchor exposing herself in the ratings story. If that happens, the ethics triangle bends out of shape and becomes lopsided, with the viewer in the middle feeling the discomfort!

You will most likely face your toughest ethical challenges during ratings periods. Remember, your own code, combined with those of the profession you honor and trust, make up only two sides of the triangle. The station or network you work for is the third side. For it to be a perfectly equal triangle—to serve the audience best (Mabel in the middle)—requires all three sides to be congruent. If the station gets "out of line" you may face your toughest challenge: Compromise your own personal code and say nothing or stand up for the professional standards to which you aspire.

The point to remember here is the viewer, Mabel, places trust in you as a news producer to design newscasts to a high ethical standard. You do this in a humble, unassuming way. Unlike anchors and reporters, producers have no daily contact with the audience. The viewer has no idea who you are. The only one recognizing your name in the credits that whiz by at the end of the newscast is your grandmother! Although your name and face may not be recognized, your influence will be felt. A keen awareness of the professional codes, spending time creating your own personal code, consulting with others from experts to fellow staff members, and finally communicating the "why" of an ethical decision will cure a producer's "professional loneliness" and help you sleep soundly at night.

Ethical Duty and the Myth of Objectivity

Whether you write them down or not, some fundamental principles should be part of your personal ethics code, including the traditional journalistic duties to be fair, balanced, and accurate. A producer's ethical duty includes striving with all your heart, mind, and might to be a fair and balanced journalist. That's the Murrow tradition and that's the Cronkite legacy.

Producer Jim Dove reviews copy with Walter Cronkite who, at age 89, still is a very active broadcast journalist.

A producer should also achieve accuracy in her or his written headlines, teases, and stories. Sometimes a fourth concept—objectivity—is tossed into the mix of good ethical journalism. But objectivity is a myth. We all come from diverse backgrounds bringing our own personal baggage to a story. Pure journalistic objectivity is a virtual impossibility. An example: If you grew up in a home where your parents were diehard environmentalists, card carrying members of the Sierra Club, and you have a lifetime of childhood memories celebrating Earth Day each Spring, it may be tough for you to see the side of big business when it comes to an environmental story. Or, if you were raised in a religious faith that opposes abortion, you must recognize there might be an internal built-in bias when it comes to producing stories about the Pro-Life movement.

There is nothing wrong with a news producer favoring the environment or being active in a religious faith. The challenge comes when you bring your personal perspective into the news decision-making process of the newsroom. Although you may *say* you leave your identity at the newsroom door, that never actually happens, nor should it. A newsroom should be a diverse place filled with journalists sharing a multiplicity of ideas and experiences, ideally mirroring your audience.

A quality newsroom is set up with a series of ethical checks and balances. A staff with diverse backgrounds, reflecting a rainbow of reasoning and perspectives, allows truth to flow through the ethical decision-making process. As a producer it is critical that you promote discussion among newsroom coworkers, especially those who may not be as vocal when a tough call comes up. You can do this by asking their opinion. Decide whether this is better in a group discussion at a rundown meeting or later one on one in the quiet of an editing booth.

Too often tough calls about ethics and the stories that impact the staff the most are processed in silence. Your audience is not much different. Individual viewers may suffer in silence, taking offense at the video used or an individual story selected. So, testing how to handle a sensitive story with the staff is the first line of defense before a tough ethical choice hits the broadcast and the frontlines of the viewer's living room.

If you are in a situation when you do have to go it alone on a story or issue that touches on a personal bias—just make sure you acknowledge your bias and then go the extra mile to compensate for it. Burying your bias under a claim of objectivity that doesn't really exist can lead to an unwitting and unfortunate lack of balance and fairness on a very sensitive story.

Ethical decisions sometimes have to be made quickly in the control room during a newscast (WHIO-TV, Dayton).

When to Warn the Viewers

Certain stories require a verbal warning to the viewer about their contents before they're broadcast. These can involve video of graphic crime scenes, "spot news" accident video, especially shots of blood and carnage, or stories requiring extra sensitivity because of the subject matter, such as pedophilia.

If you're producing an early afternoon or evening newscast special care should be taken because of who might be watching—young children, for example—and what they might be doing—such as eating dinner—while watching. However, do not assume that just because you're the late news producer the standards of ethical acceptability drop. Your audience is made up of people with a variety of values. When a story may stretch the limits of your community's standards it is wise to give a warning.

Sample Warnings.   "In our next story there will be video that some viewers might find disturbing. Key evidence in the prosecution's case at the Bundy murder trial was presented today including gruesome crime scene pictures." Note there are two sentences that give ample time for a concerned parent to protect a young child. Or, "The contents of the following story about pedophilia might not be appropriate for a youngster to hear."

Think carefully of how you tease such stories. You may want to give the warning prior to a break. Yes, you run the risk of the audience tuning out in the short term, but the viewers' overall impression of the newscast and its high ethical standards will pay off in the long term. Community image often translates into a favorable reputation of the news department. Respect for your viewers and their sense of taste and decency, although it might differ from you own, not only earns reputations but also rating points!

Crime Coverage and Family Sensitive News

Without a doubt many of your toughest ethical issues will center around crime coverage. Crime continues to be a dominant type of story as research by the Project for Excellence in Journalism (2004) shows. In the *State of the News Media 2004,* the Project noted of crime coverage on local TV:

> The idea that it has to "bleed to lead" is an oversimplification. Crime was the most popular topic—two to one over any other—but it only accounted for 24% of the stories. Add in accidents, catastrophes, fires and bizarre incidents and it still adds up to only about a third of the stories. However, when looking at lead stories, 61% were about crime or relatively routine fires and accidents. (pp. 21–22)

With its often startling pictures and sordid details crime news is easy prey for a producer looking for a hot story on a dull night. Too much crime and violence coverage in local television news spawned a particular format change on some local station newscasts in the early 1990s. The trend labeled "family sensitive" news was born in January 1994, the brainchild of John Lansing, news director of WCCO-TV (Minneapolis). Encouraging it was Lansing's news consultant, Ed

Bewely, of Audience Research and Development (AR&D, Dallas). Lansing's news staff conducted 100 community focus groups and round tables and then decided to promote WCCO's 5 p.m. newscast as family sensitive.

The movement's intent was to clean up the depiction of crime coverage in newscasts aired during the dinner hour. Nationwide media attention followed. The *New York Times* (Meisler, 1994, p. D20) reported Lansing's finding that "a distinct majority responded that the news was too violent" and the *Los Angeles Times* (Braun, 1994, p. A1) quoted Lansing as saying that "people are just tired of being afraid and tired of what we've been selling them." As many as 15 stations across the country, many of them clients of AR&D, copied Lansing's concept. AR&D's Ed Bewely became a spokesman for the movement defending it on "Nightline." As the trend spread, the family sensitive newscast caught the attention of NBC Network News which assigned their then national correspondent and now "Nightly News" anchor Brian Williams to cover the story (see accompanying box, "Family Sensitive News").

Family Sensitive News
Package Script NBC News
Correspondent Brian Williams

Williams: But the pictures don't seem to stop. Night after night television's news viewers are bombarded, some would say assaulted, by stories and images of violence. So stations in a dozen cities are now trying something new.

NatSot of station promotion: Less reports on violent crime, more positive news coverage … a newscast tailored for the whole family to watch together …

Williams: In Charlotte, Miami, and Minneapolis–St. Paul and other cities there is an experiment underway in family sensitive, early evening newscasts. Less crime, no blood, no bodies; more good news at the dinner hour. Its architects say what they were putting on the air was getting out of hand.

Sound Bite: Bob Young, former News Director in Charlotte, North Carolina at WCNC: Our decision to go in a more family sensitive direction sprung from that feeling that there was too much of a focus on violence on local television.

Williams: (Stand up) It is a fast growing trend in local television news, but one that strikes some critics as a public relations ploy by some TV stations. Others say don't question the motives. What is important is that the viewers will be better off.

Sound Bite: Newspaper critic Marc Günter: If you call public relations listening to the public and then trying to respond, ok, it's public relations. But that is not necessarily a bad thing.

NatSot from news promotion: Terror strikes the tracks again …

Brian Williams, NBC News

> **Williams:**   The temptation to hype is just too much for some stations in a business where advertising dollars are shrinking. But the biggest fear about family sensitive TV is the question that decides what doesn't belong on the air?
>
> **Sound Bite: Marc Günter, newspaper critic:**   When Robert Kennedy was killed the story was encapsulated in the picture of him lying on the floor after the shooting. That was the story. I suppose a family sensitive station would not put that on the air, and they would be missing the story.
>
> **Williams:**   If less of a story becomes profitable we will see more family sensitive news at 11.

Within two months critics accused Lansing's movement of "sanitizing the news." One outspoken critic, Terry Heaton, news director of WRIC-TV (Richmond), called the concept a "marketing ploy." In an editorial for *Electronic Media* Heaton wrote, "In stating publicly that we are part of the problem of violence in our culture, we are opening the door to a journalist's most dreaded nightmare, legal government limitations on press freedom" (Heaton, 1994, p. 8). Others raised additional concerns over the movement, including then RTNDA President David Barlett who observed, "if we're not going to cover the crime story—five people got murdered in the ghetto, because we're family sensitive—we're not going to report reality."

The family sensitive movement did not catch on. Eleven months and three ratings books after its conception, eight of the stations adopting it sustained drops in their family sensitive newscast ratings. Within 18 months nearly all the stations dropped the idea.

Some critics said the stations were not truly committed to producing news that met the value standards of their audience. Valerie Hyman, then Director of Broadcast Programs for the Poynter Institute for Media Studies, defended Lansing and the original idea:

> Private consulting companies instantly jumped on "family sensitive" and made it into a gimmick which they are spreading to clients. Now, without the months of meetings and preparations that WCCO invested in its new approach, stations across the country are making a few changes … calling their newscasts "family sensitive," perhaps devoting no more thought to the new approach then they devoted to the old. No wonder cynics are having a field day. (Hyman, 1994)

Coverage Guidelines

Although it failed, the family sensitive newscast movement did serve as a wake-up call to many local stations and news consultants that the audience had their own set of ethical standards that couldn't be ignored. An example of one local station answering that call was KVUE (Austin). For a few years after the family sensitive newscast movement KVUE had a crime coverage policy they promoted to their viewers. This is an example of Bok's (1978) public ethical dia-

WCNC-TV (Charlotte) Reporter Tiffani Helberg and Videographer Reed Bennett cover crime from an issue perspective—a protest over sentencing in child abuse cases.

logue. KVUE explained to the audience what ethical policies the station would follow in covering crime and the criteria for including a crime story in their newscast. KVUE came up with five principles to follow when covering crime as listed in the accompanying box, "KVUE Listens to You on Crime."

A second legacy of the family sensitive newscast movement is seen at the professional organization level. RTNDA modified the ethics code in part to reflect concerns over crime coverage, especially in the wake of the sensationalism surrounding the O. J. Simpson case. More recently, in the new age of terrorism and the ethical issues surrounding coverage of 9/11 victims jumping to their deaths out of the World Trade Center windows, RTNDA's educational foundation, RTNDF, issued guidelines on handling graphic images. This is just one of many sets of coverage guidelines issued by the RTNDF, some of which are listed in the box, "Coverage Guidelines Issued by RTNDA/RTNDF." This list indicates the wide variety of topics, often spurred by breaking news events, that need ethical clarification of how coverage is handled.

KVUE Listens to You on Crime

Guidelines
- Immediate Threat
- Threat to Children
- Take Action
- Significant Impact
- Crime Prevention Efforts.

Coverage Guidelines Issued by RTNDA/RTNDF

- Graphic Images
- Guidelines and Questions to Ask When Covering Funerals
- File Tape Guidelines
- Guidelines for On-Air Charitable Solicitations
- Balancing Business Pressures and Journalism Values
- Respecting Privacy
- Hidden Cameras/Deception
- Evaluating Sources
- Using Confidential Sources
- Racial Identification
- Covering a Hostage Situation
- Live Coverage
- Interviewing Juveniles
- Identifying Juveniles
- School Bomb Threats
- Telephone Callers
- Digital Manipulation
- Suicide Coverage

All RTNDA/RTNDF Guidelines can be found at: http://www.rtndf.org/ethics/ethicsguidelines.shtml

---

Chapter 4

A Higher Calling, A Professional Producer

As we've said, RTNDA defines broadcast journalism as "a duty, a calling." You need to be keenly aware of the basic duties of ethical journalism: to be fair, balanced, and as objective as possible in an overarching framework of accuracy. But duty is not enough. You must grasp a larger sense of your profession or the higher calling. To do this you must recognize an important part of ethical decision making is a big dose of humility. You don't have all the right answers and the answers you may have may be colored by past experiences. Murrow described journalistic humility with the observation that, just because your voice reaches halfway around the world doesn't mean you are wiser than when it reached only to the end of the bar (see Edwards, 2004, p. 131).

Humility is an important trait that a news producer must have to make careful, ethical decisions. One way to be more humble in your approach is to think of your work as more than just a way to get a paycheck. It's a profession or what some call a life's mission (although we will say more about the danger of being "married to your work" in a later chapter). Cultivating your profession is far more than just looking out for the chance to jump 50 market sizes once your contract is up.

Emotional Trauma
One Experience of a Network Producer

Katie Munley, ABC News, Washington experienced a personal sense of shock and awe watching incoming video feeds from the 2004 Tsunami Disaster. She first wrote a poem remembering how in journalism school they warned her of her "first body bag" story. The poem is followed by her reflections of the experience.

The Day After Christmas

I. My teacher told me about my first body.
His was in Idaho
Mine was in Indonesia
He saw his from a helicopter

II. Someone makes a joke
about not being able to get their Sumatra coffee.

III. The people who live on the islands believe
That evil comes from the ocean
And that good can be found at the top of
The mountain—water that you can drink
And that we all live somewhere in between

The people really exist somewhere in the middle of them.
He had a dark blue shirt, navy and darker
I could not separate the tears
from ocean and sweat
It was all water

IV. The pictures came out at me
similar to the wall that pushed them
to the other side of the world.
It would be dramatic
And perfect if hers
Was the only one I remember ...
Her arms didn't move
The man in navy carried her
Out of the Bay of Bengal.
The arms were fuller: heavy and immobile with water
Being warmed by the sun
But she was cold.

V. There are certain kinds of baby dolls
That have arms that just stick straight out—
That's what I first thought about when I saw
This was no doll
This was someone's baby
Maybe their first, too.

—Katie Munley

The people who live on the islands of Indonesia believe that evil comes from the ocean and that good exists at the top of the mountain (where the rainwater flows down that is ok to drink). They believe they live in between the forces of good and evil. That reflection occurred to me a few days after the tsunami hit south Asia.

On the day after Christmas of 2004, I was working in Playback in the Washington Bureau for ABC News. It was my responsibility to bring in video of the tsunami into the bureau. In Playback it is our responsibility to log what we see. The pictures that day were unlike any others that I had ever seen, in an unruly way.

When I saw the picture of one young girl being carried out of the water by a rescue worker wearing a dark navy blue shirt with letters on the back that I could not read, but I think I understood, I saw she was really more like a baby. The body-count at that point was around 8,000 people. People, said the AP, not children.

Her arms were full: heavy and immobile with water. Her face and stomach were warmed by the sun, but she was already cold. I thought about this one baby doll that I had as a child. It was the kind where the arms just stuck straight out. This wasn't a doll, this was someone's baby; she had a name. That picture really stood out the most of any, because I, myself, once was a 3- or 4-year-old girl, and I too had played in the water.

When I first heard about the Indonesian island natives believing that evil came from the ocean I thought, that's poetic, if anything. At the time, I could not begin to grasp what they, the Indonesians, meant by evil. I think in the Western world we think of evil as being a conscious decision by a person, or group of people. Out of that evil there is the hope that someone can be brought to justice. These Islanders dealt with evil on a different scale. For the people who live on those islands, there was no justice for this horror, not even a warning system.

Seeing the rows of bodies when they still had the blankets just covering them up to their shoulders, so people could identify their loved ones, really caused me to stop breathing and just type, because there was no oxygen in the stillness of those images.

It seems almost unnatural the way technology enables you to keep a tidal wave at an arm's length. You can just put the pictures on neat 60-minute beta tapes, and catalog the despair of fresh mourners, to make your life easier in accessing the pictures again later. It's easy for someone in journalism to use this technology as a sort of barrier to protect your reality from someone else's. By finding a way of describing it in terms of wide shot, medium shot or marking your ins and your outs.

For me, it's important that I understand what I'm seeing, that I don't ever just think of what I'm working on as another news story. These are real people, and they always are real people. They are not just characters we draw up to take home a paycheck. For their experience, there is no total running time. There is no outcue.

The DART Center for Journalism and Trauma is a resource to help you deal with the stress of difficult stories. www.dartcenter.org

Katie Munley, ABC News

Becoming a true "professional" means recognizing the important role journalism plays in the health of a democracy. Professional work becomes a higher, noble calling by fully recognizing the power of television. Perhaps Murrow's observation to the RTNDA convention in 1958 explains it best. "This instrument can teach, it can illuminate, and yes it can inspire. But it can do so only to the ex-

Producers at WDTN-TV (Dayton) deciding which stories from the assignment daybook will go into their newscasts.

tent that humans are determined to use it to those ends. Otherwise it is nothing but wires and lights in a box" (Edwards, 2004, p. 135).

Murrow wasn't just talking about the audience who watches your newscast but you, the producer, who decides what goes into the box—the teaching instrument—each night.

The best journalists have a sense of this professional, higher calling. In a way, like Murrow said, journalism is a clarion call to teach. Whether it is a geography lesson teaching the location of Falluja, Iraq, or an economics lesson as you work with the graphics department to explain the rising trade deficit, you fulfill a calling by producing information in a meaningful way.

Some consultants will dismiss this way of thinking and try to pound into your head you are there to inform, not to teach. By teaching we don't mean a dull college lecture, but an informative graphic, video, and sound driven story of understanding. Your students—the audience—are sophisticated enough to recognize the difference between razzle dazzle and presenting a story in a way that informs and educates. Think of the examples used during the Iraq War coverage in which large maps helped teach an audience weak in the subject of Middle East geography. Across the Missouri School of Journalism's archway entrance is this stone chiseled quote, "The schoolmasters of the people." It may seem a little noble and erudite but it is true—producers are teachers.

Get Involved in Ethics

If personal credibility is to be maintained you likely will face a tough ethical choice more than once in your career. Remember the value of time. Just as you strive not to make an ethical decision in haste, likewise do not make a career move carelessly. Weigh the options and determine if the issue is serious enough to merit a discussion with the news director or general manager or compels you to turn in your resignation notice. The last option is rare, but you should know where you draw the line and be prepared to take the most extreme step if someone demands you cross it. How do you make sure that doesn't happen?

Help build a culture of ethical thinking. Do not stay silent in your newsroom. Look for allies. Students focused on a producing career can be leaders in their campus RTNDA chapters. Producers working in their first or final positions can become active in the RTNDA national organization as well as state broadcast organizations, local press clubs, or SPJ chapters. Join an organization and deduct the professional dues on your income tax. Attend a regional or national ethics workshop at The Poynter Institute.

The Poynter Institute for Media Studies

Fast Facts

Who? The Poynter Institute is a school for journalists, future journalists, and teachers of journalists.

What? Seminars on ethical issues, news management, and a variety of journalism skills are held at the Poynter campus along with weekend workshops around the country.

Where? St. Petersburg, Florida.

When? Seminars held throughout the year. Check the web site: www.poynter.org

Why? To keep your ethical compass pointed in the right direction and the professionalism alive in your work.

How? Contact Poynter: 01 Third Street South, St. Petersburg, FL 33701. Phone: 888–769–6837.

Ask your boss if the station has training money to send you to an RTNDA national convention or regional workshop. Offer to bring back what you've learned into a staff meeting. Attend regional workshops offered by NPPA. Remember that other staff members like photographers and tape editors, as well as reporters and anchors, are keenly interested in ethical issues. Often they are the ones truly on the frontlines of ethical decision making. Be ready to assist fellow journalists tackling their own ethical dilemmas with guidelines from the professional organizations or insights from your own personal code. Above all listen.

Ethics is not just a stuffy word conjuring up endless debates. Likewise it should not be a lonely struggle in which you feel the whole burden of an ethical dilemma is on your shoulders. Ethics is a lamppost that lights the way. Learn to use and bask in this light. A wise journalist knows, when dark decision making threatens, share the struggle with others—coworkers, viewers, and family and friends away from the news business—and truly make it light. Ethics is a vital part of the profession because it leads to the noblest calling; a steward of credibility. Ethical news work, sometimes done from down deep in your soul, can bring the most satisfaction to your professional, producer life.

Sources

Announcing the 2005 Payne Awards for Ethics in Journalism. (2005). Retrieved from University of Oregon School of Journalism and Communication Web site http://payneawards.uoregon.edu/news2005.html.

Bok, S. (1978). *Lying: Moral choice in public and private life.* New York: Random House.

Braun, S. (1994, November 2). Tuning out the hype and gore. *Los Angeles Times,* A1.

Cleveland TV anchor appears nude for story about art. (2004, November 11). *USA Today.* Available at www.usatoday.com/news/offbeat/2004-11-17-nude-news_x.htm.

Edwards, R. (2004). *Edward R. Murrow and the birth of broadcast journalism.* New York: Wiley.

Heaton, T. (1994, July 19). "Family sensitive" news debate: A wake-up call. *Electronic Media,* 8.

Hyman, V. (1994). *Commentary.* St. Petersburg, FL: The Poynter Institute.

Meisler, A. (1994, December 14). Blunting TV news' sharp edges. *New York Times,* D20.

Patterson, P., & Wilkins, L. (2004). *Media ethics: Issues and cases* (5th ed.). New York: McGraw Hill.

Project for Excellence in Journalism. (2004). *State of the News Media 2004.* Retrieved from http://www.stateofthemedia.com/2004.

DEADLINES, DATELINES, AND DECISION MAKING

"I love deadlines. I like the whooshing sound they make as they fly by."
Douglas Adams, English humorist and science fiction novelist (1952–2001)

"If a reporter calls in sick, sometimes, they don't replace him. If the news director is out, they don't replace him. But if the producer calls in sick, you'd better replace him; otherwise, you won't have a newscast. The producer is the focal point; he's the strength."

Gerald Ruben, 40 year veteran of the producer wars
(*Communicator*, March 2004)

Producing a TV newscast is part art and part science—first let's examine the science. There are guiding procedures and proven formats, and you have to multitask a variety of activities under the unforgiving eye of your biggest enemy—the clock. To truly succeed you must master a keen sense of timing over both the newscast and your workday. In this chapter we'll cover timing, the selection and management of stories, determining the lead (your most critical daily decision), and the communication skills needed to accomplish it all.

Since many journalists are math challenged and often scientifically inept, we will make it easy for you to learn the science of producing by using a cooking analogy. We'll add master chef to the list of jobs—journalist, drill sergeant, cheerleader, peacemaker, maestro, strategic planner, contortionist, poet, huckster, and nitpicker—that comprise the ultimate role of the TV news producer already outlined in chapter 3.

A TV news producer master chef is a kitchen scientist who follows a winning ratings recipe, blending ingredients of factual hard items with health and consumer "news you can use," as well as the occasional fluffy soft feature stories. She also coordinates segment producers in charge of investigative franchises, sports, and weather—the wine steward, salad, and dessert cooks if you will—all in the pressure cooker of the TV newsroom that continues to steam as the clock ticks toward the inevitable boiling point, air time.

To concoct both a visual and flavorful informational feast the TV news master chef adds her own distinctive style and flair to the scientific methods of preparation. In the next chapter you'll see how producing is not only an exact science but also a loose, wild art form urging you to think outside the box. The science and art of producing combine to compose the perfect harmony of words, images, and sound, fresh and different, but above all, relevant. What it boils down to is that no viewer will watch boring news just as nobody hungry for a delicious meal wants something unappealing. The TV news producer master chef must stay focused not only on the process, as energizing as it is, but also the end product, ultimately serving up the most tasteful banquet for the audience. And the audience is one tough customer!

To keep the customer satisfied producers must serve up the choicest newscast comprised of the best ingredients created into a truly visual feast.

The Producers' Essential Utensils

A good producer, like a master chef, knows how to utilize the newsroom software tools available to the news staff:

- Become familiar with a wide range of **computer databases.** Access to city, police, and judicial public records enables you to break important stories 24/7.

- Rainbow your **Rolodex** of news sources to include lots of people of color in a variety of areas: a black pediatrician, a Latino principal, an Asian police officer.

- Know your **Graphics equipment**—what it can do and how long it takes. Brainstorm ideas with your graphic artist and/or technical director and give them map photocopies as early in the day as possible.

Adapted from Valarie Hyman tips in "The Producer's Challenge" written for The Poynter Institute of Media Studies.

The Rundown Recipe

Producers, even those who work in the same shop and use the same story ingredients, come up with distinct flavors to their newscasts. But they all begin with the same recipe. This is called a **rundown.** Some shops call it a lineup. In his book *Air Words,* Jon Hewitt (1996) describes it as "the story order for a newscast. Also called the '*stack*,' the *format*, or the *lineup*" (p. 19). Part of learning the science of producing is understanding how the rundown works. It not only helps you keep track of everything from the page numbers to the various elements associated with each story—such as the writer, story length, and graphics—but also it allows all of the other team members to see and work from the same recipe. The art of producing, covered in the next chapter, shows how you can vary the traditional format of your newscasts just like Wolfgang Puck starts with a recipe and then creatively modifies it. However, developing a style of your own takes practice and mastery of several basic skills.

The rundown is always the central controlling document so that every team member from the on-air anchor to the newscast director to those in master control running the tapes knows what is supposed to happen when. If the rundown is complete and well done, nearly everyone contributing to the newscast, except the anchors, could do their jobs with just that rundown, never needing scripts. It is your key communication tool to share your vision of the newscast with everyone else who works on your show, and everything that you want to see on the air should be indicated somewhere on your rundown.

WDTN-TV (Dayton) Video Engineer Don Jones uses the rundown to note live shots and tapes in the newscast.

Numbers in a cooking recipe indicate important information about amounts of ingredients and so on. In the newscast rundown the numbers are times, and timing is everything! In fact timing is one of the most critical parts of the science of producing—both timing your newscast and time management of your workday.

The Clock and the Computer

The clock drives every decision a producer makes including the calculations connected to timing out your newscast. When computers replaced typewriters in the newsrooms of the early 1980s writing processes went through a revolution-

A 5 p.m. news rundown example.

ary change. Today a producer can simply change a word or sentence without the hassle of retyping a multiple-carbon paper script. Producing has warped into hyper drive, partially because the computerized rundown now allows for split second decisions and incredible flexibility. This allows for fast paced *Breaking News* formats with "live shot" driven stories that can be brought back multiple times within a newscast.

Before computers, **backtiming** the broadcast was a fundamental skill to master. Adding a story to the rundown late in the afternoon or even during a live newscast forced you to recalculate the impact this would have on the overall show timing—suddenly shrinking the weather segment or feeling the wrath of the sports anchor when you had to cut his segment. Producers in the old days went through lots of erasers making changes to paper rundowns and retiming the show by hand every time a change was made.

Newsroom software systems automatically adjust the timing of the individual news stories, such as an anchor reader or a reporter package (even compensating for different reading rates), and instantly show on the screen whether the newscast is "under," meaning not enough time to fill the "news hole," or "over," indicating it is time to cut something. The systems also make it painless to instantly change a rundown—deleting and adding stories, moving stories, or even manipulating entire blocks of stories can be done with the click of a mouse. The computer software system does it all.

Many newsroom software systems automate other technical functions of the newscast such as automatically loading some graphics, putting video on the air, and even rolling commercial breaks. As the production processes of television become more automated, even more production elements of your newscast could be run through your newsroom software and your computer rundown.

Key Ingredients in Newsroom Software Programs

We asked Professor Ken Fischer, who has taught broadcast journalism at The University of Florida, Ohio University, Southern Illinois Carbondale, and Central Florida University, to identify the key ingredients in any good television newsroom software program. Ken's list is below.

- Script-writing tools.
- Show rundown
- Prompting capability.
- Archiving.
- Wire access.
- Assignment desk functions.
- Archive and wire word search.
- Interface with automation systems (closed captioning, CG control, etc.)

Newsroom Software Quick Links

AP ENPS	enps.com
NEWSKING (Comprompter)	comprompter.com
EZ NEWS	eznews.com
AVID iNews	avid.com/products/inews/index.asp
BURLI	burli.com

Chapter 5

Newscast rundown on computer.

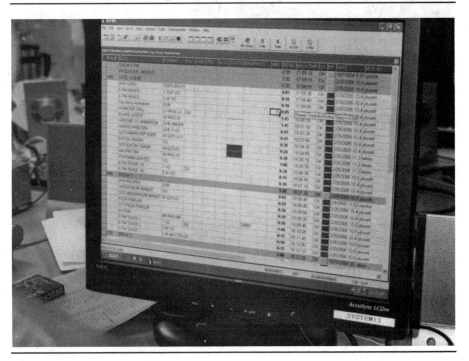

Learn your newsroom software system as quickly as possible. A good scientific news producer will take the time to read the manuals and take advantage of any training offered. It's the fastest way to master the clock and computer world of your newsroom. Then customize the desktop to fit your own style.

But learning the timing functions of producing is not just a matter of key stroking your computer. Planning out your day or time management to meet the necessary deadlines is critical. Back to our cooking analogy—if you don't calculate exactly how long it takes to unthaw the meat or peel the potatoes you won't have a clue how much total time you'll need to prepare a seven-course meal and serve it on time!

Backtiming the Day—Time Management of Datelines and Deadlines

"A producer's day is all about deadlines," observes Katie Brown, who has produced in Kansas City and Des Moines, Iowa. "Knowing when to turn in graphics requests, when to get stories written, when to print the news scripts." The quick advice from Chris Schlemon, who works in Washington, DC for Britain's global news organization ITN, is "get in early, get organized." Schlemon, whose bureau position requires daily tape editing of the network correspondents packages, notes, "it takes a good video tape editor usually about one hour per minute of package editing time, so a 3-minute package could take three hours of editing. So backtime from there and get your reporters, interns, (photographers, etc.), organized and get going." Schlemon has the luxury at the network level to craft a

Chris Schlemon, ITN, at a political convention.

news package over a period of two to three hours. That is never the case in local news except perhaps for special projects.

We asked a variety of producers in a cross section of newsrooms for their tips on how to manage the workload they face each day. Katie Brown is now the 10 p.m. producer for the Edward R. Murrow award winning KCCI-TV (Des Moines), and promotes staying ahead of the game. "It's always best to get things done early—then change them around in the event of breaking news. If you procrastinate, and breaking news happens, you could be in over your head." Producing in a large market like Phoenix, Arizona, Michelle Frey learned how to backtime her morning routine to give her plenty of breathing space to respond to changes.

> If my newscast started at 11 a.m., I wanted to be finished with everything by 10 a.m. That left me enough time to change the rundown if breaking news occurred. It also gave plenty of time for PAs (production assistants) to print scripts, for the anchors to get them ahead of time, and the tape editors to have more than enough time to complete the editing process for voice over stories.

Backtiming the day means getting organized by mapping out a time management plan so that everything flows smoothly. It begins when you first wake up.

Jump Starting the Day

Many producers speak of how their day actually starts before they even enter the newsroom—waking up to a radio newscast or watching a network morning broadcast while eating breakfast and getting ready for work. For "producer commuters" in large metropolitan areas, reading the local papers during the ride helps them jump start their work day. An important routine for a producer to develop is creating and sticking to a well-balanced **media diet.** The journalism profession necessitates your being current on all the news—that means not just hard news, but sports, weather, pop culture and entertainment, and so on. Having a well-balanced media diet ensures that.

How do you start a well-balanced media diet? It's just like going to Weight Watchers, where you start a new program, and the counselor asks you to track your eating habits for a week. Your media diet starts the same way. Pay attention to what you listen to, read, and watch.

Everybody's diet will be different. This adds diversity and broadens the collective newsroom knowledge when you hold story conferences with reporters and select which items will go into your broadcast. Matthew Felling, the director for the Center for Media and Public Affairs (www.cmpa.com) argues that the protein for your media diet comes from print. Felling discussed the importance of print news with a *Portland Oregonian* newspaper ombudsman and noted that "newspapers are the protein in news diets." If print is protein does that make television news the carbs? Critics of TV news would argue yes and urge everybody to go on a low-carb diet. We, of course, disagree pointing out the unique power that television news has to provide the most compelling array of visual images and natural sounds that transport the viewer to the scene, the event, the action in a way no print article ever can.

The important thing to remember about your media diet is variety. But don't feel guilty if you can't make it through everything every day. The rest of the newsroom will bring into the editorial discussion meetings their own digested knowledge of story ideas and angles fresh from their own diets. A wide variety of reading makes for a diverse newsroom. Hopefully, someone in your shop will read and watch Hispanic news or BET and read magazines like *Vibe* or *Ebony*. Check with the local library to gauge what newspapers and magazines are accessed the most in your community. Stretch your own taste buds and subscribe to a magazine out of your comfort zone.

A Sample Media Diet

Just like your personal trainer or dietician suggests a well-rounded food intake, so we suggest you carefully think through a well-balanced media diet. The list below is just a sample diet. Design your own. Mix it up. But stay informationally healthy—it is vital if you're going to keep your viewers informed. If you're producing the 10 p.m. news or the morning show adjust accordingly!

Daily Routine

Morning Before Work
- Wake-up to NPR's "Morning Edition" listening through a news block at the top or bottom of the hour.

While You Dress and Eat Breakfast
- Watch through the first commercial break of a broadcast or cable network morning show. This not only gives you the headlines but some in-depth perspective on the day's big stories.
- Glance at a local newspaper—you can read it fully once at work. Note the letters to the editor. They give you a good feel for the audience's attitudes and sometimes provide great story leads for your reporters.
- Quickly check web pages of a national newspaper like the *New York Times or Washington Post* and your competition across town on television. Check for stories your newsroom missed. Sites like BBC.com provide a different slant on international news not covered by the American television morning news magazine programs.

At Work
- Besides the constant monitoring of wires, network video feeds, and web sites like CNN and MSNBC also find time to read snatches of print journalism.
- Reading for depth and understanding is limited at work. Save the perspectives for nighttime absorption. But do read the newspapers at work; not only the local newspaper but *USA Today*. Pay attention to visuals and headlines, which can give you jump starts for your teasing and for the pictures people will be talking about.

After Work
- On the drive home listen to a local all news radio station and/or scan the hot music stations to stay current on entertainment trends (don't forget music styles that you may hate but your audience loves).
- Read through a national newspaper for depth and perspective.

- Watch PBS's "The News Hour with Jim Lehrer," CNN's "Newsnight," or ABC's "Nightline" to receive analysis on the headline stories.
- View the "Daily Show" or another late night comedy (Leno or Letterman) to catch the pulse of what America's laughing about.

Weekly Basis

- Read one news magazine—*Time, Newsweek,* or *U.S. News & World Report.* Or for a real change try Britain's *The Economist* (about far more than financial matters it has one of the best global news digests published).
- Read a national Sunday newspaper with its opinion and perspective pages. The *New York Times* or *Washington Post* or even the *Wall Street Journal* weekend edition would be good picks. If you live on the East Coast try to see a West Coast paper (even on line) weekly.
- Read fiction. The latest Tom Clancy or Annie Proulx novel. Her advice "My feeling is that the best way to learn how to write is to read—widely, deeply, omnivorously." (www.Annieproulx.com) Short stories from *The New Yorker* work well. The key here—as a wordsmith—read, read, read!

Chapter 5

Don't Binge on Blogs

As the new "fast food" in your media diet, blogs can be fascinating and an easy way to digest information (by letting someone else select for you), but relying too much on them can be detrimental to your informational health. Steve Outing of The Poynter Institute interviewed a public relations executive, Steve Rubel, who tried a "blog only media diet." Outing quotes Rubel as saying he received the basics "but not the real meat" of the week's news. After a weeklong blog only media diet Rubel offered these tips:

- Many blogs lag a day behind discussing news stories.
- Blog aggregation sites like Blogdex, Technorati, Memeorandum, Daypop, Popdex, Blogsnow—link to the most popular news stories of the day as ranked by the number of bloggers who link to the stories.
- General news headlines came from such blogs as Drudge Report (and Drudge Retort) and Instapundit.
- Political blogs, like Electablog and Political Wire.
- Entertainment blog Defamer turned out to be the best.
- For sports, Rubel found SportsBlog to be excellent, as well as Baseball Musings, Notes From a Basketball Junkie, and ThePostGame.
- Business news blogs turned out to be slightly less useful. Tech headlines come from Gizmodo.

Steve Outing (2004), *The Blog-Only News Diet.* Retrieved from Poynteronline at http://www.poynter.org/content/content_view.asp?id=66794

Read not just for content and story ideas but pay attention to the way magazines are formatted and how they tease and promote their stories on the cover and inside. Develop a voracious appetite for written news in good newspapers and informative magazines. Some like *The New Yorker* showcase contemporary fiction writing while journals such as *Foreign Policy* add depth and perspective you'll never get from a diet of news wire reading. Reading rounds out the links to the news constantly at your fingertips in the newsroom via newsroom software hooked into news wires, network video feeds and information sites, and downlinks like ABC's News One, CBS's Newspath, CNN's Newsource, Fox's NewsChannel, and NBC's News Channel.

Add to the written word the power of the spoken word via all news radio. Tune into talk shows like NPR's daily "The Diane Rehm Show" interview program. Pay attention to language and how it sounds. Remember, we are writers for the ear!

Timeliness

We've talked about timing your day and paying attention to your own news diet. While living with and by the clock protects the producer from failure, and having a healthy personal media diet brings confidence to your day, remember,

WHIO-TV (Dayton) Videographer Gar Brown downloads video from CBS's Newspath.

there is a big difference between the clock and the concept of time. Sociologist Michael Schudson observed, "What is most striking in journalists' attitudes toward the use of time is that the timeliness they seek operates not by Greenwich Mean Time but by a cultural clock, a subtle and unspoken understanding among journalists about what is timely and what events are genuinely 'new'" (Schudson, n.d., p. 3).

Knowing the shelf life of a story is critical. When the news is stale the audience turns up their nose. Old, moldy stories cannot be hidden with fresh toppings. To keep news fresh you must get a handle on identifying and selecting the main ingredients of the newscast.

Picking the Freshest Ingredients for Your Newscast

You bring to the newsroom a data bank of stories that you think are interesting and relevant—**local** being the key ingredient. Always keep the viewer's tastes and appetites at the forefront of your mind, but remember to make sure they have a well rounded news diet. The assignment desk and your own team of reporters also will bring in fresh, local stories. Bring in at least two new local stories yourself each day.

Much of the work of picking national and world stories is done for you. Your network affiliate feed channels predetermine what they think will be the big stories of the day and dispatch crews for live shots. You access other top story possibilities from your desktop, tapping into the most experienced overall source of news judgment and often the one with the highest trust factor—the wire service.

Discovering Cupboards of Content

The fundamental source of news on a worldwide basis is the wire service. Before computers wire machines hummed in the corners of newsrooms. Interns or associate producers quickly learned their first newsroom duty was to "rip the wire," or cut up the various stories printing out on reams of teletype paper, and "peg" them on the wall by category—state, regional and national news, sports, the stock market, weather, and so on. Today software systems in your newsroom allow you to collect, organize, and customize stories on every topic. If you produce an afternoon 4 or 5 p.m. newscast with large health blocks, for example, you can have all the medical stories you need sent to a particular file.

Determining the Lead

The most important decision you make as a producer is what story will begin the newscast. Luckily you don't make the decision alone. The lead says to the viewers, this is the biggest news of that day. The debate over whether to "lead local" or with a national or world story depends on two factors: (1) the time of the newscast and (2) the impact of the story. Of course it also depends on your target audience.

Wire Services Worldwide

Although your newsroom probably only subscribes to the AP (Associated Press) wire service be aware of the wide variety of news wires worldwide. Some, like UPI (United Press International) have faded in popularity over time but have played mighty roles in the history of broadcast news. Part of your producer's bank of news knowledge includes knowing these potential story sources. Bookmark their Web sites!

Who	What & When	Where & How to Contact
AP (Associated Press)	1,700 newspapers, in addition to 5,000 TV and radio outlets, use AP's news. Claimed as the world's largest wire service, it was founded in Manhattan by six local newspapers.	http://www.ap.org Headquarters in New York
UPI (United Press International)	Global news agency filing stories in English, Spanish, and Arabic. Walter Cronkite and Helen Thomas among two of its most famous reporters.	http://about.upi.com Unprofitable for many years and hurt by the closing down of afternoon newspapers, UPI had seven owners between 1992 and 2000. Acquired by News World Communications, owner of the Washington Times. UPI's White House correspondent and most famous reporter, Helen Thomas, promptly resigned, complaining about the Times having links to the Unification Church.
Reuters	Operating in 200 cities in 94 countries it delivers financial items and news stories in 19 languages. Almost every major news outlet worldwide subscribes. Reuter's agency built a reputation in Europe for being the first to report scoops from abroad, like the news of Abraham Lincoln's assassination.	http://www.reuters.com Headquarters on London's famous Fleet Street, once home of all the major English language newspapers.
AFP (Agence France Presse)	Oldest wire service in the world, founded in 1835. The third largest service sharing stories worldwide, AFP sends out news in French, English, Arabic, Spanish, German, Portuguese, and Russian.	http://www.afp.com/english/home/ Headquarters in Paris

At the network level, Av Westin (2002), who for a number of years was the executive producer for "ABC Evening News," asked three questions to determine the lead story: Is my world safe, are my family and home safe, and, if so, then what has happened in the world that affects them? Chris Schlemon, of ITN, a global broadcast that always leads with the highest impact story observes, "It seems for the last few years, anything concerning the war on terror has been our lead. So that is pretty much a no brainer." But on days where there is "nothing new" in terrorism, Schlemon believes "whichever story is going to grab the viewer at the top of the show and make them want to watch for at least the next (few) minutes" will be the lead.

The Three "Eyed" Test to Determine the Lead

1. Which story has the most INTEREST to my audience?
2. Which story has the most IMPACT to my audience?
3. Which story has the most EYE CATCHING elements (sound or picture) to my audience?

Adapted from A. Westin (2002), *Best Practices in Broadcast Journalism.*

At local stations, early newscasts such as the 4, 5 or 6 p.m. nearly always lead locally. The audience has heard the national and world headlines on the drive home or will watch them on one of the network's national newscasts or cable news. Producers for early morning or late evening newscasts need to give equal consideration to whether the story originates locally or globally to determine its placement. Just waking up the audience wants to know if anything significant happened overnight at home or abroad. Don't forget when it's 6 a.m. here, people in many other parts of the world—7 to 9 hours ahead—are well into their workday. "Most of the time at local news stations the lead should be a local story," advises

---

The Great Dateline Debate

Do I lead local, national, or global?

Caught in the crossfire between the consultant who says lead "live, local, and late breaking" and your own news judgment that believes your audience *does* want to know about a major famine in Africa? You're not alone. A 2004 study by RTNDA revealed local TV news viewers do want more global news; the trick is they want a local angle. Time for you and your reporting team to develop a new recipe!

Among the study's findings:

- 64% of news directors say their station integrates world news into its rundown.
- 61% of the material aired as global coverage comes from network news feeds to local stations.
- Of the international stories covered, 24% directly relate to coverage from Iraq.

Click on http://www.rtndf.org/resources/globalperspectives.pdf to read more.

Michelle Frey, who produces and anchors for NTV-Nebraska Television. "However, if something major is happening nationally—that should go first."

At the center of your decision about what to lead with should always be your audience—which story has the greatest impact on the viewers who will be watching this newscast. But four other factors frame that audience picture, influencing a producer's decision-making process in determining the lead story as well as what other stories to include in your newscast. The factors are (a) your past experience making news judgments, coupled with your own journalism education; (b) the influence of news wire services and network video feeds, including what stories competitive channels covered and what the cable news channels cover; (c) influences from your News Director and other leaders, as well as your peer producers and the other news staff—reporters, photographers, assignments editors, and so forth; and (d) print influences.

Determining the lead: Factors that influence choice.

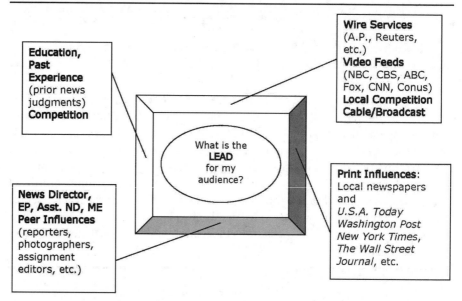

The Rundown Meeting

Because your news department's credibility is at stake, determining the lead is a very serious decision and you should be ready to defend your lead choice at the Rundown Meeting. The Rundown Meeting usually happens three to four hours before the newscast, and it's the time when the producer goes through the proposed rundown for the newscast. At that meeting the news director, or someone he or she assigns such as the assistant news director or executive producer, usually has the final word.

Stacey Woelfel, news director for KOMU-TV (NBC, Columbia) and Missouri School of Journalism faculty member reminds his producers, "The news director has 1,000 votes." At the rundown meeting in Woelfel's shop everyone

Early news producers at WCNC-TV (Charlotte) meet with Assistant News Director David Kirkland to decide which stories lead which newscasts.

has input from the producer to the assignment editor and the reporters but his ultimate authority resolves disagreements. The same is true at WHO-TV (Des Moines) where Dave Price, a senior reporter who has produced and anchored notes, "As with most things in the newsroom when it comes to the lead, the News Director or the Assistant News Director has the final say." ABC's Av Westin (2002) expands on the need for the news director to set the vision for the newscast which includes the lead, "The news director and the executive producers should have criteria for a broadcast's content. This vision must be shared with everyone on staff in order to maximize their editorial and production expertise" (p. 55).

In a quality newsroom the decision about the lead story is not determined by a dictatorial news director but unfolds in a spirit of teamwork and vigorous debate during the lineup meeting. As producer you're in charge of this meeting. Be a leader. Be organized. Be prepared to answer questions about the stories—the video as well as editorial content—and be prepared to justify your decisions, such as lead choice.

At the lineup meeting expect to be peppered with questions as the team focuses on the ingredients you've selected for the main course. Those questions don't necessarily mean that managers or others disagree with your decisions, they often just want to know why and how you came up with your rundown choices. Katie Brown, 10 p.m. producer at KCCI-TV, the CBS affiliate in Des Moines, Iowa, explained for us how she determines the lead and leads the lineup meeting.

I always decide what the lead will be, after I've checked in with my reporters in the afternoon. Occasionally my news director will want to lead with national news, if something big has happened. To help a producer determine what he/she thinks is the lead story, ask: what has the widest appeal to the audience? What will generate the most viewer interest? What is the "hardest" news story happening locally (even nationally)? Next, the producer should discuss what he/she thinks is a good lead—with the newsroom managers (i.e., executive producer, assistant news director, news director). Have a discussion—if they disagree, the producer should explain why he/she picked the lead. Be willing to fight—but also be willing to listen to other points of view. It's always better to have more than one "leadable" story than to be searching for a lead. The news director usually runs the afternoon meetings. We go over what stories are in the 5 and 6 p.m. shows, then discuss what we KNOW is happening that evening. Then reporters pitch their ideas ... usually along with a healthy discussion from other reporters, photographers and anchors. It's obvious when one idea generates a lot of reaction we are onto a good story.

KCCI-TV (Des Moines) News Director Dave Busiek and Producer Katie Brown discuss stories of the day.

Katie's station, KCCI (Des Moines), won the 2004 RTNDA Edward R. Murrow Award for Overall Excellence including producing. Her boss, News Director Dave Busiek, says, "We're especially proud of the Overall Excellence award this year, because it recognizes everyone on the team, in all departments." Busiek has spent 25 years at the station as a reporter, anchor, and for the last 15 years as news director. His perspective on how the lead story is determined and the lineup meeting unfolds is:

The lead story usually pops to the top. I urge them to use common sense. What are most viewers interested in? What's the most visual story? What has some emotion? What has impact in our viewers' lives?

Dave Busiek, KCCI-TV

Is it a dry, government story, or something with some emotion? If the lead doesn't naturally pop up, then we open it up in our afternoon meeting and get a bunch of viewpoints on the table. That always leads to a better decision. We're lucky to have an experienced staff with a lot of tenure in the market. I urge producers to take advantage of that expertise. The same is true in most other newsrooms.

We have a 12:30 p.m. meeting where we divvy up the leads for 5 p.m. and 6 p.m. The producers of those newscasts take part in the meeting, which we do around the assignment board. The meeting includes the EP, Assistant News Director, assignment editor, and me. We find different leads for the 5 p.m. and 6 p.m. more than 90% of the time. The exception would be on a day where there's a huge local story that dominates, and needs to lead both newscasts.

Across town at the competition in Des Moines, WHO-TV, Dave Price adds that a lineup meeting can become pretty elaborate. "Photographers, managers, reporters, anchors and even other station employees are invited. Each person gets the chance to give ideas or give feedback. We go over several 'lead-worthy' ideas and then decide which one could be the best." Often those who know which is the best story for the lead are not those working inside the newsroom but your reporter/photographer teams out on the community frontlines of broadcast journalism.

Joyce Brewer, who taught producing at the Missouri School of Journalism before returning to the anchor desk at WAPT-TV in Jackson, Alabama still teaches this maxim, "If the story reaches or effects a large number of viewers—that is a good reason to lead with it, if the story is unfolding while you're on the air that is a great reason to lead with it!"

Unbundling the Lead

This is a producer driven technique that breaks the lead story up into its many different angles and varies how those angles are presented, sometimes using two reporters in a team coverage style, an anchor "explainer" at the chroma key wall with maps and graphics, file video and graphics for background and context, and often a promotion for further coverage. "We look for 'break out' elements and sidebars" observes Price. Katie Brown told us, "There are so many elements that go into creating a news block. Definitely the most important is to have a good lead. Build the lead story—sell it—and make sure to wrap it up nicely." Adding in the production elements of a live reporter on location at the lead story (if it makes sense) or finding a guest expert for the anchor to do a "talkback" interview makes a lead compelling. Not all lead stories merit this kind of full court press, but always look for something extra that you add to build up your lead.

For example, suppose your lead story is the announcement of a multimillion dollar modernization at a local manufacturing plant that will ultimately lead to a hundred laid off employees. Here's how your lead might play out:

- Reporter Live with basic story of modernization and layoffs.
- Anchor VO Graphics with a timeline of the modernization and lay-offs.
- Reporter Live with employee reaction.
- Anchor VO Graphics listing some job resources and retraining.
- Live Talkback interview with someone from Chamber of Commerce about good/bad economic news.

Likewise these producer add-ons can flesh out other stories in your newscast as well. Typically you can add sources for more information, history or background, and context as producer add-ons to many stories that will give your newscast more depth.

Breaking News and Live

Many station formats demand that the producer find the freshest live action and, even if the story is less significant than others, lead with it. We argue that although the audience does respond to live shots and dramatic chases viewed via helicopters, viewers are smart enough to realize hype. In the book *Best Practices in Broadcast Journalism* Westin (2002) urges producers to "create a consistent tone of quality for the newscast. Diminish the use of the police scanners as the principal source for a broadcast's content. Encourage the staff to connect with the community, giving people information that affects their quality of life" (p. 55).

Smart news consultants recognize going live for the sake of live can turn off the increasingly sophisticated news audience. As CBS news sage Charles Kuralt observed, "Razzle dazzle is razzle dazzle and many a viewer is smarter than a television news consultant." We'll talk much more about managing live and breaking news in a later chapter.

Story Management

As an organized, effective producer you should always manage and stay on top of your reporter/photographer teams. Don't simply rely on communicating with the team through the assignment desk. Their frontline perspectives on stories can get muddled in the communication flow between the assignment desk and the producers' hub. When quizzing producers about what elements and angles were included in a reporter's news packages veteran Salt Lake City Anchorman Phil Riesen long preached, "To assume is to sin."

WDTN-TV (Dayton)
Reporter Libby Kirsch and
Videographer Dan Yoney
shooting a stand-up.

Sometimes a story assigned by the assignment desk sounds like a compelling lead, but a producer who doesn't follow through is frustrated when 30 minutes before air time the video tape editor finishing up the package tells her, "This is a pretty boring story, you know." The time to find out about the elements in a story is always before you lock it into a position in your lineup. Check in with the reporter/photographer teams in the field. As they return to the shop ask the photographer to cue up the most compelling images and quiz the reporter on what is new with this story. Good reporting teams will work hard for you as a producer when you respect their news judgment.

Recognize that some ego-driven reporters will always sell themselves rather than the story in fighting for the lead spot on your lineup. Good reporters know the better balance, as Investigative Reporter Denise Eck at WSLS-TV, (NBC, Roanoke), points out:

> As a reporter, I sell my story and myself. What does my story bring to the show that no other reporter in the market (even my colleagues) brings? Maybe it's a great live shot idea, or late breaking information or news you can use. A great way to grab the lead is to have information that impacts the most viewers. If it doesn't impact everyone, perhaps your story has exclusive information the competition doesn't have. Beyond that, I sell my own storytelling skills. Sometimes a well told, interesting story will grab a viewer.

Eck, who has done it all—produced, anchored, and reported—believes in constant communication throughout the day. "A good reporter keeps telling the producer, 'this is how my story is developing.'" The communication flow allows the producer to brainstorm live shot locations and graphic ideas with the reporter and photographer throughout the day rather than be swamped and presented with surprises at 4 p.m.

A Most Satisfying Feast

The science of news producing requires producers to obtain a precise knowledge of the technical aspects of the job such as timing the newscast, software literacy, maintaining a healthy media diet, and backtiming the day's workload to be ahead of the deadlines and ready for change. Change is the nature of news. The science of producing also requires that you accept the fuzzy logic associated with people working in fast change environments. Communication is the key. "Communication is the beginning of understanding" was once the motto of the Bell telephone system before it broke up.

Sharpen your written and spoken communication skills to handle the fuzzy logic of scientific news producing so you do not drown in the details. Let go of duties that others can do—associate producers, interns, and the assignment desk—so you can stay focused on the big meal and getting it served on time.

Sources

Hewitt, J. (1996). *Air words: Writing for broadcast news* (3rd ed.). New York: McGraw Hill.
O'Malley, S. (2004, March). Powerful producers. *Communicator.*
Schudson, M. (n.d.). Occasional paper No. 4. Gannett Center for Media Studies.
Westin, Av. (2002). *Best Practices for Television Journalists,* The Freedom Forum's Free Fair Press Project, 2002.

THE ART
OF PRODUCING

"We are all looking for ideas large enough to be afraid of again."
Ken Burns

"Bobby, Bobby, Bobby, Bobby, Bobby, Bobby."
Holly Hunter in *Broadcast News*

In the film *Broadcast News*, there's an amazingly funny scene that rings true to anyone who has worked at a television station. With less than five minutes to air, the field producer (played by Holly Hunter) gets creative and wants to add a visual from a Norman Rockwell painting as a final touch to a reporter's package. We laugh as her assistant producer dashes to Hunter's office, finds the book, races back to the editing booth so the painting can be taped and the shot inserted at the last minute into the package. Exuding nervous energy, catching their collective breath, and urging on their teammate, editor Bobby, to finish the story on time everyone joins in the chant ("Bobby") while the clock ticks toward the deadline. With the ejected tape in hand, the assistant producer races through the obstacle course of the newsroom and the control room bypassing reporters and ducking around doors in time to toss the tape to the playback operator who pops it into the machine just as the anchor finishes the intro. Whew!

Creativity under deadline will bring you many rewards in producing. In the last chapter we focused on the more exacting science of producing including developing an internal clock—a sense of timing—so you know whether at the last minute your decision to add a creative, artistic element like Holly Hunter's clip of the Norman Rockwell painting can be pulled off. In this chapter we will focus on some of the finer points of putting the rundown together including **formats, story clusters, pace and flow, anchor blocking,** the unique worlds of **weather** and **sports,** and even designing **a newscast mission statement** for each show.

Holly Hunter, who plays a producer in the film *Broadcast News*, takes charge creatively. *Broadchast News*, Holly Hunter, 1978. TM and Copyright © 20th Century Fox Film Corp. All rights reserved. Courtesy: Everett Collection.

Whoops there goes that word "show" again. Even when you're working your creative magic, try not to call your broadcast a show but rather a "newscast." Here's why. The tough balance you face as a producer between journalism with a capital "J"—your duty to bring facts and perspective to the audience—and entertainment—the race to beat the competition in a ratings-ranked environment—forces you to sometimes call upon show business elements.

The figure below illustrates the point. Show biz pressures might include choosing "live for the sake of live" with no journalistic value or using pop music to spice up a news story. The newscast is nearly consumed already by show biz aspects such as the color scheme of the news set, the "professional costumes" worn by the anchors and reporters, the graphics package, and the catchy newscast theme music.

Ron Harig, News Director at KOTV (Tulsa) teaches new producers to keep a distance from show business. Harig always corrected his producers if they referred to the broadcast as a "show"—as we mentioned above. "It is not a show," Harig would say, "It is a newscast." His emphasis helped the producers keep the credibility scales tipped toward journalism.

Formats

Just as an art museum has different galleries displaying renaissance,

Balancing your newscast.

impressionist, and other styles of art, each newscast (morning, noon, early afternoon, dinner hour, late, weekend morning, weekend night) will have its own unique style or format. Much of the format will be preprogrammed into your newsroom software system making it easier to build various blocks— news, weather, and sports, plus your franchise material.

The number of commercial breaks, special franchises, or features such as I-team investigations and health segments, along with your target audience watching at different times of the day—Mabel and Henry waking up in the morning versus college student Mitch at 11 p.m. flipping between ESPN and your local news to catch the headlines before playing late night on-line video games—all factor into the newscast format. The news director and her leadership team— assistant news director, executive producers, managing editor combined with the station's marketing department—devise and develop the formats. Ask questions and get involved in any permanent format changes to be made to your newscast.

The standard basic half-hour format developed in the late 1950s on local television stations for newscasts near the dinner hour and late at night simply called for the broadcast of "news, weather, and sports" in that order. As news consultants came along stations found ways to distinguish themselves. The **Eyewitness News** format involved reporters closest to the story appearing on camera at the location to "take the viewer there." There was also the **Action News** format that used fewer reporters and was distinguished by high story count and fast pace. As gender prejudices changed and women began to appear as credible newscasters in the late 1960s and early 1970s the concept of local anchor teams came along. Irving Fang's (1985) book *Television News, Radio News* described the **happy talk** format that ensued, which included time for the anchors to chit chat about the news and with weather and sports anchors.

In the snappy format of many a modern newscast, the co-anchors still chat back and forth between stories. Happy talk is a proven method of attracting viewers, for viewers seem to like getting to know their newscasters through snippets of conversation and quick repartee. Some viewers dislike it and some just live with it, but many people watch it (Fang, 1985, p. 380).

Technology frequently drives format changes. This happened in the 1970s when videotape replaced film speeding up the process by which stories went from field newsgathering to the on-air broadcast. It happened again in the 1980s when live technology—using ENG (electronic news gathering) from minivans and helicopters, and eventually SNG (satellite news gathering)—enabled producers to bring multiple live elements to their broadcasts. The legacy of the technology changes—the dominant emphasis on "live reports" as a staple of the news format—became embedded into local television news formats and an important part of the station's brand image. In the late 1990s many stations, influenced by news consultants like Magid Associates, urged their stations to brand themselves as "Live, Local, and Late-Breaking." We'll talk more about the use of live and news branding in later chapters.

Formats are designed to be flexible. At KCCI (Des Moines) Producer Katie Brown notes, "The producer can decide what to put where and for how long. There are standard amounts of time given for weather and sports, but the producer can change that time if needed."

priority

The important thing to remember about formats is they are simply the canvas on which you paint your newscast. They can be stretched into hour-long formats or even wall-to-wall coverage during a major story like 9/11. But always keep in mind that **news dictates format,** not the other way around. In other words, let the news of the day ultimately decide how you format your newscast.

WCNC-TV (Charlotte) 5 p.m. Producer Melody Freeman begins to add stories to her newscast format template.

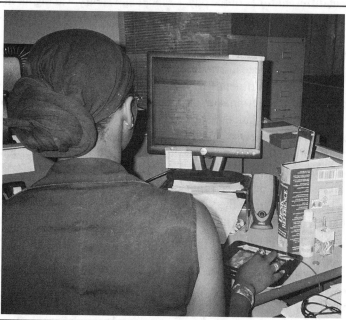

Once you've identified the format you can begin to paint the various stories into a coherent, credible picture of what happened in your viewer's world that day. Again it is important to emphasize that no two producers will take the exact same set of stories and come up with the same rundowns just like no two artists will take the same palette and canvas and come up with the same picture. Lineups will be similar—for instance selecting the same lead—but the transitions between stories and how similar stories are clustered together will be different. That is how it should be. As Tom Phillips wrote in an RTNDA *Communicator* article, "There is no formula for the order of stories in a newscast. That's because every story is different and every news day is different, making out a lineup is an art, not a science" (Phillips, 1985, p. 6).

Building Credible News Blocks— No Stacking and Packing

Perfecting the art of the lineup involves the careful and creative building of news blocks. Clusters of similar stories in a variety of forms from readers to packages comprise news blocks. Sometimes filling in the rundown with the stories you've selected is referred to as stacking the newscast. John Hewitt in his book *Air Words* defines the story order for the newscast as the "stack" or the "format" or the "lineup" (Hewitt, 1996, p. 19). No matter what word you use to call the rundown it all means the same thing. But two words used together—stacker and packer—stereotype the type of producer you do not want to become; a producer who cannot think on her own and just follows a formula stacking stories and packing them into the news hole.

Instead, think of yourself more like a producer–artist, disciplined in decision making and in command of the scientific aspects of producing we shared in chapter 5, yet staying open enough to let your creative juices flow. The combination of these two traits is what made Holly Hunter's producing character so successful in the movie *Broadcast News*.

Avoiding the stack and pack syndrome requires avoiding the rut of routine in building news blocks. As KCCI's 10 p.m. producer Katie Brown notes, "Once you feel yourself falling into a pattern with your news blocks that's a definite sign that you should try something different." Theories about building news blocks have been articulated by journalism professors in the academic laboratory and TV news consultants in the corporate boardrooms. We've combed through the best of them and boiled down the building of credible news blocks to five important principles.

1. **Journalism is job # 1.** Base your decisions on solid news judgments rather than cute little connections (story transitions) you can write between stories. Too many producers see a relationship between two stories that only they would ever understand. That brings us to principle 2.

keep in mind

2. **You produce for the audience, not for yourself or other producers.** Select stories the audience needs to know and may want to know. Don't assume just because you once lived in Germany any story from there will be of interest to your audience in Great Falls, or since you have seen every Ben Affleck film, and consider yourself a loyal fan, that your audience will await any news about him with baited breath. In many ways producers are like teachers and need to educate and expose viewers to various issues across the continents. Don't let the only time news comes from Indonesia—a vast and complex multiple island nation with millions of inhabitants and the largest Muslim country in the world—be when a tragic but freak tsunami washes ashore killing thousands.

3. **Lead with the most important story, save a second block lead, unbundle it, and win that lead!** Jon Hewitt in his book *Air Words* explained that research shows the audience gives more importance to stories in the lead positions in newscasts. Hewitt writes:

> They assume that if you think it's important you put it first. For broadcast, the positing is a bit different. You should have major breaking stories at the top of the newscast. That's expected. But at commercial stations, because of 2:00 ad breaks, you also have several segments in a newscast, and so you'll have an additional segment lead, as well as an overall lead. Therefore, you'll have to select several other stories to lead segments. (Hewitt, 2002, p. 22)

Brown at KCCI notes, "Be sure not to 'waste' all the interesting stories in the first news block. You want to spread out those gems throughout the show."

4. **Story form is determined by content.** As a producer–artist you have an array of brush strokes to use to tell your story. Long form reporter packages and short anchor readers provide the extremes with a wide variety of VOs, VO/SOTs, and so on, in between. You frequently are the one to determine whether a story is worth a package or can be collapsed into a simple VO/SOT. Reporters are trained to argue and sell their stories, as they should. Your task as producer is to determine how individual news items fit into the overall framework of the newscast you are trying to create. As mentioned previously, don't be glued to your format or habits. Valerie Hyman, formerly of The Poynter Institute's urged: Be flexible with your format. When a reporter comes up with an enterprise story and it's compelling, let it run long. Break out an important element with an anchor voice and a graphic. Tease a side bar to the lead story for after weather. Be open to 45-second packages from reporters on matters that require no more than that to make their point. Remember: let the content determine the form.

5. **Cluster stories to communicate important content.** Placing stories of varied lengths (package, VO/SOT, readers, etc.) but of a similar subject together in your news block is called story clustering. Clusters can be determined by subject (all economic stories) or geography (all local stories), but subject content should come first—don't fall into the trap of always clustering local with local, state with state, national with national, and world with world stories. Viewers think and process information topically first and geographically second.

Air Words author Jon Hewitt (1996) points out some dangers in clustering including "that minor stories derive too much importance from being joined to major stories, even if the theme or topic is similar" (p. 202). Hewitt does admit clustering stories together "helps the audience focus on the issues and allows a producer easy segues" (p. 201).

A first cluster often follows the lead story that itself could have included a cluster of multiple break out angles and side bar stories. "After that, " observes Brown, "Go for some other related stories. Related in the sense that they are on the same topic (politics), happening in the same place (Kansas City) or are of the same genre ("hard news"). The producer quickly finds all the economic stories or crime stories and can even figure out which is the most important within the cluster but then becomes frustrated asking, "how many stories of a similar nature can I group together? Do I group stories by subject matter—all crime stories in a row—or by geography?" The answer lies in the art of producing flow and balance.

Remember in chapter 2 we talked about how viewers pay attention to the news? They tend to monitor the audio until they hear something interesting or relevant and then that brings their visual attention to the television. Once we have that visual attention, we want to keep it with a good sense of flow from

WHIO-TV (Dayton) Producer Quincy
Wallace checks a script for flow.

story to story. It's easiest and quickest for a viewer to process similar information, so when you cluster topically similar stories together, you help the viewer
process those stories.

However, while keeping some logical order in building news blocks helps
viewers process more information and keeps their attention longer, Tom Phillips
notes "it can turn into bad journalism if applied to rigidly. There are some producers who feel that every story in a newscast should have some relation both to
the story before and the story after it. Each section of the newscast should be an
unbroken skein—and the only way to go from Main Street to Afghanistan is to
find some connection between them" (Phillips, 1985, p. 6).

Finally, in his excellent article for *Communicator,* Phillips strives to find a
balance between too much clustering in building a news block and "bombard-
ing the audience with stories in random order so they never know whom they'll
meet or what they'll see next" (Phillips, 1985, p. 6). He offers the idea of
clumps. "The best producers and editors ... think neither in rigid blocks nor in
garments, but in clumps—small groups of stories that do have something common, either geographically or theme or personalities, but with clean breaks between the clumps" (p. 6).

Creating story clusters is a creative process. A longtime leader in local television news innovations, former news director and now WZZM-TV General
Manager Janet Mason believes a good producer has two critical skills sets—conversational writing and creativity. "Part of creativity," Mason told us "is being

able to understand that you have to have some memorable moments within a newscast." Memorable moments often are the result of the perfect balance between two key concepts—pace and flow.

Pace and Flow

The delicate decision of how to balance your story clusters is one of many that contributes to two major concepts in the art of newscast producing—pace and flow. These two words describe the relationships among individual stories and blocks of stories within your broadcast, your anchors, graphics, and sports and weather. It is difficult to explain these terms because they often relate to an overall subjective feeling or sense about your newscast.

Pace and flow are natural processes that the audience does not even notice—unless they are missing. Pace is the rhythm of the overall broadcast while flow focuses on how the stories roll from one to the next.

Pace and Flow–A Party Definition

Denise Eck of WSLS (Roanoke) explains the relationship between pace and flow in a newscast as good conversation at a party.

A good newscast is like a good party. You start talking about the new information you can hardly wait to tell your friends, and it flows from there. Sitting and chatting with your friends, you wouldn't tell a funny story about a water-skiing squir-

Denise Eck, WSLS-TV

rel followed by one about the major having an incurable form of cancer. That's flow. When an anchor says "switching gears" or "on a lighter note" your attempt at flow has failed. At that same party, if you are stuck talking with a long-winded guy who just goes on and on, that's bad pace. News stories should flow from one to another so naturally that you almost don't realize it's happening. It should be a 30-minute conversation. A good party, and a good newscast offer a variety of stories, short ones and long ones, serious and light hearted. At the end of the night, everyone goes home happy and says, "Can't wait to do that again."

We asked Katie Brown who produces at an RTNDA Edward R. Murrow award winning station to explain the difference between pace and flow.

> Flow is usually not difficult to understand. Make sure you don't put two completely unrelated stories back-to-back. By this I mean don't put a story about flooding in China that has killed thousands of people right before a cute V/O of a local dog competition. The emotions that the first story generates are so intense (hopefully because of good writing to

video) that taking the viewer immediately to a different emotion with a
dog story is jarring and unpleasant.

Pacing is a bit more difficult to understand and is not entirely determined
by the producer. Pacing is making sure a show stays fast enough to keep
the viewer interested. It involves looking at the actual number of stories as
well as their type (Package, V/O/SOT, V/O, Reader, etc). TV is the best
combination of sight and sound so make sure that you are using both to tell
good stories. Running lots of VOs together might make for a higher story
count, but it also can be monotonous to hear the anchors talking for a long
time without some interesting soundbite to break it up.

Story Format

So story content is where you begin to create flow, but then, as you build your
news blocks you need to think about pacing, and story format is a good place to
begin for that. The more variety you can provide in the types of stories, live locations, and story length, the better pacing your newscast will have. Ultimately the
length of any given story is determined by the amount of information that has to
be presented, but here are some general guidelines for lengths of various story
formats:

Reader	:15–:20	(any story that needs more than :20 shouldn't be a reader—the viewer's attention is more likely to wander on this story format than any other)
Voice Over	:20–:30	
VO/SOT	:35–:45	
Pkg	1:40– 2:00 (including intro and tag)	
Live Pkg	2:00– 2:15 (including intro and live in/tag)	

Sound

The more sound variety—two anchors, soundbites, natsot breaks, reporters—
the better your pacing. As Katie Brown mentions above, variety in sound can
keep viewers from being lulled into monotony.

Graphics/Production Techniques

Working closely with story format and the use of sound to create pacing is
graphics and production techniques. The trick to good use of graphics and production tools is to find the right balance between enhancing your newscast and
overwhelming it. One of the first things you should do as a new producer at a station is visit the graphic arts department and talk with your director and/or technical director so you have a good idea of the graphic and production capabilities
available to you. Make sure you know about any limitations in numbers or types
of graphics used on a daily basis. Know how much preproduction time is available for your newscast to put together headlines, teases, and any other daily pre-

Chapter 6

production (or *preprod* as it's often called) and how much is left for special projects you might want to do. Find out how much lead time is needed for any extraordinary production or graphics you want to do for special coverage, such as a presidential visit, election, Iraq invasion, or other major story that you know about in advance.

Let's start with graphics. First some basic tips on using graphics well:

- **Good graphics always reinforce and support the story.** Viewers can't easily process multiple messages, and if the graphic is sending a different message than the story copy they will tend to pay attention to the visual and lose the story. Make sure any words on the graphic are the same as those in copy, and present information on a graphic in the same order it appears in the story.

- **Don't make viewers READ the news.** Simply use key words or phrases on graphics—don't use complete sentences unless you're displaying a quote.

- **Keep it simple—no more than three points per graphic.** If you have more than three bullet points, numbers, or scores, use a second graphic. You need space, called "white space," around words or numbers and want a font large enough to read even on a small TV.

- **Three or more numbers in a story should be put on a graphic.** People don't "hear" numbers well. Too many numbers make a story difficult to follow, so if you have more than two numbers in a story, use a full screen graphic to support the story.

- **Any phone numbers, addresses, or Web sites should be put on a graphic.** You can use a full screen graphic or a lower third super, but make sure you always reinforce phone numbers, addresses, and Web sites with a graphic.

- **If the information on a graphic is important, give the viewer a second chance to write it down.** Most viewers aren't prepared to write down information during a newscast. But if it's important, such as a product recall, they may want to. So, you may want to put up the graphic again as a bumper coming out of your tease at the end of the block in which the story aired. Then let the viewers know you'll do that in copy with a simple, "We'll show you that recall information again in a couple of minutes if you want to grab a pen and paper."

Now let's consider specific types of graphics you can use to help the pacing and visual appeal of your newscast.

- **Lower third graphics (supers, fonts, chyrons):** Lower third graphics are the information graphics in your stories, most often used to identify video—location, name/title, date, live, and

Lower third graphic or super.

so on. But you might also use a lower third banner with a phrase titling the story, known as a cutline. If your graphics format does call for banners on stories, try to match your cutline to copy so the viewer isn't reading something different from what they're hearing.

Over the shoulder graphic.

- **OTS (over the shoulder graphic):** These graphics can enhance any story that has an on camera component. If you happen to end up with two or three readers in a row, you can break them up by doing some with straight on camera shots and some with OTSs. As the producer you won't typically design the graphic, but you will likely need to indicate what words you want on your OTSs. Again, check the copy and choose one or two words from the first line of the story to make sure your graphic supports the story. Some graphic formats also allow you to add bullet points to an OTS graphic, which can be a nice variation to always using a full screen graphic, but keep in mind you'll only get two to three words per bullet point.

Monitor graphic.

- **Monitor or chromakey wall graphics:** An alternative to an OTS graphic is a television monitor or chromakey wall graphic. Depending on how your news set is designed, you might have a variety of shots for your anchors to deliver stories, including a television monitor shot or a stand-up position at a chromakey wall or big monitor. The philosophy and design of these graphics is exactly the same as an OTS—they should support the story and use words from the copy.

Keywall graphic.

- **Double box graphic:** A double box graphic is used to transition from the anchor desk to a live shot out in the field or in the newsroom.

Double box graphic.

It is exactly what it sounds like— usually two boxes side-by-side with the anchor on screen left and the reporter or interview guest screen right. Sometimes if you are introducing team coverage with multiple reporters, you might use a triple or quad box to show the extent of your coverage.

- **Maps:** We use map graphics for two main purposes—obviously, the first is to illustrate a location where a story happened or to help with the progression of a story with multiple locations. But maps can also be used as another way to get into live shots, especially if a reporter is in an outlying area of the market or outside the market area. It can provide some variety in the way you get to

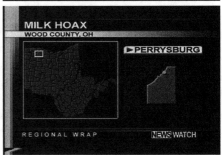

Map graphic.

live shots, as well as reinforcing that your reporter has traveled to a particular area for the story.

- **Full screen graphics:** Other than maps, there are many other uses for a full screen graphics. As mentioned previously any story with three or more numbers should use a full screen to display those numbers. Likewise you typically would use a full screen for contact information such as phone numbers, addresses, and/or Web sites. If you have a list of some kind in a story or a picture or de-

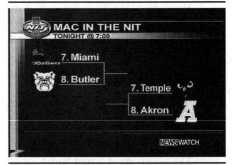

Full screen graphic.

scription of a suspect or missing person you would use a full screen. The truth is nearly any copy story can be made into a full screen graphic story with bullet points reinforcing the information. Other than those times when you definitely should use a full screen graphic, you may choose to add a full screen to a reader story to dress it up.

- **Animated graphic opens:** Animated opens are typically used to set apart special franchise stories, lead stories or team coverage, ongoing special coverage, breaking news, weather, and/or sports. They are usually short, :05 or less, and have music or a stinger of some sort. Some examples of when you would use an animated open would be health or consumer segments, investigative reports, a world wrap of stories, special coverage such as election stories, big trials, the Iraq War, major flooding or other natural disaster, and so on. If you have daily coverage of something or know the story will last several days or weeks and you want to set your coverage of that story or topic apart from the rest of your newscast, an animated open can help. Just use animated opens judiciously because they can break up the flow of your newscast or lose their uniqueness if every other story has an open with music.

- **Tickers:** Many of the cable networks now use graphic news tickers constantly to provide additional news headlines at the bottom of the screen. Fortunately most local stations don't use tickers during their newscasts except in certain situations, because they distract viewers from the newscast. You will likely have a ticker running during sports for scores. You may also use a ticker to run school and other closings during severe weather or results on election night. Just remember if viewers are reading a ticker, they're not listening to your newscast.

Again, the key to successful use of graphics for your newscast flow and pacing is moderation and support. Avoid the temptation that just one more graphic will make it better. Less is more when you're talking about graphics. Don't let a fancy graphics package overwhelm your newscast or try to use them to make up for a poorly produced show.

The same is true for **production tools** such as wipes. Just because your switcher will do a star wipe transition between two pieces of video, doesn't mean you should. Here are some basic production tools you can use to help the pacing of your newscast:

- **Cold open:** This is one way of opening the newscast with video first and natural sound, a soundbite, and/or an anchor read. This is how *The Today Show* begins each newscast and many local newscasts are formatted to begin this way instead of coming straight out to the anchors. The cold open video can come before or after the standard newscast open with announcer's voice, music, and the identification of the talent.

- **Wipes:** When you have a couple of stories with video that are somewhat similar, for example two fires, two court stories, or multiple sports highlights, and the same anchor is reading both or all of them, you can use a wipe between the pieces of video. A wipe is a visual transition that shows a change between the two pieces of video without coming back to the anchor. Typical wipes used in news are the page wipe or a push off/push on wipe. Wipes should be limited to stories that are topically related. They work nicely because they allow more video to get on the air since the video for the second and third stories starts right off the top.

- **Video off top:** You can also bring in video sooner even if you can't wipe. If you have a reader story followed by a VO, for example, why not take the video at the beginning of the VO if it is any good at all. If you are going to use this technique, the same anchor should read the VO as read the prior reader story. You don't typically want to take video off the top of a story if you're changing anchors, too.

- **Warm open:** A warm open comes in the middle of the newscast as opposed to a "cold open" at the beginning of the news. A variation on video off the top is a warm open. This is when you come back from a commercial break and go directly to video and/or sound instead of starting with a shot of the anchor. You can do this after the first block because both anchors are well established at this point. If the video is good, why not get as much of it as possible on the air?

- **Video box:** If you have additional information you want to get on the air at the same time you are showing video, you might use a video box. In this production tool you squeeze your video into a graphic box which usually has an area at the bottom for words or other information. For example, suppose you had a series of arsons in one area. After you do the main story on the most recent fire, you might want to recap the previous fires. You could do that with a video box, squeezing the video from the other fires, wiping in between them, and putting the dates and locations graphically on the box. A video box is also a nice way to set-up team coverage of a story, previewing the elements to come.

Production tools and graphics are pacing elements, but they are also important parts of the visualization of the newscast. The key element for visualization, though, is the video and how it's used.

Building News Blocks for Visualization

Claude Monet didn't paint water lilies at his garden in Giverny, France just because they were an interesting subject. Lavender hues and unreal gossamer greens filled the palette in his mind impassioning him to paint. In television news video is the passion element. Three principles are important when considering the visual aspect of building news blocks.

1. Place pictures based on their context.
2. Pictures can generate powerful emotions.
3. People need breathing space after certain pictures.

Point three recognizes that some dramatic pictures literally elicit a gasp from the audience. The viewer mentally continues to process the startling images—corpses in a mass grave, for instance—while the next story unfolds. Give your audience breathing space. This may include the anchor adding additional facts to the story on camera after the video—a concept news consultants developed that became known as the "command anchor" function. The anchor's tag to the story gives the viewer the impression the anchors are in full command of the facts and in control of the newscast because they are the ones providing closure. For sensitive stories, the practical application is that anchor tags give some needed space for the viewer to process and catch their breath before the newscast moves onto the next topic. Disturbing or emotional video may also need a viewer warning or alert before it airs so viewers can prepare themselves for startling images.

Katie Brown of KCCI-TV also noted the important role of the director and the anchors to help with the visual flow between stories and the overall pacing of the broadcast stating, "having a confident and knowledgeable director can do wonders to speed up the pace of a show, as can a quick-tongued anchor." We'll talk more about the relationship between the producer and director in a later chapter.

Producer and director at WCNC-TV (Charlotte) during the Midday news.

Anchor Input in the Art of the Lineup

A seasoned producer working in harmony with the anchor team will soon realize the importance of the interplay in the relationship between anchor and producer when it comes to the flow and pacing of a rundown. Dave Price of WHO-TV (Des Moines) says to achieve flow producers should pay close attention to "transitions to guide one story to the next and one anchor to the next anchor." Michelle Frey, who produced in Phoenix and now anchors in Nebraska, told us

> I wish every producer could honestly look at a newscast from an anchor's perspective. Each story should flow seamlessly, one to the next. As an anchor, nothing is more frustrating than trying to make a transition from jury selection on a grisly murder case to what the latest trend is in holiday gift buying. It just doesn't work. I think some producers are lazy and do not take the time to think through each and every transition their show will have. Many just group "local" and "national" news giving no thought only to the story that will transition between these two blocks.

We'll give you some examples of how to write good, but not overdone transitions coming up in chapter 7 on writing.

Anchor Blocking

In addition to how your stories flow and the transitions you write, it's also important how you assign stories to anchors. That can influence their performance as well as your flow and pacing. Just as you have grouped topically similar stories together, you want to reinforce that story flow with your anchor blocking. If you have a group of three education stories, assign them to the same anchor to read. Likewise when you change story topics, changing anchors gives your viewers a visual and audio transition for that change.

Anchor blocking to support story clustering also avoids one of the more annoying and lazy ways of assigning anchors—ping ponging back and forth between anchors after every story.

In addition to making your newscast feel very choppy, ping ponging is the worst possible performance situation for your anchors. They never get the chance to develop a good rhythm because they are constantly stopping and starting. If you've never sat at the anchor desk, think about your car. Where does it perform the best—on the open highway or in stop and go city traffic?

The question usually arises at this point, how many stories in a row should one anchor read? Your first determining factor is how your stories are clustered—change anchors when you change story topics. The second factor is balance between your anchors. Usually your goal is an equal balance between the anchors. However you won't achieve that balance by numbers of stories. What you are really trying to balance is time in control of the newscast. Since stories can range in length from :15 to 2:15, you would hardly have balance if one anchor had three :20 readers and the other had three 2:00 live packages. You may not achieve perfect balance in every block, but over the course of the entire newscast, you want a good sense of balance.

The other thing to keep in mind is from the viewer's perspective the anchor who introduces a reporter package or live shot is in control of the show during the entire story—even when the reporter is actually the one on the air. Although the anchor may only be on camera for a :15 intro and :10 tag during a 2:10 live package, from the viewer's perspective that anchor is still in control of the show during the entire story. So packages and live shots give you an exemption from ping ponging because for the viewer the anchor who intros that reporter story has been in control for quite some time. In fact you probably wouldn't want to do more than one additional, short, related story with the same anchor who intros a package/live shot before changing anchors. Otherwise the co-anchor will disappear from the newscast for too much time.

Two-Shots

Two shots with both anchors on the air at the same time are typically used at the beginning of the newscast, going into teases and for tossing to weather and sports (three shots). But you may also choose to use a two shot in the middle of a news block. Keep in mind that a two shot will always slow down the pace of your newscast. But if you've had several very short stories in a row, that may be your goal.

When blocking into and out of two shots there is a simple technique that can smooth that transition and help your flow. It's called the stair-step technique, and basically it works like this:

Anchor Sue reads the story before the two shot.
Anchor Sue reads the first line of copy on the two shot.
Anchor Bob reads the second line of copy on the two shot.
Anchor Bob turns to a one shot and continues the rest of the story.
    | Sue
    | Sue/Bob
        | Bob

If you are going into a tease then obviously you wouldn't have to worry about the bottom of the stair because after the two shot tease your newscast will go to a commercial break. This is a very subtle anchor blocking tool, but it does help smooth out your flow.

The other thing to watch when you use two shots is, don't leave either anchor sitting for very long without something to say. That is the most awkward moment in anchoring—sitting on a two shot while the other anchor talks. So keep the copy on a two shot short, so no anchor sits more than :05 without something to say.

The on-air talents of your sports and weather anchors play a vital role in the pace and flow of the newscast as well. Next up, we will talk about their unique

WCNC-TV (Charlotte) Anchors Bobby Sisk and Colleen Odegaard before Midday news.

contributions and offer some solutions to frequent pitfalls producers face in working with these talents.

Weather—Your Best Friend

Research reveals local weather is often the number one reason people tune into your newscast. In the morning they want to know if they need an umbrella or if the rain will scuttle the morning commute. Parents need to know if they have to insist the kids wear a coat to school. Global weather can be visually interesting providing startling pictures of a tsunami sweeping across East Asia or mud slides cascading over million dollar homes on a California cliff side. Most formats predetermine a specific allotted time for weather. Sometimes popular weather talent have a guaranteed amount of time built into their contracts. But many producers quickly learn that a weather person can become their best friend.

Weather talent often are willing to be flexible and can shrink their 3 minute segment if a live shot "went long" in the A block of news stories. Weather talent usually have the best ad lib skills and also can be called on to stretch 30 seconds for you if the package you wanted to kick your newscast with suddenly collapses, leaving you scrambling to write up a quick reader as a substitute kicker.

Get to know your weather talent. Leave the producing pod and go to their weather center. Ask questions about the forecast in the way the audience might. Learn what an isobar is, and make sure you understand the difference between weather watches and warnings. They will welcome your interest since they often feel ignored unless weather becomes the lead story.

WCNC-TV (Charlotte) Meteorologist Larry Sprinkle prepares the 5 p.m. forecast.

Getting to know your weather anchors will give you an appreciation for the science of what they do and help you resist the temptation to hype the weather. Most weathercasters are meteorologists, which means they are scientists who do their own forecasting and their credibility is as important as their on-air talent. Just because weather may be the number one reason people watch and the one story that affects everyone, you don't want to make it sound like the sky is falling if a dusting of snow is predicted. Learn to trust your meteorologist, and don't hype the weather until he or she tells you it's severe enough to hype. We'll get back to this topic in a later chapter when we talk about breaking news.

Many a producer has found weather to be the lifesaver of a newscast providing the most flexibility that is often needed in the creative art of producing. Sports, on the other hand, can be the opposite story.

WOUB-TV (Athens) weather anchor Ethan Huston provides forecast during 6:30 p.m. news.

Sports—Your Worst Enemy?

The sports team has it tough. Research shows an erosion of their audience in local newscasts as the diehard sports fan turns to cable or the web for the quick stories. No need to stay up to 11:25 p.m. to find out who won the game. In addition, their traditional place in the last third of the newscast means that all of the "slop time" built into your rundown is often taken up by a long-winded reporter live shot or too much chat time during the weather toss, so if you're running over on time, sports gets cut.

Research has even prompted some stations to drop a local sports segment from their early evening broadcast all together. The bottom line with sports is that about one third of the audience cares passionately about it while two thirds could care less. One third of your audience is too much to ignore completely, but you must be balanced and find creative ways for the two-thirds of the audience to care about the stories.

The best sports anchors understand that the advantage they have over the sports cable nets, like ESPN, is local coverage. Strong coverage of high school sports and the recreational sports that your viewers participate in, along with the college and pro sports in your region, will help broaden your sports viewership. But bunches of professional scores and highlights for nonlocal teams won't even keep sports fans watching your local sports coverage.

Sports can become your worst enemy if the sports anchor's ego prevents him from feeling part of the team and causes him to be unwilling to bend if you face a time crunch. If you're not a sports fan personally, recognize as a producer you must work extra hard to gain an appreciation for those who live and die for sports. By the same token it is unprofessional for a producer to have the attitude "Well, I can always cut sports a little." If the sports anchor has to constantly fight for his 3:00 he will feel picked on, isolated, and not part of the team. Recognize your attitude towards sports is the first and most important step in building the relationship of trust with the sports department. If you're a sports fan already the challenge is far less. But if not, work to find ways to connect on an interpersonal level with the sports department so they feel part of the team, insolated and ready to help you when you need to cut their segment and toss back for an update on a breaking news story.

Look for opportunities to pull sports into the news block. In large markets with major sports franchises there will be times sports stories lead a newscast, and in this case the story moves from the sports domain into a news item of general interest. Your sports anchor is the content expert over this beat so if a story

WOUB-TV (Athens) sports team prepares for its Emmy award winning Friday night high school football show, *Gridiron Glory*.

about major league franchises becomes news do not assign a news reporter but let the sports staff handle it. This will go a long way toward building a relationship of friendship and trust with the sports department. It also helps build the credibility of your sports anchor.

Learning to appreciate sports is really no different then learning to appreciate an art form you do not like. You may think that all Jackson Pollack did is throw cans of paint at his massive canvas, and it may be hard to see any "art" in the splashes of colors. Indeed, you may never like Pollack's paintings, but you can gain an understanding of why others might admire his work. The same is true with sports. Find a connecting thread to the wide world of sports. This attitude shift alone can begin to dissolve your inner prejudice and perfect the art of producing. Understanding is an important stepping-stone to reach that desired performance level.

The bottom line is weather and sports are part of your newscast, not just six minutes you don't have to worry about. Embrace weather and sports, and take care of your weather and sports anchors. Build in news stories around weather and sports so the viewer perceives them as still part of the newscast. If you approach weather and sports with this attitude on a daily basis, when one is the big news story and you need them at the top of the newscast, they'll be ready to work with you.

Newscast Mission Statements

One final idea in the art of producing worth sharing is a concept borrowed from the management field. Mission statements proclaim principles, which motivate and provide vision to a company. A newscast mission statement acts in the same way by articulating principles that will govern how your newscast is conceived, constructed, and coordinated by the various members of the newsroom team and communicated to the audience at such a powerful level as to become a ratings winning success story.

WZZM-TV General Manager Janet Mason speaks to the value of a newscast mission statement:

> If your station does multiple newscasts back to back. For instance, if your 5 o'clock newscast and your 6 o'clock newscasts have different missions, then you could potentially bring more people to the set. If your 6:00 mission is local, local, local but maybe your 5:00 newscast is more a "look around the world," not only in our backyard, then this helps the producers distinguish the differences.

Former director of the program for broadcast journalists at The Poynter Institute for Media Studies, Valerie Hyman urged those she taught to "write a mission statement for your news program, in keeping with the overall mission for the newsroom and the station. Include such things as your target audience, the program's general pace and style, and mix of local, national and international news."

At KOMU-TV (Columbia) students learning the art of producing at the Missouri School of Journalism had the newscast mission statement placed next to their computers at the producer's pod. Any mission statement becomes stale if unheeded and ignored.

Ask yourself at your station if a newscast mission statement might make sense. Ask the news director for a staff meeting or a retreat during which various members of your newscast team—the anchors, field teams of reporters/photographers, assignment editors, video tape editors, and the graphics folks—might brainstorm and articulate on paper the mission of each newscast. The newscast mission statement can help when deciding what stories to lead with, which to include in a rundown, where stories should be placed and why, and even how to handle tough ethical calls. Don't forget to bring the production crew—the director and technical director—into the process. Perhaps others from across the station in promotion or sales or even engineering could help shed light on what might attract an audience to a newscast. A newscast mission statement provides the producer with a clear vision of the newscast sketched out and articulated on paper. Then the pure artistic joy begins every day when you as the producer–artist receive a fresh 30 minute canvas on which to paint the day's most powerful and interesting events for viewers watching from their living room galleries.

Sources

Fang, I. (1985). *Television news, radio news* (4th ed.). St. Paul, MN: Rada Press.

Hewitt, J. (1996). *Air words: Writing for broadcast news* (3rd ed.). New York: McGraw Hill.

Hyman, V. (n.d.) *The Producer's Challenge* [Handout]. St Petersburg, FL: The Poynter Institute for Media Studies.

Phillips, T. (1985, December). The art of the lineup. *Communicator,* p. 6.

WRITING WELL

"Television has raised writing to a new low."

Samuel Goldwyn

"Vigorous writing is concise."

William Strunk Jr.

"If you don't have the time to read, you don't have the time or the tools to write."

Stephen King

"Without words, without writing and without books there would be no history, there could be no concept of humanity."

Hermann Hesse

"A word aptly spoken is like apples of gold in settings of silver."

Proverbs 25:11

A t its most basic level television is pictures, sounds, and words. Producers can have some influence over the pictures and sounds, but they spend a huge amount of time writing and reviewing the words. Throughout the day, most show producers are either writing stories and teases or reviewing other people's writing. So having an excellent grasp on good broadcast writing is essential if you want to be a newscast producer. In this chapter we're going to review some of the basics of broadcast writing and talk about some of the aspects of writing that are particular to producing.

TV Is Personal

Why do you watch the newscast you watch? In other words, of the newscasts in your hometown, why do you pick one station over the others? When most people are asked, it comes down to anchors. Why are anchor people so important to viewers? Primarily because, as we've discussed, TV is a very personal medium. If you read the paper, there's nothing personal about a byline, but in television (and sometimes in radio, too) by choosing a station you are inviting someone into your home. You are watching primarily one or two anchors give you the news each night, so what you think of them becomes important. You want to connect with that anchor. It's personal. As producers, if we understand the personal aspect of television, then we can incorporate that into the way we write news so that the news fits the medium.

We still have important information to tell people. But if we can tell it in a personal way that's meaningful to viewers, it has a much greater chance of getting noticed. That's why when we talk about broadcast writing we really emphasize **conversational writing.** In other words, we want anchors, when they read stories, not to sound as if they are reading, but we want them to sound instead like they are simply talking to us, speaking to each of us personally.

Most of our lives we're taught to write in a more formal style—a style that will be read, not heard. When you write a paper for college or a report for work, you most often aren't planning to read that piece of writing aloud. There are rules and structures that work well for the written word. However, in television and radio news, we read aloud what we write. So a very different set of rules applies to broadcast writing than does to traditional writing.

One other thing to keep in mind: when you read a sentence on a page, if you don't understand it, you can simply reread it. You can even stop for a moment and think about it. Not so when you are watching a newscast. When people watch a newscast, they have to understand everything immediately, the first time they hear it. There are no second chances. Think about that for a moment. Do you know anyone who records the news and watches the stories over and over? When we write for broadcast, we must write with ultimate clarity, so people don't have to stop to figure out what we meant or what that unusual word was they just heard.

What follows are some of the rules or guidelines we use when writing broadcast stories.

The director/technical director follows the script closely during the newscast (WHIO-TV Dayton).

Short Is Better

First and foremost in broadcast writing we like things short. We like them concise. We like things that get to the point quickly. If you think about it, that's the way we talk, too.

That means we use short words that are easy to understand. Long words, words that aren't well known, and jargon are things we should try to avoid. When we write a sentence we could use words like flagellate, fustigate, bastinado, fillip, or smite. But if what we mean is hit, we are better off just saying hit. If you do use a word people might not understand, you better offer an explanation in the story itself and that explanation better come quick. In choosing words for broadcast stories, we've heard it put this way: use nickel words, not quarter words. The fewer syllables the better.

Short sentences are also essential. This has a lot to do with how we speak. Because we breathe and speak at the same time, if sentences aren't short, we run out of breath. Plus a long, convoluted sentence can be very hard to follow. A good rule of thumb is around 15 words a sentence. If your sentence runs 20, 25, or 30 words, chances are you need to split that sentence up into several shorter sentences. Another good guideline here is one thought per sentence. If you get one idea in and communicate it clearly in a short sentence, you've done well. One other good rule is to avoid dependent clauses in sentences. A dependent clause is a part of a sentence that won't stand on its own. Here's an example: *Alexandra Johnson, who has served the city of Cedar Park as mayor and also as a council person for the past 24 years, announced today she will retire at the end of this year.* The dependent clause here is *who has served the city of Cedar Park as mayor and also as a council person for the past 24 years.* Long clauses often make listeners forget what the beginning of the sentence was about in the first place. That original sentence is 36 words long, which is tough to read without losing steam, or without losing breath. This particular sentence would be more effective as two sentences: *The mayor of Cedar Park says she will retire at the end of this year. Alexandra Johnson has served the city as mayor and in the city council for two-dozen years.* These two sentences are easier to read aloud and easier for listeners to understand than the one long sentence we started with.

Simple Is Good

Another way we try to make things easy to hear and understand is to simplify things that might be complicated. In the sentence above we changed 24 years to two dozen. Two dozen is just easier to comprehend than 24. Many times we will simplify numbers in broadcast copy, but it's important not to change the meaning or accuracy of those numbers. So *$1,062,000* becomes *just over a million dollars.* If we had changed this to just *a million dollars,* it would not have been accurate. Instead of writing *32.3% of people in the city support increasing taxes to help schools,* it could be *nearly one in three people in the city support increasing taxes to help schools.* One in three is much easier to digest than 32.3%. We call this mental math. We use it all the time in daily tasks when we have to deal with numbers, but can't write them down. For example if you're in the grocery store with ten bucks and you have three items to get, you'll calculate price totals as you go. But you won't think—bread, $1.46; milk, $2.19; cookies, $2.89. You round the numbers in your head—bread, $1.50; milk, $2.25; cookies, $3.00—so you can do the mental math easily. Viewers need the same help if they are only going to hear a number in a story.

There are times we want to use the exact number. *Governor Dickson beat his opponent by just one-hundred-13 votes.* You could also say just over a hundred votes, but sometimes giving the exact number illustrates a point and in this case, 113 isn't hard to hear and understand quickly. *Police say seven people were killed in the accident.* In this kind of story, the number might be very important. We wouldn't want to hear *around a half dozen people were killed in the accident,* we'd want to know the exact number, if that information is available. These are examples where the exact number is central to the meaning of the story.

You may notice some other things going on in some of these sentences. The way we write numbers is different, as is the way we deal with symbols, like %. Each place you work may have its own rules for writing scripts, but a general rule is you want to write in a way that an anchor can read the sentence clearly the first time they see it. In general, numbers 1 through 9 are written out, one, two, three, and so on. For numbers 10 through 99, we just use the numbers because they are easy to see and identify. For numbers over 100, we often mix elements, but connect each part with a dash, for instance *one-hundred-72.* We generally do NOT use symbols, so % is percent, $ is dollars, and so forth.

Write Like You Talk

Broadcast writing should emulate talking. In other words, it should look and read more like something you'd hear than something you'd read. Another general rule to help that happen is to **use contractions** whenever possible. So *will not* becomes *won't,* *she will* becomes *she'll,* *that is* becomes *that's.* The exception may be if you really need to emphasize one of the words that would be contained in a contraction. For instance *John Mogley says he did **not** kill his wife. The president says she will **not** send troops to Haiti.*

Another way we try to write conversationally is we try to write in the **present tense** whenever possible. When friends call you with some exciting news, they generally speak in the present tense. They usually say *I'm getting married* rather than *I decided a week ago to get married.* Since news is supposed to bring people current and late breaking information, present tense is always preferable. So instead of *the city council decided today to fund a new light rail system,* it might be stronger to write *the city council will fund a light rail system.* Or instead of *police today arrested the man they say robbed 17 local banks,* it could be *police are holding the man they say robbed 17 local banks.*

In almost every story we write, we can use present tense, but there is at least one exception. One classic example is when you are writing a story about someone who died. It's virtually impossible to write a sentence about a death without writing it in the past tense, because by the time you report the story, the person has already died. But in almost every other case, we try to write in present tense.

Here are some examples of sentences written in past and present tense:

Past Tense
The university has decided to renovate its football stadium at the cost of 40 million-dollars.
Present Tense
The university will spend 40 million-dollars to renovate its football stadium.

Past Tense
Houston Astros pitcher Ralph Parillo pitched an almost perfect game today against the Colorado Rockies.
Present Tense
Ralph Parillo is winning games for the Astros. Today's victim; the Colorado Rockies. Parillo was almost perfect.

Past Tense
Three people were killed and seven others wounded when a man jumped on stage during a rock concert and opened fire on the crowd.
Present Tense
A gunman charged onstage at a rock concert, opening fire on the crowd, killing three people and wounding seven others.

Another tense to avoid in broadcast writing is **past perfect.** This tense is most often identified with the use of *have been* and *has been.* Past perfect is meant to be used when you're talking about something that's happening over time. *City council has been discussing the smoking ban for a month.* Unless you're talking about an action that has been happening over time, leave the has or have been out and just use straight past tense, or as discussed above, find a way to make the sentence present tense. When you use past perfect tense for an action that happened once, you take away an important piece of information— *when* did it happen. For example: *City council has passed the smoking ban.* Better—*Tonight city council passed the smoking ban.* Best—*Starting tonight smokers in the city have to light up outside. About an hour ago city council passed the ban on smoking in public places.*

Another technique you can use to make sure your stories are conversational is to write in **active voice.** Think back to when you learned to write sentences. You might remember that sentences have a subject and a verb. To write in active voice you want the subject of the sentence performing the action of the verb. Let's find an example, like *a rabid dog bit and injured a local man today.* The subject in the sentence is usually the actor, the one initiating the action. In this case, it's the dog. This sentence is written in active voice. An example of the same idea written in passive voice is *a local man was bitten and injured today by a rabid dog.* So in each sentence in a news story, you have to ask yourself, who is the actor, who is initiating the action? Then look at the sentence; the person or thing initiating the action should be at the beginning of the sentence. If it is, you've most likely got an active voice sentence. It the actor is later in the sentence, you need to think about whether the actor can move up closer to the front of the sentence. Another way of putting it is you try to see whether the actor is acting (the dog is biting) or whether the actor is getting acted upon (bitten by the dog). So, in active voice, the subject performs the action expressed by the verb. In passive voice, the subject receives the action expressed by the verb.

Here are a few examples of sentences written in passive and active voice:

Passive Voice
The bank was robbed by two masked gunmen.
Active Voice
Two masked gunmen robbed the bank.

Passive Voice
Much of lower downtown was flooded as water from the Colorado River spilled into the streets.
Active Voice
Water spilled over the banks of the Colorado River, flooding much of lower downtown.

Passive Voice
John Frangole was sentenced to life in prison by Judge Sandra Flynn.
Active Voice
Judge Sandra Flynn sent John Frangole to prison for life.

Passive Voice
The layoffs of 1,200 workers were announced today by the Condata Computer Corporation.
Active Voice
The Condata Computer Corporation will layoff 1,200 workers.

You'll notice in most of these examples there are a couple of clues to passive writing: a form of the verb to be—*was* robbed, *was* flooded, *was* sentenced; use of *by*—*by* two masked gunmen, *by* Judge Sandra Flynn.

Phone Mom Theory

How do you know whether your story is written conversationally? Call your mom, read the story to her, and see if she understands it. Or call your brother, sister, father, spouse, or roommate. Do they understand the story the first time they hear it? Or, just read the story aloud and listen to your own voice. A newsroom full of good writers should sound like a bunch of people talking to themselves as they read their copy aloud.

The Good Writer's Dazzlin' Dozen

Mackie Morris is a long time journalist, teacher, and legendary writing coach. For many years he has been teaching broadcast journalists to use his dazzlin' dozen tips for better broadcast writing. Here they are:

1. **Write factually and accurately.** The best technique and the finest form mean nothing if your copy's wrong.

2. **Write in the active voice.** Do everything reasonable to avoid the passive voice. Active writing is tighter, complete, easier to listen to, and more interesting.

3. **Write leads in the present or present perfect tenses.** Those tenses connote action and immediacy, and they enliven your copy. Avoid the "false present" tense. Use fresher, more immediate time references than the generic "today."

4. **Keep your writing simple.** Choose positive forms over negative forms; the former requires fewer words. Write conversation, not literature. Don't waste time searching for synonyms, since repetition is not a sin. Don't use complicated, "intellectual" language.

5. **Be complete and clear.** In your quest for brevity and conciseness, don't omit necessary information. Write for the listener who is hearing the information for the first time.

6. **Be creative.** Stick to the rules, but develop your own style. Try to write the same old thing in a different new way. Use the *Rule of Threes* and other devices that make writing more rhythmic, easier to listen to, and more interesting.

7. **Write to be heard.** Avoid confusing homonyms. Avoid tongue twisters. Always, always test your copy by reading it aloud.

8. **Avoid interruptives.** Don't force the listener to make difficult mental connections. Place modifiers next to what they modify.

9. **Avoid commas.** Commas often indicate compound or complex sentences, which the eye can read but the ear finds difficult to hear. Good conversational style contains simple sentence structure.

10. **Avoid numbers.** The listener has trouble remembering them.

11. **Avoid pronouns.** If you must use a pronoun, make sure the pronoun agrees with its antecedent and appears close to the antecedent.

12. **Write to the pictures, but not too closely to the pictures.** Remember that more specific video requires general writing and vice versa. Utilize the *Touch & Go* method wherein you write directly to the video at the beginning of a passage and then allow the writing to become more general with background information and other nonvisual facts as the video continues.

13. **Write a beginning, a middle, and an end.** Effective story writing boasts that structure.

From © 2004, Mackie Morris.

Clichés

In broadcast writing we try to avoid clichés like the plague. Seriously, so the *like the plague* part of that sentence should be avoided. Strong broadcast writing is fresh, concise, direct, and original. Clichés are often well-worn phrases that have lost their meaning over time. So as you write your own stories or edit other writers' stories, look for clichés and try to replace them with stronger writing. Don't get caught up in the use of news clichés, either. Using them is just lazy writing. Here's a hit list of four most overused and meaningless news clichés:

"Parents' worst nightmare ..."
"Only time will tell ..."
"One step closer ..."
Adding "gate" to every political scandal since Watergate.

Broadcast News Clichés

Abe Rosenberg is a writer at KTTV in Los Angeles and a writing coach. He has compiled a good list of clichés and other terms to avoid as a broadcast news writer. Here are a few of what he calls "groaners":

Area Residents
Shhh, Tommy, don't play the drums so loud, you'll wake the area residents!" Normal people don't refer to their neighbors this way. Why should we?

Campaign Trail
What, exactly, is a campaign trail, anyway? Are there covered wagons? Does Campaign Cookie rustle up Campaign Grub? Do folks munch Campaign Trail Mix as they warble yippie–i–o–ca–yay through the precincts? Why do writers feel a compulsion to use this terrible term? Just say where the candidate is, and get on with it.

Death Toll
A silly way to refer to the number of dead. Does someone ring a heavenly bell every time a person dies? Does a heavenly nickel get dropped in the fare box on some celestial highway? Maybe "up there." Down here we speak plain English.

Firestorm of Controversy

Whoa! Get out the flame-retardant umbrellas! Non-conversational, and bad hyperbole, all rolled into one. Just explain what the controversy is without the brimstone.

Flurry of Activity
Not unless you're the weathercaster, and it's beginning to snow. There are plenty of less stuffy ways to say someone's busy.

Heating Up
If you're referring to soup, maybe. Unfortunately, this term seems to show up every time we get

Abe Rosenberg, KTTV-TV

within three weeks of an election. Don't insult people's intelligence. They understand what a close race means. If it's not a close race, don't say it is.

Killing Spree
Webster's says a spree is "a lively frolic." Mass murder is not a "spree." It's mass murder.

Major Breakthrough
Seems some folks can't write a medical story without this little bit of redundancy. By definition, there's no such thing as a minor breakthrough, any more than there's such a thing as a miniature Sumo wrestler.

Officials Say
Don't cheat the audience with this cheap trick, or its tacky counterpart, "Authorities say." WHICH officials/authorities are saying it? Name a name, give a title, or just find another way. This overused piece of news camouflage only tells viewers, "We didn't bother to find out." Is that what you want to say?

Plagued
Isn't it funny how politicians aren't troubled by scandals anymore? They're plagued! Pharaoh seeing frogs in his oatmeal ... that's a plague. Anywhere else ... dump it.

Team Coverage
Stuffy, pretentious, and about as nonconversational as you can get. News managers think it conveys a sense of importance. Wrong. Committing the resources to cover the story does that. If your news operation is known for effective coverage of big stories, the hyped language isn't necessary. David Brinkley understood that. His version was short and simple: "We have two reports, beginning with Marvin Kalb in Washington." Beautiful, isn't it?

Wreak Havoc
Bad enough this overblown term shows up in stories about earthquakes and hurricanes. But traffic jams? Do fender-benders really wreak havoc with the morning rush hour? Just tell folks how long they'll be sitting on the Interstate.

You can find more at http://www.newswriting.com/

What Goes Where?

In newspaper writing, writers often used what's called the inverted pyramid style to structure a story. The idea is that you put a lot of the most important information up top in a story, because a reader may stop reading at any time and skip to another story or headline. In broadcast news, we do not use inverted pyramid style.

Perhaps the best way to think about broadcast structure is to think about all stories having three things: a beginning, middle, and an end. The beginning part of the story needs to grab the viewers' attention, the middle gives the basic information and background, and the end wraps the story up. You could argue that all broadcast news stories, whether they run twenty seconds long or five minutes long, still basically follow this structure.

Leads

A lead sentence should jump out of the TV set and slap you. Leads may be one of the most important parts of broadcast writing. If a lead is not excellent, viewers might click over to another station, they might get up and leave the room, or they might just turn the TV off. Lead sentences should grab the viewer's attention and give a little information about the story to come. Leads should be short and to the point and almost always written in present tense. Producers often spend quite a bit of time each day writing leads and rewriting leads.

There are different kinds of leads. For instance, there is what's often called a **direct lead.** A direct lead has a direct appeal to the viewer. Often direct leads have the word *you* in them. *You may soon be paying more tax on food if the governor signs a new bill into law. You might want to find a different way to work Monday if you travel on Interstate 70.* Direct leads take into account how the viewer may be impacted by a story.

There also are **blind leads.** A blind lead is intriguing but keeps viewers blind when it comes to certain information. Here are some blind leads: *he didn't mean to stab his wife* or *it's more than eighteen feet tall, purple, and smells good.* A blind lead is followed by a sentence that puts that sentence into context. *He didn't mean to stab his wife. That's what defendant Robert Brandon said today during his trial for the murder of his wife. It's more than eighteen feet tall, purple, and smells good. We're talking about a new float, designed for this year's Christmas parade.*

There are also **question leads.** As you might have guessed question leads contain a question. *Tired of all this rain? Are you planning a trip this summer?* A couple of guidelines for question leads: They should be used infrequently and whatever question you pose should be answered by most viewers with the answer yes.

The Middle

The middle part of the story is where most of the information goes; you might think of it as the meat and potatoes of the story. The story still has to move, keep a viewer's interest, and be well written. Don Fry of The Poynter Institute likes to say that in a story you need to place gold coins along the path. What he means is there should be treasures along the way in every story, reasons to keep watching a story, reasons that viewers will stick around. In the middle of your story, are there some gold coins, some interesting story elements that will keep viewers interested?

Video Referencing

This might be a good point to talk about writing to pictures. One of the toughest things to do consistently in television is to make sure the words you are writing have a relationship with the pictures viewers are seeing in video stories. Paying

WCNC-TV (Charlotte) Reporter Lisa Rantala borrows the prison control tether that's the focus of her story for her liveshot to help tell her story.

attention to the relationship of the words and pictures is often what makes the difference between a dull newscast and a newscast that really keeps viewers interested and engaged. That means every piece of video—whether it's a short voice-over, where the anchor reads while the viewers see video, or a video tease—should have a lot of thought put into whether the words and the pictures match.

Words and Pictures: The Coordination Challenge

Lee Hood is an award winning news producer who now teaches at the University of Colorado at Boulder. She offers these suggestions for writing to pictures.

Good broadcast-style writing is clear, concise, and conversational. Adding video to the mix requires additional skill, but it's well worth the effort for more effective television presentations. It's also a balancing act between two extremes: on the one hand, not writing closely enough to the pictures, and on the other, writing too closely to them. In the first extreme, the viewer is bound to get lost, hearing words and seeing pictures that have little or no relationship to each other. But write too closely to the video and the story becomes a shot-for-shot recitation that states the obvious rather than taking advantage of opportunities to augment what is shown on the screen. The most important thing to remember is to enhance the video

Lee Hood, University of Colorado

rather than narrating it. Allude to what we're seeing, but add information that helps us understand it.

Here are a few guidelines to help you coordinate words and video effectively:

- The first essential step is to **watch the raw video** *before* **you start to write.** Without this step, the coordination will be a guess rather than a process.

- Video should be **referenced within the first two to three words,** both at the beginning of the story's video portion and when you change scenes.

- Plan on most referenced shots or scenes lasting at least three seconds. **Don't try to reference each word with another shot.** This only works—sometimes—in packages, never in stories that are played live, such as voice-overs and vo-sots. Think of it this way: Most video references should get their own sentence. You can't do a list of different items and have each with a different shot.

- If you have distinctive shots or video of **recognizable people, reference them** or ask the videotape editor to leave them out. For example, it's distracting for a viewer to see a celebrity in the video and not have any mention of it in the script. ("Was that Brad Pitt at the parade? I wonder what he was doing there?")

- If you have **aftermath video** and are describing what happened, **start with the end result** to make the referencing closer. One example I use in classes is the story of a tanker truck that overturned after being cut off by a car. It's unlikely you will have video of an accident as it happens; in this case, the video is of the overturned tanker (i.e., aftermath). If the video portion of the script starts with a description of the car cutting the tanker off, that's not coordinated with what we see in the video. So you start with the end result: *"The tanker overturned* when a car cut it off." Notice how this follows the rule at the beginning of the list and references the video within the first two to three words.

- For the best coordination, **video on live-rolled stories** (voice-overs and vo-sots) **should not be edited before the story is written** and timed (preferably by the anchor or reporter who will read it on the air).

- Visuals are a great tool that add value to what television news offers. Yet many stations do not pay adequate attention to the coordination of words and pictures. Perfecting this art will make your writing, and your newscasts, stand out.

The End

This might be the toughest part of a story to write. The end of a story must offer some closure to the story; it must wrap things up. It's often also the point in the story where it's easy for writers to show their own bias. In other words, often when we conclude a piece we unconsciously put a slant on the story rather than trying to continue to be balanced. The end must wrap things up but not give a definitive opinion about the story.

There are some good strategies for ending a story. Here are a few:

- Save one fact for the end of the piece. It can't be the most important fact, but something that will add something to the story.

- Look to the future. In other words, what happens next in the story? Is there a public meeting ahead, or has a trial date been set?
- Look at how you started the story. If you posed a question, did you answer the question? If not, do it now. Did you start with an example? It might be good to come back to that example here. This is the place where you should tie up those loose ends or answer any unresolved questions.

Copy Editing Tips

Deborah Potter is a former network correspondent and news producer who now runs Newslab, a resource for broadcast journalists. Deborah says the key to broadcast writing is learning to edit and rewrite, or as she puts it: Revise and Conquer. Here are some of her best tips for editing copy:

- **Wait** at least five minutes before beginning to revise your copy. If you start revising immediately, you may read what you thought you wrote or meant to write, rather than what you actually put on the page.

- **Read** your copy aloud. OUT LOUD. Not under your breath. Listen for sentences that are too long, for awkward phrases and for double meanings.

- **Replace** jargon, "cop-speak," and "journalese" with more everyday language.

- **Derail** freight trains. Break up long titles and awkward strings of modifying nouns ("the 6-year-old Boulder area girl").

- **Remove** shopworn adjectives ("tragic," "stunning," etc.) whose only purpose is to tell viewers what to feel. Retain or add specific details instead.

- **Look** closely at transitions in and out of tape. Be sure the lead-in sets up the tape and explains any pronouns, but doesn't just restate the bite. Be sure the tag follows logically from the tape. Remember: a well-written story is seamless. There are no sections that can be lifted out.

- **Police** for spelling (especially common mistakes) and grammar (especially subject–verb agreement and subject–pronoun agreement). Make sure your verbs are in the right tense, and look for any use of the passive voice that is not deliberate, which may signal missing information.

- **Double check** for accuracy: all numbers and calculations; names and titles; date and time references; superlatives (Is it really the first? The biggest?)

- **Edit** backwards. The last word is the most powerful. Do you need that last sentence? Those last few words in each sentence? (A chrysanthemum show featured 51 varieties of the flower.)

- **Listen** to the story without looking at the video. Make sure all the sound is clear and understandable.

For more excellent resources about broadcast journalism, visit the Newslab web site at http://www.newslab.org/

Deborah Potter, Newslab

Assistant producer edits copy and checks rundown for proper script commands (WDTN-TV Dayton).

Writing for the Anchor

As you get experience writing and producing newscasts, you can begin polishing your skills. One of the more advanced skills that many producers develop is the ability to write for a particular anchor. As producers work day after day with an anchorperson, they get to know how that person speaks and how they read the news on the air. In other words, as a producer writing a sentence, you can imagine the anchor actually reading the sentence you are writing. As you write you can ask yourself: Can I picture Jennifer reading this sentence this way? Or would Hernando actually ever say anything like this? Excellent producers begin writing sentences that are tailored to a particular anchor. This helps the anchor, as well, because now what they read sounds more like something they might actually say, so delivery can be even more conversational.

The Seamless Show

One goal many producers work toward is to have a show that flows well from one story to the next. As mentioned in the previous chapter, this is also important to an anchor's performance. Most of this is controlled by the order in which stories run. But it can also be helped along with some good writing. Producers sometimes use **transitions** to help the newscast flow from one story to the next.

Let's say in a newscast you have two stories you have blocked together because they are both about disasters that have hit local businesses. One is about a water main breaking and flooding a downtown business. The other is about a fire that seriously damaged a local restaurant. Firefighters had a hard time containing the blaze because of a fire hydrant that had no water. After the flood story you might write a transition something like: *it wasn't too much water, but not enough water, that caused problems at a local restaurant today.* This kind of contrast transition can help link together stories and make the newscast flow.

Another more subtle transition can help you over a bump in your show flow. When you have to change story topic and have two unrelated stories together, sometimes you can pick up a word or phrase from the end of one story and use it in the lead to the next story. For example: Last Line—*The school board **still has to decide** if it will put the bond issue on the May ballot.* First Line—*The District Attorney **is still deciding** who he'll charge in last night's bar brawl.* This technique is effective for writing out of sound bites as well as to help an individual story flow better. Most producers do not feel the need to link each and every story with transitions, but it can be an effective way to help a show move along.

What Makes Good Writing Good?

The big ideas to take away here are that **good writing**:

- **is clear and concise.** Word choice is very important—make sure you take the time to find just the right word to communicate clearly and accurately. Use simple language and make sure stories have a clear point. Avoid complex sentence structure.
- **grabs and holds our attention**. Good leads are essential, but stories should not drag or be filled with incomprehensible information. If you don't understand a story, the viewer will not understand it either. Good stories go somewhere—they have beginnings, middles and endings.
- **teaches us something.** Well written stories offer us new information. Good writing teaches and informs. Good writing is accurate.
- **rarely is a first draft.** Very occasionally you can sit down and write a good story on the first try, but that's not the norm. It's more usual to write something, leave it alone for a bit and then come back and improve it.

Becoming a Good Writer

How can you improve your writing and become an excellent writer? First, as the quote from Stephen King suggested at the beginning of this chapter, most good writers read. Any reading is helpful, but to learn about broadcast writing, you should read good broadcast writing. You could read scripts written by Edward R. Murrow (http://www.jewishvirtuallibrary.org/jsource/Holocaust/murrow.html) or by Charles Kuralt (there are several collections of his scripts in

Chapter 7

book form). You can watch good network newscasts and good local newscasts and pay attention to the writing. Learn what others are doing well.

Ultimately the best way to become a good writer, though, is to write. Write as often as you can. The more you write, the better you will become. You can also ask people you respect to critique your writing.

Good writing is essential to good television news. Without words, without writing, there is no news.

PUT ON YOUR MARKETING CAP

"If your newscast is a wardrobe ... then a tease is a negligee."
Bob Clinkingbeard, WOFL-TV News Director, during tease workshop
at The Poynter Institute

Think about that for a minute and it will put you in the right frame of mind to think about newscast promotion. A negligee entices attention by showing a little and promising a lot without giving everything away. That's exactly what good headlines, teases, and promos do. They show and tell the viewer just enough about upcoming stories to entice them to watch or continue watching your newscast.

Promos, teases, and headlines are one of the most important parts of your newscast, but unfortunately they're often left until the last minute or treated as simply another task to do as quickly as possible and cross off your list. However, the truth is you can work all day on a show and end up with a newscast that just jumps out of the gate and races to the finish line, but you'll never cross that finish line if people aren't watching. Good promotion can get them to watch and keep them watching!

Types of Promotion

There are two broad categories of promotion: image and topical. **Image promotion** sells the news brand, talent, weather, or resources (i.e., live, bureaus, radar). In other words, what is the image of your news in the viewers' minds, and can we influence that image? Image promotion typically reinforces viewing decisions for people who consider your newscast their favorite—your loyalists. **Topical promotion** sells the viewer on specific stories for an individual show. Audience research has shown that viewers use topical promotion—whether it's preshow promos, headlines, or teases—to decide if they're going to watch a given newscast and how long they'll watch. A good topical promo can influence a viewer to watch a newscast other than their favorite. Good headlines and teases can keep viewers tuned in longer than they had planned to watch or keep them from switching during a commercial.

WHIO-TV (Dayton) Anchor Cheryl McHenry stands in front of a green chromakey screen to record a topical promo for the 11 p.m. news. The green screen is replaced by a promo graphic.

In a 2003 study of news viewers, more than half reported that seeing a promo for a newscast they don't usually watch would cause them to stay tuned to that station so they wouldn't miss the promoted story. When asked about a specific promo, a third could recall the promo content, and 64% of those were motivated to watch the newscast (Albiniak, 2003, p. 5). In a 1997 study, more than 70% of viewers said they pay attention to topical promos and teases, and 40% said the most useful information in any promotion was information about upcoming stories (Magid Associates, 1998).

As a newscast producer, you will be focused primarily on topical promotion—both outside and inside your newscast. You will likely always write the headlines at the beginning of your show and the teases inside the newscast. You may or may not have to write the promos that air in the lead-in programming. These promos can include pretaped or live 30 and 15 second spots, as well as 4 second station IDs. At many stations the promotion department will write and produce these promos, but even if there is a news promotion producer, you will likely be asked which stories are the most teasable.

Is It Teasable?

When marketers are promoting a product they don't focus on the product, they focus on the consumer. What is it that the consumer wants or needs from their

---

Show Me the Money

How much would it cost you if you had to **pay** for promo time like any other advertiser in your show? Check with the sales department and find out what the 30 second spot rate is for your newscast and then:

	Example 11 p.m. News
ADD up the seconds you use inside and outside of your newscast for promotion	180 seconds
DIVIDE by 30	6 spots
MULTIPLY by spot rate	$6 \times \$800$
EQUALS the dollar value for your newscast's promotion	$4,800

That means that you are spending a few thousand dollars every night to promote your show. You can bet advertisers give lots of time and attention to the message they put in those 30 seconds. Why shouldn't you do the same?

---

product? How does their product meet those consumer wants and/or needs better than any competing product? You should approach marketing your newscast the same way. You make decisions about story selection for your newscast with viewer relevance in mind; you should make decisions about which stories are teasable the same way. The attributes you have to sell your newscast are your stories, so choose the ones which best meet your viewers' wants and needs.

Just as you ask yourself which stories have the biggest impact on the largest number of viewers when choosing your lead, ask that same question when choosing which stories to tease. That often means choose local stories first. If you want to tease a national or world story—make it directly relevant to your audience.

Example:
Any Viewer
Congress tackles the president's new prescription drug plan ... find out if it will really lower drug costs for seniors when we come back.

Your Viewer
Will Athens County seniors really end up with lower prescription drug costs under the president's new plan? See what your local lawmakers think when we come back.

Make liberal use of **you** and **your** in tease writing. It's another way to make your promotion more focused on your viewer. It's much easier for a viewer to ignore a message directed at generic "residents," "citizens," or "consumers" than it is a message directed at "you."

There are other things that make one story more teasable than another:

It's the Video, Stupid!

Nearly half of news viewers report that what makes a promo memorable is the video, compared to a third who say it's the words (Magid Associate, 1998). Look for your best video when selecting stories to tease, and use it. There's no good reason to "save" the best video for the story. If the video is good enough, don't you think the viewer will want to see it more than once? Talk to the photojournalists who shoot the stories. They are the ones who will tell you what the best pictures are. They might even give you the angle for your tease based on the video. The biggest mistake many producers make in writing and producing teases is not finding out what video is available for the story.

> Count on your video journalists to let you know what the best tease video might be for their stories (WCNC-TV Charlotte).

GET IT *ONLY* HERE

Any marketer will tell you if your product has an attribute that no one else has, that's the selling point. When you're choosing stories to promote, sell your exclusives—not just exclusive stories, but story elements.

Example:

> State police issue an Amber alert for missing 4 year old Lisa … Tonight at 6 you'll hear the story behind her disappearance that only police know. Lisa's mother talks for the first time only to Newscenter 7.

Promotion consultant Graeme Newell puts it this way, "When most people do teasing what they end up doing is selling the news instead of selling their coverage. They're encouraging people to watch the news, which you can get from any station" (quoted in McGaughy, 2003, p. 21).

One important thing to keep in mind when teasing exclusives—be absolutely sure that what you think is an exclusive is in fact one. Viewers don't like to be lied to, even if it is unintentional.

Sell your coverage

When, Where, and How Often?

Once you have selected your most teasable stories based on viewer relevance, best video, and exclusivity, there are other considerations to get the maximum strategic value out of your newscast promotion. These are questions of placement. Where will a story tease do the most good, and how often can you tease a story before you drive the viewer crazy?

What Are They Watching?

When selecting stories for promos outside of the newscast, know your audience here as well. If your lead-in program is a prime-time news magazine, chances are those are news viewers. You should choose your hard news stories, enterprise stories, and investigative pieces to tease in those promos. But if your lead-in program is a sitcom or drama, many of those viewers will not be news viewers. So you need to select stories that might appeal to a non-news viewer in the show's target demographic. And don't assume you know who the target audience is. At least one executive producer at an ABC affiliate made that mistake assuming *NYPD Blue* was a cop show primarily targeted at men. She was quite surprised to learn that the network considered it a relationship drama and targeted women in much of its promotion. Once she reflected on the show she had to admit, *NYPD Blue* wasn't showing Jimmy Smits's bare butt for male viewers.

   Likewise, promos for the 5:00 p.m. news often appear in soap operas and women's talk shows such as *Oprah*. The audience here is typically stay-at-home parents and women, so they are a great place to tease health, consumer, and education stories. But don't avoid teasing the big news of the day for these viewers—5:00 p.m. viewers want the hard news stories as well. They don't like to be treated as second class viewers who have to wait for the 6:00 p.m. newscast to get the "real" news of the day!

Emotional Rollercoaster

You also have to keep the program environment in mind for your in-show teases. When you decide on your story order, editorial flow is foremost in your mind. But you usually select which stories to tease separately from that process and, in choosing stories to tease, you're looking ahead in your newscast to what's coming up. You're not looking at the story leading into the tease. That means if you're not careful you can set up your anchors and viewers for a very awkward moment.

   If you end a block on a serious story, you don't want to tease weather or something light first in the tease. You're asking your anchor and viewers to make a difficult left turn. You make your anchors appear very callous as they try to transition from a story about death and destruction to a "Gee, what a beautiful day!" weather tease. Be aware of the story going into your tease as you choose the stories for that tease, and the order those stories will go in.

What's Next?

When you're working on in-show teases and headlines, don't make your viewers wait too long for stories after you tease them. Make sure you choose at least one story for your headlines and each tease that's coming up immediately or within one story after the commercial break. Understand that viewers have very specific expectations when they hear the word **next.** So don't say "next" unless you mean the very first story they will see when the newscast continues.

There's nothing more frustrating for a viewer than to hear a tease for a story that interests them and then have to wait 20 minutes to see that story, but we do it all the time. That's called **deep teasing.** It's a good way to get viewers to stay through the newscast, but you need to tell them what you are doing. Don't be afraid to say, "Coming up later" or "Later in this half hour."

Cross-Show Promotion

Many promotion consultants believe the best place to tease your next newscast is inside the current newscast. One of the keys to making cross-show promotion effective is separating repeated stories from new stories. To do this right, producers need to communicate with each other.

Most shows will have a stand-alone tease inside the previous newscast, often done by an anchor for the next show, which promotes that upcoming newscast. This is the place to tease fresh stories that viewers will see in that upcoming newscast. Stories that are being repeated from the current newscast are best teased forward at the end of the story in that newscast. You want to tell the viewer exactly what will be new in the version of the story they'll see in the upcoming newscast. These forward teases can be done by the reporter or as a separate tag to the story.

Now, obviously, you can't do this for every story or you will have a lot of repetition. If you do, the viewers of the current show will begin to feel cheated—as if they're not worthy of getting the whole story, or they'll think there's no reason to watch the next newscast because they've seen all the stories. But forward teases tagging new angles for a couple of stories can be very effective in warding off complaints of repetition.

Repetition

Repetition is an ongoing complaint of viewers, and teasing does contribute to the perception that there's a lot of repetition in local news, especially across 90 minute early local news blocks. When you know you have a very teasable story, there's a strong temptation to promote it as much as possible. Repetition may work well for product advertising, but it can work against you in topical promotion. Once you've promoted a story more than twice, you may build up expectations beyond what the story can deliver or the viewer may think they've already seen the story. This can be especially true when a story is not only promoted within its own show but, as mentioned above, when it's also cross promoted in other shows.

Beating the Repetition Rap

A station in Dayton, Ohio found out the hard way that promotion can contribute to repetition complaints. The station was trying to build a stronger carryover audience from its 5:00 and 5:30 newscasts to the 6:00 p.m. show. One of the reasons viewers gave for not staying with the 90 minutes was repetition. So the news staff worked very hard to present a completely different newscast at 6:00 p.m., but viewers still said there was too much repetition. When the astounded staff took the question to focus groups, it became clear that there was so much promotion for the 6:00 p.m. show in the 5:00 and 5:30 news that viewers heard the 6:00 p.m. stories teased up to four times. So by the time they got to 6:00, viewers thought they'd already seen the stories.

If you do have to tease a story more than once, make the teases as different as possible. Choose a different angle, different video, and definitely write the tease differently. Remember you're selling your **coverage** of the story, not just the story alone.

Example:

Tease 1

You'll hear how last night's mysterious downtown inferno got started from the lead investigator tonight at 6.

Tease 2

SOT *"I didn't think there'd be anything left, but I found this." Next, walk through the apartment fire wreckage with one young mother who managed to find a small treasure in the ashes of her life.*

Tease 3

A surprise finding from arson investigators ... We'll tell you who they're pointing a finger at for last night's downtown apartment fire when we come back.

Let's Write

As you sit down to write your promos, headlines, and teases, always keep in mind that you are no longer writing a news story. You are writing an ad. But that doesn't mean that the rules of good journalism go out the window. Many stations have found themselves in legal trouble, not because there was a prob-

Chapter 8

lem with a story, but because of a tease or promo for the story. Rules of accuracy, balance, and fairness—and not editorializing—apply to promotional copy in the same way they apply to any news story. If the promotion department writes the topical news promos, the copy should be checked by a news manager to make sure it meets legal and ethical journalism standards. If a story has been checked and approved by your station lawyer, make sure all the promos and teases are too. Also beware of file video! Just as you have to be careful with use of file video in stories, so too you have to watch how it's used in promos and teases. You don't want an editor grabbing generic playground video for a promo about a story on child abuse!

There are two elements that every tease needs: **context** and **reason to watch.** Now the second one is obvious. If a tease doesn't give the viewer a reason to watch the story, then why bother? But the first is not always so obvious, especially to a producer who knows everything about the story before writing the tease.

Context

The easiest way to think about context is to think about a good joke you heard. Remember the punch line? Now imagine if you only heard the punch line without the rest of the joke. Is it still funny? A tease that provides a great reason to watch without some context is like a great punch line without the joke. Much of the time it doesn't make sense. The viewer only has a matter of seconds to get your message and make a decision to watch or not—don't make them work for it. They won't do it.

The viewer also doesn't have the benefit of knowing what the story is about, so you can write the cleverest play on words, but if the viewer needs to know what the story is for that play on words to work, you've lost them. You can pretty much guarantee that after they hear the story (if they even stick around for it) viewers won't be thinking back to the tease and saying to themselves, "Now I get it! What a clever writer!"

Example:
Story—Local McDonald's worker wins millions in the lottery.

No Context
There will be no more "Fries with that?" for this Pittsburgh man.

With Context
There will be no more "Fries with that?" for this Pittsburgh McDonald's worker—he's now a Mac-millionaire.

You can see it only took replacing "man" with "McDonald's worker" and adding a phrase about millions to give the tease context and make it understandable to the viewer. But we still leave the viewer wondering how he got millions. Often it's the case that a simple word or phrase is all that's needed to give the viewer some meaning to hang the tease on.

Reason to Watch

The other key thing to remember when you're deciding how you're going to sell a story is **don't give it all away.** While it's important to give the viewer some context so they understand your reason to watch, that doesn't mean you tell the whole story. If you tell the viewer everything they need to know in the tease, they have **no** reason to watch.

Example:

Giving Away Too Much:
We have a major safety recall of Brand X child car seats to tell you about. Details coming up.
(What more details do we need?)

Giving a Reason to Watch:
Parents you might want to grab a pencil, we've got some important safety information you need to know coming up next.

The other thing to note about the first tease in the above example is it limits the audience for the story much more than the second tease. If a viewer hears the first tease and doesn't own a Brand X car seat, she's not interested in the story. But the second tease is going to attract any parent, and probably grandparents or aunts and uncles too.

Reason to Watch Toolbox

There are many ways to create a reason to watch as you write your teases. Here are a few of the best:

- **Create a question** in the viewer's mind that the story will answer. This doesn't mean you need to write the tease as a question. Look again at the example above on the safety seat recall. The first tease doesn't create any questions in the viewer's mind, but the second certainly does.
- **Promise a benefit.** Give the "what's in it for me" to the viewer. This is especially useful for health and consumer stories.

   Example:
   Gas prices jumped another nickel this week. We'll show you where to find the cheapest gas in town.

- **Go for the unusual.** Hopefully you've already done this when you selected which stories to tease. Now make sure you follow through in your writing. What is it that makes the story unusual? What makes it news?
- **Sound/natsot.** The most underused tool in teasing is sound. If you have compelling, emotional sound in a story, use some of it in your tease. Don't **tell** viewers they are going to hear the mother's emotional reaction, let them hear a sample. The same goes for good natural sound. It's what view-

Chapter 8

ers hear that brings their attention to the television—good natsot can be a surprise and an attention getter.

The Devil's in the Details

Writing headlines and teases is much like every other part of producing. It's the details that can get you, and in promotion writing "details" is a dirty word for more than just that reason. We use the word details all the time in tease and headline writing, but what does it mean? "More Details Ahead"; "The Details Coming Up"; "Stay with us for the Details." Be specific. "Details" doesn't tell the viewer anything about what they are going to get from the story. And quiet frankly in broadcast news, "detail" is not what we do best. We rarely provide all the details of a story. That's what print stories do. So attend to the details, don't write them.

Video Reference

This is crucial. Video is your best weapon in your tease arsenal, but it must be referenced. Again remember the viewer only has 4 to 7 seconds to get your tease message. If the pictures and words don't match, you create confusion. With good video, the tease can write itself—just link the words to the pictures. Always know what the video is before you write the tease, and then be specific in your instructions to the video editor—make sure you get the video you reference!

Video Reference Oops!

A producer in Green Bay learned a tough lesson about communication in tease video editing. She wrote the following tease:

Hundreds of people came out to honor Green Bay's most beloved former mayor. We'll take you to the memorial at City Hall ... Plus it's the biggest and ugliest catch of the day.

Unfortunately the video editor mixed up the video, so as the anchor was talking about the former mayor, viewers saw a very large, ugly sturgeon fish laid out on the dock, and when the anchor referenced the fish, there was the mayor lying in state!

Sense of Immediacy

When writing any tease for a story, make sure you are teasing the newest part of the story. Ongoing stories sound stale to viewers when they are part of teases unless the tease is specific. And don't fall back on the old trite words, "we'll have the very latest on … ." It's the news; of course you're going to give people the latest information. Give the viewer a **good** reason to watch the next update on a story you've been covering for awhile.

Red Flag Words

Start your teases just as if you were starting a news story. Don't start a tease with a red flag word or phrase. These are words such as "when we come back," "coming up," "ahead at 5," "next at 6." When you start your tease with those phrases it's like holding up a big red flag that signals "commercial break." The viewer may hear "Stay tuned for …" but they're thinking "go to the bathroom," "check out the fridge," "change the channel." Save your tease words and phrases for the second or third story of the tease. You may be able to keep the viewer's attention through the tease if you do. The viewer will realize it's a tease soon enough on their own, you don't have to wave that red flag in their face.

Reporter Teases

Using your reporters to tease their own stories live or on tape can be effective, but only if the reporter knows how to tease. So many reporters simply do another version of their stand-up and tack an "I'll have that story at 6" to the end of it. Just as you work through story angles with your reporters, talk to them about their stand-up or live teases. Make sure they understand the difference between a stand-up in the middle of their story and a stand-up tease.

We're in the Communication Business

One final note about writing teases. As with almost any other part of producing, the key to successful newscast promotion is communication. You can't sell the best video, sound, and story angles in your newscast if you don't know what they are. That means you've got to talk to your reporters, photographers, and editors. Can you imagine an advertising agency not knowing absolutely everything about a product before developing an ad campaign to sell that product? The same goes for selling your newscast. You need to take the time to know what you've got to sell before you craft your promos, headlines, and teases. And believe it—good promotion writing is a craft.

News Branding

No discussion of newscast promotion would be complete without a few words on branding. The last several years branding has become a buzzword when talking about promoting the news and the station. In fact we've been branding the news for a long time. The earliest branding we simply referred to as formatting.

WCPO-TV (Cincinnati) Traffic Reporter Cindy Matthews looks for good video to tease her segment.

There was the *Action News* format and the *Eyewitness News* format. But essentially these were brands that set up newscast reputations and viewer expectations as explained in chapter 6.

More recently news brands have come in the form of slogans, such as "Live, Local, Late Breaking," "Hometown Television," "Coverage You Can Count On," and "Where Your News Comes First." The problem is in too many cases, stations have assumed they could create instant brands like you make instant pudding. Take a box of unidentifiable powder, add milk, and—voilà!—you get pudding. You can't take a mish-mash of news, weather, and sports, add a slogan and—voilà!—you get a news brand!

That doesn't mean that television news can't be successfully branded. It just requires approaching the process in the same way marketers have for years. First let's define what a brand is. Here's a marketing textbook definition:

> A brand is a name, term, sign, design, or a unifying combination of them, intended to identify and distinguish the product or service from its competitors. Brand names communicate attributes and meaning that are designed to enhance the value of a product beyond its functional value. The basic reason for branding is to provide a symbol that facilities rapid identification of the product and its repurchase by customers. (McDowell & Batten, 1999, p. 17)

This definition makes it clear that a simple slogan is not a brand. First what's promised in the slogan has to be valued by the consumer, in our case the viewer, and second, the newscast has to live up to the slogan. Do you really think viewers will believe your news is "Live, Local, Late Breaking" just because you tell them it is? Stations that have successfully branded themselves started with audience research to find out what viewers valued in their news and what they might be missing from the news they watch. Then those stations took a realistic look at their product and resources to see which of those values or niches they could deliver.

Typically that's where news producers enter the branding process. It's unlikely you will be part of the decision to create the brand, but you will likely have to implement it in the way you produce and promote your newscast. It's important to find out what the brand means in terms of added value for your viewers, because that's the product you need to deliver if the brand is going to be successful for your station. What does it mean to be the station "Where Your News Comes First"? News and promotion managers should be able to answer that question with concrete things you can do in your newscast and promotion every day to serve your viewers. That's how you turn a slogan into a brand that can set your news apart from the competition in a real way.

Two Branding Successes

The Dayton Ohio market has two examples of branding success. WHIO-TV has been the longtime news leader in the market. As a Cox station, it does a lot of audience research to support news and promotion. The station has used the brand "Coverage You Can Count On" successfully for years. The brand was developed from research that showed people in Dayton highly valued hard news coverage in their newscasts. WHIO committed to a coverage position with the largest staff of reporters, four bureaus including the state capitol, and a strong special projects and investigative unit.

The number two station, WDTN-TV, tried for years to also develop a coverage position, but to no avail. They tried multiple slogans and graphics—some a close derivative of "Coverage You Can Count On". But inevitably research showed that viewers didn't identify good coverage with WDTN. In fact some of the station's slogans were more often named as WHIO slogans than WDTN. So the station did audience research of its own to find out what viewers weren't getting from WHIO and what they perceived were the best attributes of WDTN. The station struck gold. It turned out that WHIO was considered weak in weather coverage and WDTN had the top two weather talents in town. The station invested heavily in state-of-the-art weather equipment and began selling itself as "Your Weather Authority." Within eight months of focusing nearly all promotion on weather, going all out with severe weather coverage, and looking for weather related news stories, nearly 90% of viewers surveyed recognized WDTN as their "Weather Authority"—an incredible turnaround from brands that fewer than 60% of viewers associated with the station.

Ethics of Promotion and Branding

There aren't many absolute rules in television news, but this is one. **Don't over-sell your stories**—never exaggerate the importance of a story and don't promise something the story doesn't deliver. The idea of newscast promotion is to entice viewers to watch, not drive them away. Overselling stories in teases and promos will drive viewers away. If you don't believe that, think about the last time you bought a product based on promises made in an ad. If the product didn't perform as promised, what was your reaction? Chances are you took it back. Certainly you didn't buy it again, and you probably told your friends not to buy it either.

Viewers unfortunately can't take back the time they invested in watching your newscast to see a particular story if it isn't as advertised. However they can and will decide not to watch again if you make them promises or set high expectations for a story and then don't deliver. They also will be happy to tell others about their dissatisfaction.

The Sales Rule of 150

Most people know 150 people they'd invite to their wedding or who would come to their funeral. They'll tell all 150 if they have a complaint about a product or service. And those 150 will tell their circle of 150, and so on.

Word of dissatisfaction spreads!

Sometimes you don't have to exaggerate to oversell a story. You can simply over tease it. Perhaps you have a really cool kicker story with fun video so you tease it two or three times. But when you get to the story, it's a short story, as many kickers are. So you may have spent upwards of 25 seconds teasing a story that's only 20 to 25 seconds long. The viewers are disappointed because their anticipation has been built up for something more.

The other big no-no in teasing and promotion is sensationalism and fear mongering. Here's one of the worst examples of fear mongering that came from a New York City station:

> 10:30 p.m. Promo—*Baby formula sold locally kills two infants ... Details at 11.*
>
> The station received a dozen calls from worried mothers concerned that the baby formula they were about to feed their babies would hurt them. It turned out that the story happened in California and that's the only place the formula was contaminated, but the *brand* of formula was also sold in local stores. Needless to say, there were many parents who complained they'd been frightened for no good reason.

Sensationalism most often happens when teasing crime and/or tragedy. Typically these stories don't need any additional hype to get people to watch, the stories "sell" themselves. Here's a really tacky example from a station in

Lexington, Kentucky teasing a story about a big increase in traffic fatalities over a holiday weekend:

> Headlines—*Kentucky ... there's blood on your highways tonight!*
>
> Just a little over-dramatic, don't you think?

The bottom line is good teasing and promotion gives viewers a reason to continue watching your newscast without promising something you can't deliver, manipulating viewers' emotions, or lying to them. Any of those things might get a viewer to stay for a particular story, but in the long run cheap tricks will drive them away from your newscast.

Sources

Albiniak, P. (2003, June 9). Coming up at 11! Viewers don't care. *Broadcasting and Cable,* p. 5.

Magid Associates. (1998). *Strategic Teasing Workshop.* Minneapolis, MN: KSTP-TV.

McDowell, W., & Batten, A. (1999). *Branding TV: Principles and Practice.* Washington, DC: National Association of Broadcasters.

McGaughy, C. (2003, May). The big tease. *Communicator,* 19–22.

The Poynter Institute. (1995, August). *Producing seminar.* St. Petersburg, FL.

Chapter 8

LIFE IN THE BOOTH

"Reality is the leading cause of stress amongst those in touch with it."
Jane Wagner and Lily Tomlin

Going into the control room to begin a live newscast always feels a bit like being at an amusement park and boarding a rollercoaster. When you go to sit in your chair in the control booth, you should be required to put on a safety belt. Those minutes before you go live are like slowly climbing up a large hill; you can almost hear the tracks sharply clicking underneath the car you are riding in. You know the inevitable is coming. You know it's already too late to stop, and once you reach the top of the hill, or the top of the hour, you're going to be off for a ride.

Once a newscast begins, it can either be a smooth and exhilarating experience, or it can be full of unexpected turns and dips, jolting you from one moment to the next. This chapter will help you to achieve the former rather than the latter. But one thing is certain; with live television, almost anything is possible.

Getting Oriented

The first key to learning how to "booth" a newscast is to learn what's in that booth: What are the tools at your disposal, and what is all that other stuff in the room? The booth or control room is that room in a television station or cable outlet where people congregate with equipment to put a newscast or any locally produced program on the air. It's often dimly lit and over air-conditioned.

Generally everyone has an assigned spot in a control room. The two people that control most of what goes on during the newscast are the director—that's the person in charge of all the technical aspects—and the producer. Often these two sit in close proximity, sometimes next to one another; sometimes there are two rows of seats, with the director in front and the producer not far behind them.

Once you find that producer's position, take a look around. Usually there will be some kind of console in front of you, often with a small microphone attached and some buttons that seem to be related to that microphone. In some control rooms, there will be a headset with a microphone attached that plugs into the console. Whichever, this is designed to let the producer communicate with different people in different parts of the building. For instance, in most cases, the producer can push a button and speak into an anchorperson's ear through a system called an IFB, or Interrupted Feedback. Push a different button and you can talk to the assignment editor in the newsroom. Push another and you may be able to talk to someone in video editing, to see if a tape will be ready in time for its proper time slot in the newscast. Press yet another and you should be able to talk to a field crew standing by to do a live report from a breaking news story. And there may be others. All of these allow you to be in contact with different people involved in the newscast, and, in return, it allows them to be in contact with you.

Producer and director at WDTN-TV (Dayton) sit next to each other during noon news.

Most control rooms also are outfitted now with a computer terminal linked to the newsroom through the news producing software. This means that a producer from the control room can change scripts, times, technical information, or even rearrange elements of a show if needed. The newsroom software also can help in backtiming the show and allows the producer to follow along seeing the same copy the anchors see in the studio. In addition, a computer can allow a producer to look up a fact or two on the Internet quickly or even e-mail someone with a question to verify information if needed.

Most control booths also are equipped with some kind of clock, digital or otherwise, that producers can set or watch to help keep the show on time, to monitor how long stories or segments are running, or to help give time cues to talent. In most cases, for instance, weathercasters are given a set time for their segment, but they ad-lib most of the content. It is up to the show producer to make sure they get time cues—signals telling them how much time they have left in their segment—so they know when to stop talking and toss it back to the anchors. The

IFB/ communications panel in WCNC-TV control room.

producer usually passes on these cues to the director, who tells the floor director, and then a hand signal is given to the weathercaster.

Control rooms have lots of other equipment as well. There's the video switcher, a huge piece of equipment with lots of illuminated buttons that allows a director or technical director to choose from an array of video sources and also allows them to add special effects when called for. There's often an audio control board, also with lots of switches and sliding bars, that allows for different audio sources to be selected during the newscast. Most control rooms also have some type of computer character generator, which is the device used to create titles and graphics that appear during the newscast. It's good to be aware of what these pieces of equipment do, although the producer is primarily concerned with the news content of the show, not overseeing the technical aspects of the show.

The director also technical directs (TDs), working the switcher, during a newscast at WHIO-TV (Dayton).

Chapter 9

Audio engineer in a sound proof booth behind the control room works the audio board during a newscast at WHIO-TV (Dayton).

The control room is the place where a group of people work together to put a newscast on the air. The other people you might find in the booth include

- The **Director:** The person responsible for the technical aspects of the newscast.
- The **Technical Director:** The person who pushes buttons on the switcher and other equipment, usually based on cues given by a director. In some stations the director and technical director are the same person.
- The **Audio Technician:** This crew member generally sits in front of the audio board and controls all of the audio sources for the newscast.
- The **Character Generator Operator:** As the title implies, this person helps with titles and graphics that appear on the air during a newscast.

Outside the control room there may also be

- The **Floor Director:** Who works in the studio and gives talent cues.
- The **TelePrompTer Operator:** Who scrolls through scripts as the anchors read copy.
- The **Camera Operator:** Who runs the studio cameras.
- The **Tape Operator:** Who loads and rolls tapes to be aired during the show.
- The **Video Engineer:** Who monitors camera color and brightness levels, video tape levels, and locks in and monitors live shots.

Some stations now have installed systems in which a director may handle some or all of these jobs from the control room. In these systems cameras are now robotic and tapes are preloaded. Or a station may not use tape at all, storing all the stories digitally on a hard drive. Because of these computerized systems, some of these jobs have been eliminated and now fewer people control more aspects of the technical execution of the show.

The Producer's Role in the Booth

The producer's job in the control room is to oversee the newscast. The producer makes all decisions concerning the content of the newscast, what stories air where, how long segments should run, which anchors read which stories, which stories should be cut. What's a little ironic about being a producer is when you come to the control room, you have worked all day to execute this newscast, yet once the show begins it will be up to the technical staff and the people who are on the air to make it all work. In some regard you will be a like a coach, monitoring what's happening, making some decisions, but not executing what happens by being on air or pushing any buttons. The fruition of your work for the day is primarily now in other people's hands, and you must do all you can to see that it goes smoothly without actually doing any of it yourself. So what should you do in the control room?

Arrive Early

If possible, it's helpful to arrive in the booth more than a moment or two before the show begins. If you can arrive 10 or 15 minutes early, you can double-check certain parts of the show. A primary job of the producer, especially in the booth, is to anticipate problems and troubleshoot or, when something goes wrong, do damage control. Anticipating and correcting in advance is always much easier than trying to fix things after they have crashed and burned, so troubleshooting is a big part of a producer's job. Arriving early can give you a chance to foresee any problems that may be coming.

- **The director.** For instance, does the director, having now looked through a rundown and scripts, need anything from you or have any questions about what is ahead?
- **Live shots.** You can see if the technical crew has the live shots up and running in TV monitors in the control room. Check to see if technically these live shots are running smoothly, or, if there's a problem, what can be done to fix it. Is there a good, clean video and audio signal? Is the reporter on hand? The photographer? Can you talk to the field crew and make sure everything's going according to plan? Another question you might ask is, if there's a problem, should the live shot be moved down to a later slot in the newscast or will it have to be scrapped entirely? If you lose a live shot, that means your newscast timing will now be off, so you can begin planning how you will fill that time. If a live shot is not going to work and it involves an important story,

Chapter 9

you'll need to think about how you can still get that information on the air, even without a live shot.

• **Are the stories ready?** It might also be helpful to check with the editing area and see how stories are coming along. Is the lead story edited and ready for air? If not, will it be done in time for its slot in the show? If it's going to be close, you must begin thinking of contingencies. Should the story be moved down? Should you alert the anchors and let them know there might be a last moment change?

• **The anchors.** It's always good to just say a quick word to the anchors, including the weathercaster and sports anchor. Do they have any quick questions? Is there anything different or unusual you need to alert them to? Any potential rough spots? At the very least you need to double check and make sure the IFB is working and you have good communication with them.

• **Technical crew.** As well, you might ask the technical crew if they have questions or concerns, and ask yourself if there's anything they need to be alerted to in advance like the possibility of a late story or breaking news.

WDTN-TV (Dayton) Videographer Dan Yohey communicates with the producer from inside the live ENG truck before a liveshot.

Married to the Director

News producers, to be successful, have to nurture and maintain good relationships with a lot of people on the staff. Relationships with the bosses, the news director and/or the executive producer are obviously important. Earlier in the book we wrote about the important relationship between the anchors and the producer. Producers must have good working relationships with most everyone in the newsroom. But in the booth during the newscast, the producer's relationship with the director is crucial. These two people are in charge of the show: They are both calling the shots. If one of them isn't doing a good job, or if the two of them are not getting along, it can wreak havoc on the staff and the show. The relationship between a producer and a director is often a close working relationship. Some have equated it to a marriage, and as we all know, there are good and bad marriages. The key in most of these situations is communication. If there are honest, open, and direct lines of communication between the director and the producer, things are generally good. One of the worst qualities in a producer is not communicating important information to other people, especially the director.

Before and during a newscast, it is essential to keep the director apprised of what is going on. If there will be a change of any sort, the director is the person that will have to make that change happen technically. If a story will be dropped, if there's a late-breaking story, if a story won't be done on time, the director needs to know. When a producer and director are in tune with one another, chances are much better that a successful newscast will result. In fact, some producers and directors get to know each other well and can begin to anticipate what the other will need so that these two are working in excellent accord. As a producer, you will begin to appreciate outstanding directors because of their skill in negotiating different crises and their ability to stay calm and help get your show on the air, at times flawlessly. In addition the best directors also are great sources of ideas when you want to add that something extra to the production value of your newscast, and they appreciate being brought into the planning process early enough to make those special touches happen.

The director marks scripts for the noon news at WHIO-TV (Dayton).

Producer/Director Relationship

Bob Pusatory is a newscast director at KUSA-TV (Denver) where he has worked for the past 23 years. Bob has won two Heartland Emmys for directing and one for technical direction. We asked Bob to list some qualities he has found in excellent producers who are especially good in the control room. Here's his list.

Ten Qualities of a Great Booth Producer

• **Have a back-up plan:** If it looks like the lead story is in jeopardy. Make this plan known to the director early.

• **Know the technology:** Have some understanding of the equipment, its capabilities, and its limitations.

• **Be knowledgeable of other people's jobs:** The best producers have done other jobs such as studio camera, tape, audio, and so forth. This helps them understand the effect of their decisions on the crew.

• **Stay calm in tense situations:** A calm voice in the director's ear can make a huge difference in the execution of breaking news or a newscast that has a lot of changes.

• **Communicate to the director at the proper time:** Wait to talk to the director if he or she is giving instructions or otherwise busy with the crew. Always confirm that the director has heard and understands.

• **Give the director time to make changes and relay them to the crew:** Last second changes can make a segment go bad real fast if the crew doesn't have time to react.

• **Be in control during breaking news:** The producer should be the only one to make content decisions during breaking news situations. Too many cooks …

• **Be confident:** With decisions made before and during the show.

• **Be accurate:** Call remotes by their technical name, for example "We're going to Cheryl on Remote 1 next" not "We're going to Cheryl's live shot next."

• **Be patient:** Don't rush to get a story on NOW. Better clean and accurate.

During the News

Eyes Go Where?

Once the show begins, producers spend most of their time trying to pay attention to several things at once. Among those, what's going on the air? Is the show proceeding the way we had planned? Is what the anchors are saying correct? How does the show look and feel? Remember, you know the show better than anyone, so you have the best chance at catching mistakes or even preventing them. If you're checking the graphics monitor, you can catch a wrong graphic or misspelled super before it gets on the air, or if you're checking the tape monitors, you can catch wrong video cuing up before it gets on the air.

Producers are watching the television monitors but also referring to their rundown, the blueprint for the newscast. Why refer to the rundown? Because most good producers anticipate what's ahead. KOAT Producer Leslie Garza says when in the control room it's crucial to, "know what you've done, where you are, and what's coming up next."

Troubleshooting

Part of being a good troubleshooter in the booth is always thinking a step or two ahead. Most producers know within their show where the particular spots are where there might be trouble. For instance, do we have a tape that's coming in late? Or is there a tricky live shot ahead? Producers think ahead not to give themselves more stress but to try to think through what they might do should things go wrong. If the tape is late, then what? If the live shot runs longer then we allotted, then what? If the anchor reads something incorrectly, then what? Producers are often planning contingencies in their head while watching the newscast, trying to be ready to react if a problem comes up. This skill takes some time and experience. Unfortunately, you often learn the most from mistakes, even though your goal is a mistake-free newscast. But as a producer, if you can learn to anticipate problems, you will be well on your way to being a good producer in the control room. It will make the difference between sitting and observing your newscast—almost feeling helpless when things go amiss—and being in control no matter what happens. The longer you produce, the more you feel you are driving the roller coaster, rather than being taken for a ride.

Time Flies, Really

Another key element for the producer to monitor during the news is the time. It is the producer's responsibility to make sure that the newscast ends on time. Newsroom computer programs help a lot, showing a producer whether the newscast is running on time. However, if any times have been inputted incorrectly into the computer, these mistakes will affect the backtiming. Some producers like to print a rundown and backtime the newscast on paper as a backup to the computer, or keep an eye on the control room clock as a double check for the computer timing. Either way, it's vital as the news progresses to monitor how you are doing on time.

Time during a newscast is kind of a funny thing. You would think that if all the times are correct—the time it will take for anchors to read stories, the time it takes for edited stories to run, the allocated time for weather or sports—you could figure out exactly how long a newscast will run. But the reality is much different. Anchors, while often consistent in their reading pace, can at times read a script or two faster or slower. Ad-lib times between anchors are unpredictable because they are unscripted. Edited stories often come in at a slightly (or significantly) different time than what you had allocated. Weathercasters and sportscasters can go long or short, even if you are giving them time cues. So producers monitor the time as the show goes along and make decisions and adjustments as needed. A producer may be able to add time to a newscast if things run short by adding a bit of time to weather or sports. Or a producer may be able to make up time by cutting a story along the way. No matter what adjustments are made, it's crucial to communicate to the director and all involved (anchor, weathercasters, sportscasters) what decision you've made.

Often commercial breaks become natural places to make these adjustments, because they are brief pauses from the newscast when you can give out instructions without as many distractions. Some producers always go into the newscast light—in other words, with some extra time unaccounted for—because things generally go longer than expected. Good producers also get to know the talent. They learn which folks consistently go long and which go short. With this knowledge, a producer can plan, anticipate, and adjust accordingly.

The Big Finish

Timing becomes increasingly important as the newscast moves along, because the producer is trying to hit a precise end time. What a producer has planned for the end of a newscast becomes very important. To have some flexibility in what you've planned for the last minute or so of the newscast can help significantly. If you need to fill a bit of time, or if you need to end earlier than expected, it's good to have some options open. Most stations have several speeds at which the end-

WHIO-TV (Dayton)
Producer Quincy Wallace
decides what to drop when
the newscast is running
long.

ing credits can be run. Credits identify the crew by name and position with electronic graphics. In addition, most newscasts end with some type of copyright. So if you need to get out of the show quickly, you can choose just to show the copyright. If you are coming out of the show just a bit short, you may be able to pick a slightly longer version of the credits, and so on.

The last story in the newscast is usually called the kicker story. It's often a lighter story to end the newscast on a happier note. Producers can build one or two of these stories into the newscast with the idea that one or both might have to be dropped depending on the timing of the show. Other things that often run in a final block of the newscast are promos—short teases that highlight what's coming up in a future newscast—or some stations let weather and/or sports have another few seconds for a recap of the forecast or another brief sports story. Again, a producer could keep these in or drop them as needed according to time. Since most newscasts end on a shot that includes all the anchors together, they often can ad-lib a bit to help make up time, but asking them to fill for more than 10 or 15 seconds may be risky.

One thing to keep in mind about timing is if you go into a show heavy, or over time, or you start picking up too much time early in the show, don't panic and start dropping stories in the first or second block. These are the heart of your news coverage. As mentioned above, there are usually plenty of places lower in your newscast to skim time if you're running over—try to stay away from cutting your essential *news* content.

Professional Demeanor

As a newscast producer, you are the person in charge of the newscast. That means people are looking to you for leadership. Leadership not only in what you say and what decisions you make but also in the way you carry yourself and behave. In other words, your demeanor, the tone of your voice, and your behavior send a message to people in the newsroom, in the studio, and especially in the control room about how the newscast is going. Often excellent producers are people who seem not to get easily ruffled. This is one job where a poker face, the ability to look calm even if you are not feeling calm, is a valuable asset. People don't want hysteria in their leader. They don't want fierce anger. They don't want paralyzed silence. People generally want calm assurance. This doesn't mean you have to be devoid of any emotion whatsoever. But it does mean that, especially during a live program, high highs and low emotional lows probably are not a good idea. News Director Jim Ogle says: "Think air traffic controller: calm, confident voice. You might not have all the answers. But you will keep it together because you sound grounded and in control. Don't yell!"

Control rooms during newscasts are often places of seeming chaos. Several people are talking at once, maybe even in elevated tones. There's also the sound of what's going out in the air. Often you can hear people talking over the intercom from another location. People rush in with last minute information. The director is barking out cues. There is usually a palpable energy or excitement in the air. Many good producers say they thrive in this atmosphere. They are self-described adrenaline junkies. The job of a producer in the control room is to bring order in the midst of this chaos. Keeping a calm head, anticipating what's next, making sound decisions in the midst of crisis, dealing with spontaneity, and helping relax others who are angry or stressed: these are all the marks of a good newscast producer. We'll go into some of the tips described in the accompanying box, "Dealing With Stress," in more depth a little later in the book.

Dealing With Stress

Newscast producers face stress every day, with deadlines and uncertainty of news. But often times the control room is where a lot of stress happens, as the whole work day comes to a head. A few things might help you manage your day-to-day stress and allow you to enter the control room with a clear head and a calm mind:

- **Take five minutes and get out of the newsroom.** Take a walk, leave the building, get some quick exercise, all might help you relax and refocus.

- **Don't be afraid to delegate.** Are there anchors, editors, other producers, associate producers, or interns who can take on a task?

- **There are times you'll have to say no.** Protect yourself and know what you are and are not capable of. Extra shifts and extra duties may help advance your career, but they can also take a toll—know your own limits.

- **Deep breaths can help.** Using techniques from yoga or meditation may also help during the day.

- **Share your stress.** It may be helpful to have a colleague or even a friend outside of work who you can talk to about things that are causing stress in your life. Sometimes a quick conversation can really help.

- **Sleep and eat.** Getting enough sleep and eating a healthy, balanced, diet can do much to help you be prepared for stressful situations.

- **Physical activity is good.** Jogging, working out, playing basketball, riding a bicycle, and other physical activities are all helpful stress outlets.

- **Invest.** Finding activities outside of work can be very helpful, whether it's a church, synagogue or mosque, or another kind of volunteer activity. Finding a life outside of the newsroom often can help put things in a broader, healthier perspective.

- **Forgive yourself.** Many excellent professionals are their own worst critics. Understand that you will make mistakes and you can learn from those experiences, but then you need to let go and move on, not dwell on times when you weren't your best.

Talking to Talent

One of the ways in which professional demeanor can be particularly important is how, during a newscast, a producer relates to the people who are on the air. Now, in most cases, producers have the ability to talk into anchors' ears with the touch of a button through the IFB system. But that may not always be a good thing. First, very few people can be reading a story or talking live on air and not be impacted in some way by someone speaking to them in their ear. A few anchors can listen to one thing and say something different at the same time flawlessly, but it's often a dangerous idea. What may happen is the anchor may just begin repeating whatever you are saying in their ear. So if that's "Cut page B-4," that's probably NOT what you wanted the anchor to say live to the viewing audience. A general rule of thumb is to try to talk to anchors when they are not reading.

WHIO-TV (Dayton) Anchor Jim Brown listens in his IFB and checks the rundown on a laptop on the set, while the producer updates him on changes to the newscast.

As well, *how* you talk is very important. Speaking quickly or angrily is most often a very bad idea. Calm and clear should be the goal. Talking through the IFB should be kept to a minimum. So, if possible, one or two words is best. "Skip B-4," or "wrap quickly," are good short messages. A bad example: "I think the tape for B-4 is going to be late so I'm going to move it father back in the newscast." Many news sets have a phone on which the anchors can call the control room if needed so that during commercials breaks there can be a two-way conversation, which may be helpful.

Dealing With Crises

No matter how well you've prepared the script, no matter how early you arrive in the control room, no matter how much you've talked through the show with those involved, sometimes bad things happen. Live television is live, which means the spontaneous and unpredictable will happen. What separates great producers from good producers is the ability to deal with the unexpected. When something blows up, you want to stay calm, think clearly, think about what's next, and how you can recover. If you can get into a package (a pre-edited story with reporter's narration) or into a commercial break, it can be a lifesaver, because it gives you a few seconds to think, make a decision, and communicate that decision to the director and anchors. Great producers are calm and decisive under fire.

People who can suffer most in a crisis are the anchors, because they can be left live on the air with nothing to say, often with that deer-in-the-headlights look in their eyes. The quicker you can give them direction in their ear or through cues of what to do next, the better off everyone will be. At these moments, their credibility is at stake, as is the credibility of the news organization, so trying to help anchors and protect them from these moments is a good strategy, whenever possible. Executive Producer Mike Wortham offers this advice: "Take care of your anchors. The best way to foster a good producer/anchor relationship is getting them to trust you. You are often their only lifeline in difficult situations. If you can gain your anchor's trust … those difficult situations are when you both will really shine."

WDTN-TV (Dayton) Anchor Marsha Bonhart does a quick makeup touch-up during a commercial break.

Taking time during a crisis to complain, curse, scream, or moan may make you feel better, but it can be a sure fire way to lose focus. Those valuable moments when producers are expressing some emotion may be the very moments needed to make a decision and move on. It's better to suffer quietly and don't let it interfere with the newscast. One measure of your performance may not be the fact that there was a crisis but what happens next. How you recover from the crisis may be much more important than the actual glitch itself.

Post Mortems

At some stations it's common for the producer, director, anchors, and perhaps other managers or crew members to meet briefly and discuss the newscast. If there are problems, this can be a good opportunity to recap what happened and why and what can be done to improve for the next time. Good producers give out praise along with criticism. It often goes a long way if you wait and offer constructive criticism one-on-one rather than in a meeting or in front of colleagues. Likewise, listen to criticism directed your way and try not to be too defensive. It might be more productive to listen, consider what's being said, and think about ways you might improve.

Fritz Kunkel wrote that: "To be mature means to face, and not evade, every fresh crisis that comes." Learning to work in the control room during a live newscast gives you the opportunity daily to face a different crisis and deal with it head on. Hopefully some of the things we've outlined in this chapter will help you have grace under pressure in the booth.

Chapter 9

MANAGING LIVE

Joe Anchorman: "We go now to Joan Reporter live at city hall where some eastside neighbors raised quite a ruckus earlier this evening."

Joan Reporter: "It's all quiet now, Joe ... " (thinking ... No kidding it's quiet because the meeting ended three hours ago but the darn producer is making me stand out here in the cold and dark where no one can see anything except me in a black hole so she can have a live shot for her lead story!)

L ive field production and television news seem to go hand-in-hand these days. It's very rare to see a newscast in any time period that doesn't have at least one live shot from a remote location, and most have several. In fact in a study of live coverage in eight television markets, researchers found that re-porters appeared live about 40% more often than they did on tape (Tuggle & Huffman, 1999). Clearly one of the greatest advantages television has over other media delivering news is the ability to bring the viewer live pictures and sound from the scene of a story virtually anywhere in the world. And when live tech-nology is used in that way, to take the viewer to the scene of a developing story, it is an incredible tool. The problem is that's not the way live technology is used most often.

There is no doubt that as a producer live field production will be a center-piece of your daily routine. And not just in your newscast production, but also in breaking news situations where you have to produce live updates or ongoing coverage, as well as special event programming such as election night cover-age. One of the things that separates the best producers from the rest of the pack is the ability to use live technology effectively and not fall into the trap of "live for live sake."

Why Do We Go Live?

That may seem like an obvious question, but unfortunately, as mentioned above, the answer's not always the one we'd like to think—the good journalism answer. Certainly there are many times when we go live to the field because there is an immediate development in a story that we can let the viewer watch unfold as it happens. But much more often, there is no immediate development and we are live at a scene long after the reason for being there has ended. Don't believe that? Watch local television and make a conscious note of the number of live shots from the scene of an ongoing news story.

News researchers Charlie Tuggle and Suzanne Huffman did just that, examining live coverage from 120 newscasts in eight different television markets. They found that more than half of the straight reporter live shots (no videotape) and nine out of ten lives that wrapped around a preproduced reporter package had no journalistic justification for the live. The event or story was long over (Tuggle & Huffman, 1999). So why waste the resources and news time on a live shot that adds virtually nothing to the story? Well, there are two other reasons that too often trump good journalism—big money investment and audience response.

Big Money Investment

Live technology is readily available, but it isn't cheap. A microwave live truck, or ENG (electronic news gathering) truck, can cost anywhere from $150,000 to $250,000 depending on how you outfit it. An ENG truck is the one you see with the high mast pole and short yellow rods (called golden rods) or a small disk at the top. There are much cheaper portable ENG units that you can put in the trunk of a news car, but they have a very limited range. ENG broadcasts live by sending a microwave signal back to the station's tower. So the golden rods need a line

of site to the tower in order to go live, and your ability to go live is limited by distance and topography. Also you can't go live if there is lightning in the area, because that mast is just like a big lightning rod! Another way to use ENG live is via helicopter. But owning or leasing a helicopter is even more expensive.

An SNG (satellite news gathering) truck can cost a station a half million dollars. The SNG truck is the one with the big dish on top that bounces the live signal off a satellite and then back down to the station receiving dishes. There are now suitcase size portable satellite lives and satellite videophones that you saw in action during the Iraq war. Of course they too are cheaper than the satellite truck and much more practical in a mobile situation such as being embedded with a mili-

WDTN-TV (Dayton) ENG truck with mast up ready for a liveshot.

tary unit, but, again, the quality of the live picture and sound is fair to poor. You can go live from virtually anywhere with SNG as long as the dish isn't blocked from sending the signal upwards (sometimes in downtown areas surrounded by too many tall buildings an SNG signal might be blocked). Also an SNG signal might be disturbed by weather—if you have a home satellite system you know when it's raining hard or if the wind's gusting you lose your satellite signal, well, the same thing happens with SNG. It's called rain fade.

WCNC-TV (Charlotte) SNG truck with dish down, ready to hit the road.

Nearly all stations have some form of ENG, but helicopter and SNG technology tend to be widely used only in the top 50 markets.

Market Size	SNG Truck	Own/Lease/Hire Helicopter
DMA 1–25	73%	80%
DMA 26–50	62%	46%
DMA 51–100	33%	35%
DMA 101–150	20%	20%
DMA 151+	3%	6%
From *Ball State University Annual Survey* (2001). Radio-Television News Directors Association.		

So if you are the station general manager paying hundreds of thousands of dollars for one or more SNG trucks and a helicopter lease, are you going to want to see that expensive technology sitting in the parking lot during a live newscast? Chances are the answer is no. In fact some helicopter leases include clauses that say the chopper is flying during morning and/or early evening newscasts no matter what. So if your station is paying for that flying time every day, you better believe the pressure is going to be on you as the producer to find ways to use live chopper shots. That often leads to live for live sake (making up reasons to go live that have zero news value) or coverage of very minor spot news stories just because the chopper is over the scene. Every second you waste on a non-news event to showcase live technology is a second that can't be devoted to an important news story.

Audience Response

Stations wouldn't make the investment in such expensive live technology if the viewers didn't respond well to it, and, in fact, they do. Much of the audience research shows viewers rate live coverage from the scene and breaking news, which is usually live, highly as reasons to watch local television news. In the 2003 RTNDA *Local Television News Study* nearly a third of the viewing public surveyed said Live and Breaking News was the most appealing thing about local TV news. So if I'm a news director looking for ways to increase ratings, I'd look at a number like that and say, "More Live!"

The problem is, as was mentioned in an earlier chapter, broad research questions underestimate the viewing public. When you take a more detailed look at how viewers perceive live coverage, you get a very different picture—one that you as a producer should know and understand if you want to use live effectively.

Let's look at some additional research into live television reporting done by Charlie Tuggle and Suzanne Huffman with colleague Dana Rosengard (all of whom spent several years working in television newsrooms before moving into academe). These researchers went beyond the broad question about live coverage and looked in detail at what viewers perceive as good use of live and whether live makes a difference in the interest, understanding, and usefulness of a story. They found that only about 15 to 20% of viewers surveyed had a sense of which local stations did the most live reporting or which were first with breaking news stories. And as you can see below, viewers have strong positive and negative opinions about live reporting.

Positive Statements About Live Reporting	% Agreeing, Even Slightly
There are times when reporting live from the scene enhances a station's coverage of a story.	85%
Reporting live from the scene gives the story a sense of immediacy.	81%
Live reporting gives me the sense that a station is "on top of the news."	60%
Reporting live from the scene gives the story a sense of immediacy, even when nothing is happening at the time.	53%
Seeing a reporter live on the scene helps me understand the context of the story.	50%
Seeing a reporter live on the scene helps me understand the context of the story, even when nothing is happening at the time.	35%

Negative Statements About Live Reporting	% Agreeing, Even Slightly
There are times when a live report from the scene is meaningless.	88%
Local TV stations often report live from the scene for no apparent reason other than because they can.	67%
Events that would receive little or no attention had they happened earlier in the day are sometimes covered live because they happen close to the newscast hour.	64%
Once a station has committed the resources to report live from a story far from the station the live reports continue beyond the true life of the story.	58%
At times a desire to showcase equipment seems to outweigh other factors when news managers decide which stories to cover.	42%

From C. Tuggle, S. Huffman, & D. Rosengard. (2002, April). *Audience Assessment of Live Television News Reporting*. Presented at Broadcast Education Association National Convention, Las Vegas.

It's interesting to note that in open-ended comments viewers said that with the overuse of live there is too much emphasis on the "now" of stories but not much reporting on the "why" of stories and no effort to provide context. In addition to discussing live coverage, the participants in this study rated real stories in the context of a news block. Some saw live versions of three of the stories, others saw versions with the live component replaced by in-studio anchor intros and tags. The results were inconsistent between ratings of live and nonlive versions of the stories. The one story that consistently rated higher in its live version was reported live from the scene of an ongoing situation with updated information. So the researchers concluded that a live element doesn't guarantee a story will provide better understanding, interest, or more information (Tuggle, Huffman, & Rosengard, 2002).

The bottom line is viewers are smart. They're not dazzled by live technology and don't want meaningless live shots. But they do think live can enhance a story when there's something going on related to the story or the location is where new information might come from. So, how can you as the producer ensure that those are the type of lives in your show?

Producing Live Shots

The first step toward improving the quality of live shots in your newscast is changing your thinking about them. Don't leave live shot planning to the reporter covering the story alone—just as you produce all other aspects of your show, you need to work with your reporters and produce your live shots too. Start with the morning meeting and decisions about which stories will be assigned to reporters. Discussion and planning of what will be done live should begin there too. Typically you will have more reporters on stories than live trucks. So consider at that point which stories lend themselves to live shots and which are better done as straight packages or with the reporter in the newsroom or on

One-man-band Bureau Reporter Lisa Rantala also sets up her own live shot—here she's live at a prison during the 5:30 p.m. news on WCNC-TV (Charlotte).

set, maybe at a chromakey wall with a graphic. Here are some things to consider when deciding which stories are best done live:

- **What's happening at news time?** This is the most important factor. If the story is long over by newscast time, you don't want to go live from an empty scene—it simply makes no sense. But likewise don't get caught up in the trap of assigning a precious reporter resource to a minor story just because it is happening at news time. If the story wouldn't get a reporter at any other time, it shouldn't get one because some smart PR person scheduled it to happen during the news!

- **Will there be late developments in the story?** Does the reporter need to be at a remote location to ensure that she gets the most up-to-date information on the story? If so, then that's a good reason for a live shot, but make sure the reporter explains that right up front in the story so the viewer understands why she is live at that location at that time.

- **Is there some part of the story the reporter could best tell in a live "show and tell" shot?** You want to get your reporters thinking about how the live shot will be used as a story-telling technique. The best live shots are integrated into the story—just as the best stand-ups move the story along, the best live shots set the stage for the story, provide the most up-to-the-minute information, and truly take the viewer into the story as it's unfolding. They are not just a showcase for expensive technology or a way to make the story appear to be a bigger deal than it is. When viewers think, "Gee they're going live to the scene, it must be a big, developing story!" and are disappointed, it diminishes the value of the next live shot.

- **Location, location, location.** Just because the story happened at one place doesn't mean that's the best place for a live shot. For example: City council passes a spay/neuter requirement for all pets. Wouldn't it be more interesting to be live inside the local animal shelter or pet shop than city hall? City council passes a smoking ban in local bars and restaurants. The reporter could get the reaction part of the story live at a restaurant rather than on tape that is introduced live from city hall.

   Likewise if you have a reporter going live from an active scene, make sure your crew sets up in the middle of the action. There's nothing more frustrating than taking a live shot and finding your reporter standing in front of a boring background when you know nearby there's lots of activity.

- **Is the reporter traveling too far to get back in time for the newscast?** Sometimes logistics enter into the decision about which stories get done live. If a reporter is traveling for a story, he might need the satellite truck to ensure that the story gets back in time. But the fact that logistics require a story to be edited in the field and sent back via the live truck doesn't mean that you shouldn't still *produce* the live shot. Select a location in the field that makes sense with the story, which, again, may not be where the story was shot. Think about what's coming next in the story—maybe that will provide your location.

- **The black hole live shot.** If you are the morning show or late news producer, you have the added problem that it's dark when your newscast goes on the air. And early evening news producers have the same problem in the winter. There's nothing worse than the "black hole" live shot in which your reporter is standing outside in the dark and you can't see anything behind them except darkness. If you produce these newscasts, one of the best things you can do is make a list of places in your market that are well lit at night or overnight and places you can get inside access to early in the morning or late at night. Also, keep the graphics department busy—a reporter live at a chromakey wall with relevant graphics is much better than a black hole live shot.

The important thing to keep in mind always is planning. Start thinking about and *producing* your live shots early, and then keep in touch with your reporters throughout the day to make sure the plan will still work with the way their story is developing.

Chapter 10

Breaking News

One of the most exciting times in any newsroom is when there is breaking news; producers are right at the heart of this live coverage, just as they are for newscasts. There are typically no scripts and no rundowns, just a producer calling the shots of what comes next. As the producer during live breaking news coverage you have to take in information, make snap decisions, and communicate those decisions quickly and efficiently. This is where all the things discussed in the previous chapter about professionalism and communication in the booth be-

Live Shot Advice From a Veteran News Director

Jennifer Rigby is a longtime news director with Cox Communications, currently leading the flagship Cox television newsroom at WSB-TV (Atlanta). She strongly advises producers to take ownership of the live shots in their newscasts.

Jennifer Rigby

Producers, It's Your Live Shot Too!

Viewers want to see live. It's not hard to understand why. Live reports bring urgency and energy to the newscast. The active scene gives viewers the chance to join you in experiencing the action as it unfolds. It's unpredictable and that's when it's all working. Live shots can also slow a show down and leave the viewer confused and bored. Don't allow the live shots in your newscast to "just happen." Get involved in the planning and the execution and produce the live shot as you would produce your newscast. Define the value of why you're live and communicate that value to your viewers. Avoid going live for the sake of live.

Communicate, Communicate, Communicate!

- In other words over-communicate. If you do this, everything else will work.
- Brainstorm live shot possibilities with the field crew. Questions should include what will we see, why are you live at this location, what will you do getting into the live shot, and what will you do coming out?
- Help the field crew understand how they fit into the entire program. Give them the context of the newscast to ensure transition and flow.

Produce the Live Shot

- Think about the live shot in relation to the rest of the program. How will you showcase it? Is it a double box or a straight toss from the anchor desk? What graphics will accompany the story? Make sure it all ties in and it's pulled together in a well-produced manner.
- Brand it. Make sure viewers know it's live and make sure they know where you're live, both graphically and in copy.
- Keep it concise and avoid repeating information. Too often, the anchor lead and the reporter live intro repeat information. Coordinate and make sure the anchor lead is short and grabs the viewer's attention. Then work with the reporter to keep the introduction short and relevant. It should move the story forward from the anchor lead and it should be tightly focused. Long anchor leads and long reporter introductions slow the pace of the show.
- Be flexible. Be ready to throw out the planning and let that great live shot go.
- Live teases can be effective when done correctly. Help the reporter write the tease. Bring in the promotion department if needed. Know your team. Use the reporters who do this well.

Logistics and Location

- Start the live shot planning in the morning meeting. Consider the team and put the right players in the right positions. What will the scene demand of the team at news time? Is it unpredictable and may need ad-lib work? Is there historical context that will help explain the story? If that's the case, don't assign your brand new hire to the shot.

- Listen to your field crews. Don't direct, but rather listen and support. Consider the distance they need to travel, time pressures, and resources when determining the best live shot.

- Have Plan B and Plan C in place. Be ready for lightning to kill all of your live shots.

- Avoid the black hole. Evening live shots work with proper lighting, location, and props. Reporter must still establish relevance to the viewer.

- Know, understand, and produce the technology, i.e., mast cam, COFDM, chopper, et cetera.

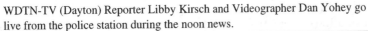
WDTN-TV (Dayton) Reporter Libby Kirsch and Videographer Dan Yohey go live from the police station during the noon news.

come twice as important, and you definitely have to be thinking two or three steps ahead. If you're not, you will face that awful moment of not having anything to go to and leaving your anchors with nothing to do but ad-lib.

Preparing for Breaking News

Now, you're probably asking yourself, how could anyone *prepare* for breaking news? By its very nature, breaking news is an unexpected news event—something you didn't and couldn't plan for. While you can't prepare for most specific breaking news stories, you can prepare for handling breaking news in general.

When a story breaks and you confirm enough information to make the decision that it's a big enough story to warrant live, breaking news coverage, the first thing you typically think of is needing a live shot or multiple live shots and videotape from the scene. It is true that your assignment desk should dispatch live trucks and crews as soon as possible, but chances are you will have to get something on the air long before a live truck gets to the scene and sets up a signal.

You can prepare for breaking news by thinking ahead about what other production elements you can use until you actually have live from the scene pictures and sound. Here are some tools you can use:

- **Maps:** Make sure your graphics department has a good set of base maps for your market area. One of the quickest things you can get on the air is a map of where the breaking news is happening if all the graphics department has to do is plop a location dot and a title on an existing base map.

- **Phoners:** Often long before you can get interviews and video from the scene you can put people on the air via the phone. Make sure that those answering phones in the newsroom know that if a witness or someone with information calls in, they should be screened as a possible live phone interview. Likewise, your assignment desk should be calling local authorities, local radio stations, and neighboring addresses (you'll need a Criss-Cross directory that lists phone numbers by address as well as by name to find numbers for surrounding properties). And when these numbers are contacted, always ask if someone has a home video camera and can start taking pictures and/or meet your station's crew when they get there.

- **Sky/tower cams:** Too often we forget about those cameras most stations have attached to the television tower and other very high places in the market. They're usually used for nice weather shots or traffic, but they may be your first visual of a breaking news story—so get them all pointed in the direction of the story location and see what you can see.

Phoner Hoaxes

Unfortunately in the middle of the controlled chaos of breaking news, sometimes people will play pranks or try to get their 15 minutes of fame. That's why it's important when someone calls into the newsroom with story information, they don't go on the air without careful screening. Here are some questions that can be asked to help determine the legitimacy of a caller:

- Get a full name and location of the caller.
- Ask for a phone number to call back in case you get cut-off—most pranksters won't want to give you a number.
- Get the full details of what the person saw/heard/knows and go back to some details checking for consistency.
- Ask if you can give the person's name and phone number to police for their information.

The bottom line is you, as the producer, don't have time to screen callers—you need to know that when a caller is sent up to you for a live phoner he or she has been screened. So make sure there's a screening process in place before breaking news hits.

- **Experts list:** Your newsroom should have an "experts list" readily available. These should be people you've contacted in advance who've agreed to supply background information in various types of stories. Make sure that you have complete contact information for these people, and when a big story breaks, get them on the phone to help provide context. Don't wait until they can come to the station or get to your nearest live truck.

- **Co-opt people from other departments:** Depending on when a breaking news story happens, don't forget there are people working in other departments that have nothing to do with the newsroom. Don't be afraid to go up to the traffic department or the business offices and ask people to come down to the newsroom and help. Sometimes just having extra help to answer the phones can make a big difference.

There are some breaking news stories that you can anticipate. If the jury is deliberating in a big trial, you know you're going to have a verdict at some point. While you're waiting, have the reporter covering the trial produce a story recapping the major testimony and arguments and set it aside so you have a nice backgrounder when the verdict comes down. If you know someone prominent in the community is ill or injured, or simply elderly, prepare a background story on his or her life and accomplishments that's ready to air when they die. This is the kind of preparation that can make the chaos that always surrounds breaking news a little more manageable.

Live Weather Coverage

There are very few stations in the country where you won't be doing severe weather coverage at some point. It's often the most important coverage you do and can make or break your station's reputation as the "go to" station for weather. That's an enviable place to be. As we've mentioned before, the one consistency from television market to market is that weather is nearly always the number one reason people watch local television news. "Think about it in your day, the impact it is going to have on your day," said Byron Grandy, news director at Channel 7 in Denver, "The news will rarely impact your day, unless it is fairly large or fairly local. The weather is going to affect how you dress your kid, your drive to work, it can be dangerous to your safety, to your property. You're not going to find anything that means more to people than weather" (Kreck, 2004).

Severe weather leads to ratings spikes. Here's just one example: In March 2004 the Cincinnati local stations had 74% of the viewers watching television tuned in to their 10 and 11 p.m. newscasts the night of a late winter snow storm. With more than a hundred cable stations to choose from, normally less than 50% of people watching television at that hour would be watching local news. And the next night, after the storm, 68% were watching a local newscast at the same hours (Eckberg, 2004). People want to know what's going on. Severe weather coverage is something you want to do right.

WCNC-TV (Charlotte) Meteorologists Larry Sprinkle and John Wendel track
Hurricane Katrina.

Here are some tips to help you no matter what type of severe weather you're
covering:

- **Trust your meteorologists.** Most stations' weathercasters are meteorolo-
  gists—that means they're not just on-air personalities, they are scientists.
  Keep in close contact with them so you're forewarned when severe
  weather is coming, but let them decide when it's time to warn the viewers.
  Don't force them to hype forecasts beyond what they believe is expected.
  Make sure they are the centerpiece of your coverage—let them explain
  what's happening and why, and let them give safety information.
- **Know your terminology.** It's absolutely vital that you know the difference
  between a *watch* and a *warning*. These are terms the National Weather Service uses to warn people about severe weather. A **watch** means conditions
  are right for that type of severe weather (i.e., thunderstorm, tornado, flooding, etc.), and it could happen. A **warning** means that type of severe
  weather is imminent—it's definitely coming your way.
- **Get crews in place.** If you get enough warning about severe weather, send
  crews and live trucks out to the places expected to be hit so they're ready.
  Once the weather hits, no matter what form, getting around is usually one
  of the first things disrupted. Don't be left out of the story because you can't
  get to the effected area. If you expect snow or flooding overnight or in the
  early morning, send photographers home with their camera gear and station vehicles so they can start shooting on the way into work.
- **Find out who has 4-wheel drive.** Have a pick-up plan for newsroom employees. Know who has the 4-wheel drive vehicles and where they live in

relation to other employees who don't. Have a car pool plan in place before your staff is stranded at home.

- **Don't just preach safety—act on it.** There's nothing more ridiculous to a viewer than a reporter standing outside in frigid temps with no hat or gloves telling viewers the cold is dangerous or a reporter wading through flood waters telling viewers to stay away from flooded areas! Make sure your field crews dress appropriately and are equipped with the same safety and survival supplies you advise for viewers. Remember you are inside the newsroom, warm and safe, but your field crews are out in the middle of messy, often dangerous situations during severe weather coverage.

- **You can have damage too!** When severe weather hits, the station is not immune to power loss, damage, and all the problems your viewers are having. So be prepared—know what station equipment operates with the back-up power source and what computers are on uninterruptible power source (USB) backups. Know which areas have emergency lighting. Also understand that your live technology is effected by the weather as mentioned earlier.

The most important thing to remember during severe weather coverage is while the video can be awesome and the people stories incredible (in other words, severe weather is often great television!), don't lose sight of what the viewers most want to know—what's coming where and when. The forecasting technology now allows station meteorologists to track storms by neighborhood and tell viewers minute by minute where the storm will be. Make sure this is the focus of your coverage—warning viewers what's headed their way and telling them what to do to stay safe.

Disaster Plan

Your newsroom should have a disaster plan for the really big breaking news story, the kind of story that's going to put you into continuing live coverage for some time—the September 11th story. Find out when you first arrive at a new station if they have one. If not, talk to news management about developing one. Consistently over the years the stations that have had the best coverage and served their viewers best during a crisis have been the stations with well-developed disaster plans that outlined responsibilities and resources and provided that initial direction amid the craziness.

Warning: Don't Be Exploitive

When breaking news happens there's a special adrenaline that zaps most people who work in a newsroom. While your viewers may be stunned or horrified or grieving—you're jazzed. It's not that news people are cold or callus; it's just that when something terrible happens, we are needed the most. You can't be an emotional basket case and calmly call the shots in the control room. So news people

Lessons of 9/11

As the first anniversary of 9/11 approached, RTNDA's *Communicator* magazine talked with news managers in New York City and Washington, DC about their reflections of the coverage that day and how their perceptions of disaster coverage, their profession, and their staffs had changed.

"'The first priority in an emergency is your safety and the safety of your family. If there are family issues or concerns, attend to them first.'—Ed Tobias, assistant managing editor, AP Broadcast News, quoting from the first page of AP's newly revised Broadcast Emergency Recovery Plan. Tobias now believes news organizations need to 'think the unthinkable' regarding terrorism coverage. 'There is biological, chemical and nuclear contamination to consider, as well as secondary explosions. ... So, we need to consider methods of covering these events from afar. I'd also like to investigate the possibility of news organizations working with public safety officials to train and equip very small reporting pools that would be rushed to these scenes, much as is the national DOD pool, to safely report from as close as possible.'

"'Have a detailed plan for covering the big stories, keep perspective in your reporting, always show compassion to your people, and recognize when you, as the leader, are too tired to make a good decision, and force yourself to get some rest.'—Katherine Green, VP and news director, WTTG-TV. Passionate about planning, Green relied on her 'continuous coverage' plan on 9/11. It outlines key positions to be covered and the specific duties of each post, and moves the staff to a 12-hours-on/12-hours-off work cycle. She brought in university experts to brief staff on Middle East relations and the Islamic faith.

"'Never underestimate the expectation of your viewers; get it right, make it relevant.'—David Roberts, VP and news director, WUSA-TV. Roberts says 9/11 reinforced the importance of journalistic experience, commitment and hard news presented without hype. Like several other news directors, he cited the value of working with a general manager (in his case, Ardith Diercks) 'who understands and supports good, sound journalism.'"

Geisler, J. (2002, September). "One Year Later," *Communicator.* rtnda.org

typically have delayed reactions to major stories—delayed until after the job is done. This adrenaline and delayed reaction are good because they allow you to take action and get information out to people who desperately want to know what's happening.

However, a problem can come when, in the middle of continuing coverage or as a story first breaks, you don't realize that you've crossed the line from providing information and reaction to invading someone's private moment of grief. You need to be constantly watching the level of emotional content of what's going on the air as you're deciding and communicating what goes next. Viewers often feel uncomfortable when someone being interviewed breaks down or when we zoom in for a tight shot on the victim's family as they embrace and cry. Often the crew in the field thinks they're getting "great stuff" because they are so caught up in the adrenaline rush of a big story, they can't see they're being

Hurricane Heroes

A good disaster plan and supportive corporate parent made WWL-TV (New Orleans) and its staff Hurricane Heroes. Knowing their city faced the worst possible scenario with Hurricane Katrina, the station worked on contingency plans to stay on the air no matter what. Because of that plan, WWL-TV started live continuous coverage Saturday morning and stayed on the air longer than any other station—until midnight Saturday. Station staff evacuated the station after midnight and headed to Louisiana State University's journalism school in Baton Rouge where they were setup to continue broadcasting starting early Sunday morning. For many hours WWL was the only television station on the air. The station also called in the troops from its parent company, Belo Corp., which owns 19 television stations. Sister stations sent satellite trucks and lots of extra staffers to keep the continuous hurricane coverage going. Belo's interactive media division kept the station's Web site up and running and constantly streamed the station's air signal. That allowed evacuees from the region to keep in touch with what was happening to their homes and businesses, as well as find lost loved ones. The Website also set up blogs in which people could ask for news about family or friends. Finally the company established the WWL-TV Employee Relief Fund to help the many station employees who lost their own homes but kept working with little thought of their own personal tragedies. Those journalists and other station employees worked for days without sleep and few other amenities to bring people the local, hometown perspective on a disaster that nearly wiped New Orleans off the map.

WWL-TV (New Orleans) broadcast signal was streamed online during and after Hurricane Katrina allowing evacuees to watch and look for loved ones and property damage.

exploitive of someone else's tragedy. Reporters and video journalists usually don't mean to be insensitive, they just aren't feeling the same things as those involved in the story because they're so focused on doing their job. So, beware of exploiting overwhelming emotions at any time, but especially during live breaking news coverage.

Teen Tragedy

One of the worst examples of unintentional exploitation involved a breaking news story in Green Bay, Wisconsin. It started during the noon newscast. A group of teens were swimming at an old quarry and two of the teens disappeared. Water rescue teams searched the quarry for hours and by the early news all the stations were live at the scene covering the search and the large gathering of friends keeping vigil. At the top of the 6 p.m. news one station was preparing to go live with an interview with the sheriff and one of the friends. As the reporter started his live shot someone passed the sheriff a note and he announced live on the air that the teens' bodies had been found. The reporter then turned to the stunned friend and tried to interview him. What followed was the most agonizing 90 seconds in television; the friend could barely say a word he was so distraught. Both the reporter and the producer were so caught up in the adrenaline of a big story and the "scoop" they were lucky enough to get, they thought they were doing a great job. The executive producer had to run all the way to the control room to pull the plug on the live shot. The newsroom received more than a hundred calls from angry viewers accusing the station of sensationalizing and exploiting the teens. The reporter and producer didn't understand what they had done wrong until they sat down and watched the tape of the show—no other consequences were needed; they both were devastated by what they'd allowed on the air in the heat of the moment.

But We Didn't Know *That* Was Going to Happen!

Sometimes it's not the emotion of the situation that gets you in trouble but the unexpected. By its very nature, breaking news is full of unexpected things that happen. When you are covering a breaking news story live, in real time, that unexpected event can put you in the difficult situation of airing something that ordinarily you'd never put on television.

The classic example happened in Los Angeles in 1998 when six of the local stations interrupted afternoon programming, including children's programming, to air live coverage of a man who was blocking rush hour traffic on a major highway. The man was firing shots into the air, and, as viewers watched, he first set the inside of the truck on fire and then ran out of the truck waving a rifle and finally shot himself live on television. Nearly all the stations were on a close-up shot of the man when he pulled the trigger, which provoked widespread criticism of the L.A. stations. Jeff Wald, news director of L.A. station KTLA-TV at the time, said after the incident:

> We've put in a number of safeguards. We literally have a breaking news policy that we put together. As a list of criteria, we first ask the question, are we in children's programming, who's the audience at that particular time, and that sort of thing, so it's that type of checklist that you go through. The bottom line is, each one of these incidents needs to be judged on an individual basis and how many people are being affected by the story? We also went through the soul-searching of could we have done a better job of cutting away quicker and not allow that to appear on our air? I mean, there were so many questions that we had after that happened. As a result of that, I can tell you that we've pretty much gotten

away from breaking into programming unless the chase is something that is affecting a lot of people at a particular time. ("The Issue of High Speed Chases," 1999)

After the L.A. suicide story, many stations put in place other safeguards during live, breaking news coverage, including a video delay similar to what radio stations often use during live call-in shows. Instead of broadcasting something live as it's actually happening, it's recorded and played back on a continuous 2 to 3 second delay. The video delay gives the producer three seconds to pull the plug on a live feed before it actually goes on air if the situation suddenly goes bad and something happens the station would not normally put on the air. Other stations have policies that limit the use of close-up shots during live, breaking news coverage. Ultimately, it's often going to come down to the producer in the booth watching the unfolding events very closely, and cutting away if it appears a situation is about to take a turn that ethical judgment and human decency would dictate you don't air on television, live or otherwise.

Live Ethics

Beyond all the television and journalism questions about live coverage, there are also ethical issues to consider. Al Tompkins of The Poynter Institute summarizes those issues in a series of questions to consider, especially during breaking news.

Al Tompkins, The Poynter Institute

Live Coverage Guidelines

Electronic journalists have a unique ability and opportunity to provide viewers and listeners with vital news information instantly. Journalists have a special responsibility in such situations to be accurate and to be measured in the tone of their coverage. A good guideline in such situations is to "over-react in the newsroom and under-react on the air."

Questions to Ask Before Going Live

Beyond competitive factors, what are your motivations for "going live?" Why do your viewers need to know about this story before journalists have the opportunity to filter the information off the air? What truth testing are you willing to give up in order to speed information to the viewer?

- Are you prepared to air the worst possible outcome that could result from this unfolding story? (Such as, a person killing himself or someone during live coverage.) What outcomes are you not willing to air? Why? How do you know the worst possible outcome will not occur?

- How do journalists know that the information they have is true? How many sources have confirmed the information? How does the source know what they say is true? What is this source's past reliability? How willing is the source to be quoted?

- What are the consequences, short-term and long-term, of going on the air with the information? What are the consequences of waiting for additional confirmation or for a regular newscast?

- What is the tone of the coverage? How can the journalist raise viewer awareness of a significant event while minimizing unnecessary hype and fear? Who in your newsroom is responsible for monitoring the tone of what is being broadcast?

- What electronic safety net such as a tape and signal delay has your station considered that could minimize harm and could give your station time to dump out of live coverage if the situation turns graphic, violent, or compromises the safety of others?

- How clearly does the technical crew at your TV station understand the newsroom's standard for graphic content? How well are guidelines understood by directors, tape editors, live shot techs, photojournalists, pilots, or engineers who might have to make an editorial call when the news director or other "formal decision maker" is not available?

- What factor does the time of day play in your decision to cover a breaking event? For example, if the event occurs when children normally are watching television, how does that fact alter the tone and degree of your coverage?

Al Tompkins, Broadcast/On-line Group Leader, The Poynter Institute for Media Studies

Know the News

Whether it's a major national story or a local story, the best thing you can do to prepare yourself for that moment when you're in the booth calling the shots by the seat of your pants is knowing the news—all the news. It's been mentioned before, but deserves repeating. The best producers are news junkies. They start their day already having a strong handle on the days' news, and they are avaricious consumers of all types of news—local, national, world, entertainment, pop culture, sports, and weather. You never know where the next breaking story might come from and what you might need background in to produce it. Certainly there were many network and local producers who had never heard of Osama Bin Laden or had no idea where to find Afghanistan on the map before 9/11. You don't know when the next person arrested in your backyard might be Michael Jackson or Kobe Bryant. The only way to be truly prepared is to be on top of the news—all the news.

Live Special Event Coverage

In addition to live breaking news coverage, there will be times when you have to produce live special event coverage. It might be a visit by the President to your town, a big economic announcement, the inauguration of a new university president, or the naming of a new college or pro football coach. Your station might decide to take your newscast out on location for a big event—in Green Bay all the stations do remote newscasts in Oshkosh for EAA air show week because it's the biggest experimental aircraft show in the world; Minneapolis stations do remote newscasts from the state fair that brings a million people into the Twin Cities. And, of course, there is election night coverage.

The thing that all these events have in common is you have advance notice and can plan your live coverage days, weeks, or even months ahead of time. After producing hundreds of live special events, we can tell you there is one absolute in this type of coverage—the better you plan, the better your program is. Here are some tips to ensure your live event comes off smoothly:

- **Script as much as possible.** Put together a rundown of what you expect to happen and write scripts or at least script outlines for as much as you can. You will always need to be flexible and go with the flow once the event starts, but it's much easier to change a plan than to have no plan and be calling the shots blindly.
- **Background material.** Make sure your anchors and reporters have plenty of background material and filler facts in case they have to cover a lull in the action. You probably should also have two to three preproduced background packages and/or interviews ready in case you need to fill time or need time to get a show back under control.
- **Communication.** Double and triple check your communication with all talent and all remote locations. Nothing will kill you faster in a live program situation than not having clear communication with all parties. In addition to IFB see if you can get phone lines installed at major remote locations and have interns who keep those phone lines open to you at all times.
- **Remote anchor locations.** If you are going to have your anchors in the field for special event coverage, make sure they are taken care of with a good setup. Anchors need a desk or table of some sort so they have a place for scripts and notes. Put scripts and notes into a 3-ring binder so they don't have loose papers that blow around. Make sure they're not blinded by the sun. If the location is noisy, get them headphones or they'll never hear IFB. And get them out to the scene early so they have time to get comfortable with the setup.
- **Clear assignments.** Make sure everyone in the newsroom knows their specific assignment for the special event, and preassign everything including equipment—live trucks, camera gear, news cars, cell phones, et cetera. The assignments should be posted so there's no confusion for anyone involved. If possible have a newsroom meeting with everyone working the special coverage the day before to discuss how the program is expected to run and answer any questions.
- **Graphics.** Work with your graphics department to create a special graphics package for the event. You should have some kind of title and logo design for the coverage. Have the graphics department create lower thirds, full screens, OTSs, and animated graphics all using that design to tie your coverage together. You shouldn't create an entirely different

graphics look from your news, because you want the special event coverage to be associated with the news department, but simply have the special logo and title added to all your news templates.

Election Night

We often refer to election night as the breaking news story you get to anticipate. And the 2000 and 2004 elections certainly gave us a lot to anticipate! Even though you typically don't know when all the results will be in and when you'll be able to call certain races or when the candidates will make their victory or concession speeches, you still should plan and script as much as possible. All of the above tips apply to election night.

If you are doing live cut-ins during election night, you should produce each cut-in. Have a mini rundown for each one—even if it's just something you write out by hand and photocopy for everyone. Make sure the anchors, director, and graphics department know which election results boards you're going to use and which live shots you will go to for each cut-in.

Most election graphics programs will automatically update results as they come in from the Associated Press or as your news people call them in. But on the air, those graphics work best when called up from a preordered race list. In other words, you give the graphics person a list of the races that you want to display results in for a given cut-in, and the graphics person creates a race list of just those results as full screens that he can advance through quickly during the cut-in. If the graphics person has to individually call up each full screen results page, it can take several seconds for those pages to come up.

If you are in continuing coverage election night, try to plan as much of your early coverage as possible—scripting perhaps the first half-hour to hour. That gets you started in the right direction and allows everyone to develop a routine and comfort level with all the elements of your coverage. Then, as races develop and change, you can go into a more breaking news producing mode. As you get to the end of the evening, and the 11 p.m. news, you should be able to head back into a more scripted mode. In fact, there should be a separate producer for the late news election night to relieve the continuing coverage producer.

Election night, as with any live ongoing coverage, can be a lot of fun, but the amount of fun and success you have will be directly proportional to the amount of planning you've done in advance.

Conclusion

The ability to take a viewer live to a story as it's happening is a wonderful and remarkable tool in television news. But as with any technology, it is just one tool in an incredible toolbox we have working in TV. Live technology isn't worth the wires it's made of if it's not used with good journalistic judgment. Resist the temptation to go live simply because you can. Use this amazing tool to help your viewers experience and understand the news—don't let it replace your journalistic values or become the reporter. Just because you can take the viewer live to a news conference or battle scene doesn't mean you've completed your obligation as a journalist. You are still responsible for providing balance, context, and sometimes criticism of what's unfolding live.

Sources

Eckberg, J. (2004, March 30). Bad weather, good ratings: No. 1 reason people watch news? Storms. *The Cincinnati Enquirer,* p. C1.

Geisler, J. (2002, September). One year later. *Communicator,* RTNDA.org.

The issue of high speed chases. (1999). *The Ethics Project.* Available from KCET.org.

Kreck, D. (2004, May 16). Taking Denver by storm. *The Denver Post*, p. F1.

Papper, B. (2003). Radio-Television News Directors Association. *Local Television News Study.* Washington, DC.

RTNDA battles to get helicopters flying again. (2001, December). *Communicator,* p. 10.

Tuggle, C., & Huffman, S. (1999). Live for the sake of … What? A study of news coverage in eight markets. *Newslab Research Report,* p. 2.

Tuggle, C., Huffman, S., & Rosengard, D. (2002, April). *Audience Assessment of Live Television News Reporting.* Presented at Broadcast Education Association National Convention, Las Vegas, NV.

MANAGING PEOPLE

"We are not trying to get ahead of others, but only surpass ourselves"

Hugh B. Brown

"Then I asked, does a firm persuasion that a thing is so, make it so? He replied: all poets believe that it does, and in ages of imagination this firm persuasion removed mountains: but many are not capable of a firm persuasion of anything."

William Blake, *The Marriage of Heaven and Hell*

Do you believe in the power of firm persuasion? The technique is a balance between issuing orders and giving people the creative freedom to solve problems. Firm persuasion is just one of the talents you can develop as you build on the other skills we outlined for you in chapter 3. Like a drill sergeant you need discipline combined with the confident command of language to sustain your authority. Like a cheerleader you need energy and enthusiasm. Like a peacemaker you need balance, perspective, and a great deal of patience. Throughout this book we've talked about the important relationships you need to cultivate to be a good producer. This chapter focuses on how to go beyond just getting along to succeeding at managing people!

Like a master chef you need to understand not only flavor and tastes but how to manage and motivate the kitchen team to serve the customer. Two critical points about communication are key—listening and trust. "Listening is the leader's way of laying out a welcome mat for the truth" (Johnson & Phillips, 2003, p. 122). For example, many producers fail to listen carefully enough to the details a reporter gives about a live shot guest's super titles. Misspellings lead to credibility gaps. Dave Price, anchor at WHO-TV (Des Moines), believes that to build teamwork between you the producer and all the staff you must communicate with requires the practice of "talking with each other and trusting each other."

Building relationships of trust with every staff member you deal with is critical as a producer. You do that by building the relationship beyond the crunch of the newsroom deadline. You don't have to hit the bar with the photog staff! But pay attention to the little things like the value of recognition through a quick e-mail or handwritten note. Be stingy with criticism, resolving differences in a private place and space. Be generous and public with praise. Compliment your colleagues with sincerity in front of the boss.

A newsroom bubbling up to air time is as frantic as a hotel kitchen before a banquet. Amid the clatter and bustle of the environment, take the time to smile and joke. And while you should never forget the appetite of the audience, take a moment to pause, sit back, and enjoy the feast. Developing a style of your own as a producer comes with time as you increase your depth of experience and carefully observe those you consider role models.

WCNC-TV(Charlotte) 5 p.m. Producer Melody Freeman discusses her rundown with anchors, news managers, and other staff members in a rundown meeting.

The key to all of these interpersonal relationships is developing trust and respect. Trust is born as someone becomes confident in your ability to do the job, so it goes without saying that managing people begins with being in command of the facts and the operations. You can't fake it. Pay the price to have total knowledge of the stories in your newscasts, where the crews are, the coverage options available, and the ramifications of tough ethical calls. As you do, you gain the trust of the news team. Respect comes from doing your job well, taking responsibility for your mistakes, and sharing the success of a good newscast. Trust and respect do not equal being liked by everyone. It is better to be trusted and respected than to be loved. Coworkers do not have to become your best friends but surely your work will flounder as a producer if any of them becomes your worst enemy.

We'll begin by managing the relationship with the most important people you come in contact with, although indirectly, each day—the viewers. Then look at the interplay between the assignment desk and the producer. The assignment desk is the heartbeat of the newsroom. We'll show you how to keep stress between you and the desk down to acceptable levels. Your interactions with reporters and their key partners, the photographers and video tape editors, begin our discussion on the art of dealing with talent. That skill rises to the level of a fine art as we talk about your relationship with the anchors—your critical partners in your newscast, but who you don't "manage" as they make two to three times your annual salary and often have two to three times your experience.

At WDTN-TV (Dayton) the "producer pod" is in the center of the newsroom with easy access to the assignment desk, reporters, and anchors.

Last but surely not least is the series of bosses you have in the newsroom and the larger station structure, from the executive producer and assistant news director to "the boss," your news director, and her boss, the TV station general manager. Managing up is one of the toughest skills to develop but clearly one of the most critical if you are to rise to positions of more responsibility and higher salaries in televisions news. Managing across the station is also vital especially in your relationship with the production team and their leader the newscast director.

Chapter 11

Managing the Viewer

As the following figure indicates, the producer is the gatekeeper, the center point that controls information and communication about all aspects of the newscast. Data flows into the producer's sphere and then out again. The ultimate focus of this information flow is straight to the audience. The challenge is that the viewer is in essence hidden from you for the most part. In many ways it can

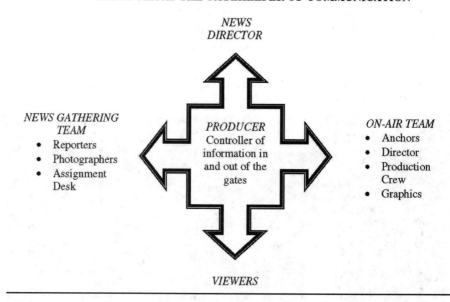

PRODUCER AS THE GATEKEEPER OF COMMUNICATION

NEWS DIRECTOR

NEWS GATHERING TEAM
- Reporters
- Photographers
- Assignment Desk

PRODUCER
Controller of information in and out of the gates

ON-AIR TEAM
- Anchors
- Director
- Production Crew
- Graphics

VIEWERS

feel like you produce news in a void. You spend your day in a building. You spend hours each day carefully constructing a newscast for an audience that never applauds when the broadcast is over. Unless you answer the phone or respond to viewer e-mail and take a complaint or a compliment on the coverage, you never truly connect with the audience.

The news director, anchor, and newsgathering teams of reporters interact with the public and bring you feedback from the viewer. The reporter comes back with insights from an interview, the anchor has spoken to the Rotary Club at lunch, or the news director, likewise, has her pulse on the public via focus groups and market data. Shawn Patrick, anchor at KTAL-TV (Shreveport), works with young producers to help them understand the audience and why they call.

> Chances are the calls you get, the e-mails you get, come from someone irate over what they thought they heard on your channel. I remind myself, most of the time, people contact you when they want to complain, but for any one of them, there are countless others who appreciated the way you handled the story on the death of a local soldier, or a mother who lost her children in a fire. After getting wrapped up in the exclusives or the slick graphics, it's easy to forget the root of it all, the story. We're talking about someone's son or daughter, husband or wife, neighbor or friend; that's a tremendous responsibility, they do notice.

Unlike anchors who get recognized in grocery stores, producers are virtually invisible to the audience. In the daily work week you take it on faith and ratings that people are actually watching your news. E-mail increasingly has added more direct feedback. But many a night you can wonder if all that effort in putting together the news was just simply for your other teammates in the news department. Unlike talk radio where listener's comments come back to you in real time, reaction from television news viewers often is not in real time.

Feedback from the TV news viewer is still very real, especially when with a click they change the channel—and don't forget those who have ratings books or their hands on a People Meter! But while those viewers remain anonymous to you, others can become very vocal through telephone calls, e-mails, and letters as they express their opinions on your news decisions. Loyal viewers take pride in the station they watch and many feel as if it is "their newscast," so receiving feedback from them should be expected and welcome. The problem comes when that phone call comes as you face a deadline crunch and you're hard pressed to put on good manners to deal with a viewer's critical phone call complaining about news coverage. And sometimes viewers even confuse something another station did with your news team, as Shawn Patrick experienced covering a police shooting.

> A young police officer responding to a 9-1-1 hang up call was gunned down at the doorstep of a home. I rushed out there and was live all day, found out the officer's name, was asked to hold it because the police had not yet notified all of the family. I respected their wishes but, a competitor did not. It didn't matter to some viewers. They saw the name on the TV news and called us to chastise us. Police ran us off the parking lot at the funeral. I felt like I did everything I could to show respect toward the situation, but sometimes you're just part of the pack of wolves whether you like it or not. A thick skin goes a long way in situations like this. You can only remind yourself, at least they're watching.

An old adage says for every one person who calls, a hundred others have the same opinion, and for every letter, which takes more effort to write and send, a thousand people may be equally upset. News directors and other managers handle most of the complaints and comments on news coverage, and during the day you should pass these calls over to them. But if you are the late news producer or work weekends when no front desk operator screen calls, you can easily answer the newsroom phone and find an irate viewer on the other end of the line. Attitude toward the viewers is a serious part of your job. Next time you take a phone call from "Mabel," the typical viewer, and find yourself frustrated, remember the 10 commandments to serve our viewers.

The 10 Commandments to Serve Our Viewers

1. Viewers are the most important people in our business.
2. Viewers are the reason for our existence.
3. Viewers do us a favor when they contact us.
4. Viewers are our business.
5. Viewers, too, are human beings with feelings and emotions.
6. Viewers have needs. We fill those needs.
7. Viewers are not people to argue with or to debate.
8. Viewers deserve our attention and courtesy.
9. Viewers pay our salaries.
10. Viewers are the lifeblood of our company.

Chapter 11

Use these rules to remind yourself when a viewer calls; he or she deserves your patience and respect. And these rules are not for the producers alone. It is a good idea to post the guidelines at the assignment desk where often the phone calls first enter the newsroom system.

News Gathering Team: The Assignment Editor— Heartbeat of the Newsroom

Your biggest partner in the gathering of news is the assignment editor. The assignment desk is the heartbeat of the newsroom. The producer's desk might be the brain of the newsroom where the hard and tough decisions are made, but the assignment desk keeps the lifeblood flowing in the daily news work. From the desk, reporter and photographer teams are dispatched out into the field, while faxes, phone call tips, press releases, and e-mailed ideas pump inward.

WCPO-TV (Cincinnati) Assignment Editor Jana Soete, surrounded by scanners and phones, updates story information in the daybook.

Back to the cooking metaphor: If the producer is the master chef, than the assignment desk is the inventory boss supervising the vast storage and staging area where all of the raw ingredients of the news are gathered, sorted, and initially prepared for the producer's shaping and arranging into the final gourmet meal of a newscast.

Most assignment editors are on an equal or in some cases higher job rank than producers, so managing the desk is really developing a strong communication relationship with a team partner. This requires verbal skills as well as understanding assignment and messaging or e-mail functions in your newsroom software system. Although most of those systems maintain an assignments' list for the day, many a newsroom has brought back the old grease board or dry erase board so that everybody passing by can see what crews are located where and what stories the news team is working on for that day.

Because many assignment desks also monitor police and fire scanners for "spot news" the desk area is often a noisy work environment. The constant ringing of phones, the drone of fax machines, even the volume from various TV news channels being monitored can strain hearing. Note this and make sure you physically face the assignment editor when you talk to him or her so your communication is crystal clear. And the rule of thumb is to always double check. Is your reporter team really on their way back? Will the video really be in house in 20 minutes? Producers need to develop a sixth sense so they constantly keep in the back of their mind a keen awareness of what the desk is doing, what the scanners might be broadcasting, and what the two-way radio traffic from a field crew might mean to a story. Being a second set of ears monitoring the police scanner for the desk is especially important since spot news is one of your key newscast ingredients and often the 10-code system used by police to identify various crime situations becomes garbled in scanner transmissions.

It's a good idea when you first begin producing at a station to spend time actually working at the assignment desk. Knowing how your mobile radio system works and where everything is on the desk can be critical in a breaking news setting. You may have to jump in and give instructions on the radio to field reporting crews while the assignment editor has a telephone in each ear trying to nail down facts and addresses to dispatch the live trucks. Working the desk also helps you master the scanner's ten-code system, contribute on conference calls for regional or network video feed services, change toner on the fax machine, and connect with viewers via their incoming phone calls.

Finally, do not just view your assignment editor as a heart without any soul—a functionary who simply dispatches crews like a taxicab company. A master of logistics, a good assignment editor also has a solid journalism foundation. They'll have their own ideas of what the lead story should be or how a cluster of stories might be arranged on your rundown. Often assignment editors develop the daily news menu by trying to think as a producer thinks, looking for ways to unbundle the lead story or find the best visuals of the day for the kicker story. Pick their brain. Ask for input. Listen to suggestions. As master chef, ultimately you decide how the lineup menu unfolds, but just like the brain cannot function without the heart pumping blood—you as the producer need all of the ideas you can get. That which comes from the assignment desk is particularly important to the overall health and viewer satisfaction of your news operation.

Managing the assignment function is ultimately building that relationship of trust with a colleague whose reward system is like yours—pride in the newscast, success in the ratings, and the satisfaction of an overall team effort. Often the personality types attracted to the desk are ideal for this type of relationship and very similar to those attracted to producing. This is in contrast to the reporters and anchors whose job reward is as much based on a self-focused ego drive as it is on working for the team. It makes them tenacious reporters and command anchors, but it also requires some special skills in working with them.

News Gathering Team: Reporters

As a producer you often have indirect management responsibility over the reporters and the photographers. While it is doubtful you will have input on their pay raises, you do have a great deal to say about how their day unfolds including what stories they cover and how they spend their time. "The best producers are those who have spent time in the field as reporters." This was the maxim from John Edwards who for a decade served as the news director for KTVX (ABC, Salt Lake City). Edwards believed that until a producer understood the obstacles to storytelling that a reporter could experience in the field—everything from bad directions from the assignment desk to dead batteries on the photographer's camera —skills were missing that allowed that producer to gain the respect and trust of the reporting staff.

WCNC-TV(Charlotte) Reporter Glenn Counts discusses his 5 p.m. story with Producer Melody Freeman.

Clear communication combined with empathy for what field crews face in their reporting is vital to your success as a producer. Empathy is the key term here. Reporters often think, "Producers sit all summer in an air conditioned newsroom sipping a soft drink and watching CNN while they write up a few teases and put together a rundown." While that's an unfair stereotype, it is true the producer stays back at the shop while the reporter is in the field sweating up three flights of stairs carrying a tripod in the July heat or freezing waiting to do a live shot on icy road conditions in January. Producers have to develop empathy with reporters in order to understand what they face in getting the story told. Knowing how long a camera battery lasts, you can understand when the reporter radios in that the "juice is all gone" after several hours in the field at a hostage standoff. A good news director will find opportunities for a job-swapping day so producers can be reminded how tough it is in the field.

News Gathering Team: The Videojournalist— The Faces Behind the Camera

While empathy for both members of the field team—the reporter and the photographer—is important, the producer needs to recognize these egos are stroked in different ways. But first recognize that all reporters are not driven by the same needs. Some are driven by an inner need to be "seen" and thus feed on compliments about how they "looked" during the story. We believe far more will want feedback on their writing, their storytelling skill to match words to pictures, as well as how well the stand-up demonstration went on the live shot. In other words, compliment them on the whole package and point out specific areas that you know they thrive hearing about.

How to Do It
FEEDBACK
Fast Facts

There are four types of feedback:

- Silence—no response.
- (Negative) Criticism—Identifies inadequate behavior: *"You did a poor job running the morning meeting."*
- Advice—Identifies desirable behavior.
- (Positive) Reinforcement—Praise!

Remember

- Silence is not always golden.
- Criticism overpowers all other feedback.
- The difference between criticism and advice is timing.
- Most criticism can be given as advice.

The focus of many photojournalists seems to be on helping others "see." Pay attention to a particularly difficult camera angle or creative execution of a stand-up. This difference between the reporter wanting to be "seen" and the photographer wanting to help others "see" has practical applications in giving feedback to both members of the field team. Remember to praise in public—in front of their peers in the newsroom—but criticize, constructively, in the quiet corners of the editing booth or privately in the parking lot where you can add concrete, helpful suggestions. Make sure you never compliment on how reporters were "seen" without also commenting on the editorial aspects of their story. Part of your job as the producer is to maintain the credibility of the newscast and make sure it remains news and not a show.

Chapter 11

Photographers tend to have far less need for public recognition than reporters. It is not that they are a shy bunch—just get a group of them together for karaoke night and see what we mean. But photographers often have a deep respect for the image and their craft of photojournalism. They take pride in their pictures. Recognize and reward this as a producer. Look for opportunities to showcase the photography independent of the reporter. On a slow news day have the photographers put together a photo essay about the season's first snow fall or a "show closer" featuring vignettes from the county fair. If a reporter package warrants it, and your news director approves, have the anchor's introduction include not only the reporter but also the photographer or see that they get a name super as an on-air credit. One of the oldest and best managing tricks in working with people is to (1) learn their name and (2) use it often.

Videographer Reed Bennett creatively shoots an interview through protest signs with reporter Tiffani Helberg (WCNC-TV, Charlotte).

Video tape editors at some smaller stations also double as field photographers. In larger markets tape editors often spent time in the field shooting before trading in their cameras for a life inside the darkened editing cubicle. Many times the motivation techniques and ego management of tape editors matches that of photographers. But there are exceptions and just like the reporter/photographer team recognizes team members are individuals, so too what motivates one tape editor will not necessarily charge up another. Even less honored and rarely recognized by the public or their peers, tape editors spend hours watching thousands of images go by.

Learn to trust your editors who can give you an objective outside opinion on the value of a story's pictures that sometimes the photographer who shot them may "oversell." It is the reporter/photographer's job to sell their story to you and argue for high placement in the lineup. The tape editor typically has no stake in story placement, and hence, their opinion is often trusted by producers when it comes to assessing the merits of the story and where it fits in your newscast.

Much of the video editors' most critical work happens in the final 60 minutes before airtime. The matching of words and pictures is vital in your newscast. Long-time CBS Correspondent Charles Kuralt was noted for saying, "I never write a sentence in television news unless a picture is there." Communication with editors is critical as changes are made in the rundown that could effect tease video or even how to manage which stories get cut first if the edit bays are backed up. Use your time management skills wisely and think twice about last minute changes that could have a ripple effect in the editing bays and spell disaster if a story misses its slot.

Special Projects Videographer/Editor Byron Stirsman uses nonlinear editing to put together a package for WHIO-TV (Dayton).

In working with video tape editors, as well as reporters and photographers, remember you are building a mutual respect among the team members. Michelle Frey, who produced morning news in Phoenix before moving to on-air work at NTV-Nebraska TV KHGI/KWNB, says respect is the main ingredient to team building and quoted the Aretha Franklin song.

"R-E-S-P-E-C-T find out what it means to me." Make that, mutual respect. As a producer I was frustrated when reporters would not give me roll cues or teases that I needed. As a reporter, I get frustrated when the producer is not clear with me on what they need. Anticipating and over-compensating is always good. As a producer, I learned to over-communicate my needs to the reporters. I would tell them the same thing every day that I needed. As a reporter, I remember that feeling and try to anticipate what my producer will need. I always keep her up-to-date on my times, where I am, what I am doing so there's no need for frustration.

In summary, managing those team members who find, gather and package stories—the desk, the reporters, photographers—and the team members who remain in the shop with you—the video tape editors and those in graphics and production (more on these key players later)—requires a healthy dose of humility on the part of the producer.

Michelle Frey, NTV

(Michelle Frey now works as an anchor/reporter for WMTW (ABC) Portland, ME)

Humility is not a weakness. Humility is a willingness to recognize you don't have all the answers and you won't get all the answers unless you ask questions.

Are You Actively Listening?

Checklist

We believe active listening involves three steps that happen quickly and process interactively. Our thoughts move about four times as fast as speech. So, with practice, while you listen you can also run through a checklist to make sure you're actively listening with your EARS, MIND, and HEART and ready to give excellent feedback!

✓ **Ears.** Did you hear it correctly? By repeating a fact, you prove you have heard what is said. Example: *"So you're saying the reason you couldn't make the live shot slot is the live mast wouldn't go up on the truck because the hydraulics were stuck?"*

✓ **Mind.** Your brain is where the understanding of the facts is processed and you make judgments about what has been said. You might think, *"So you weren't slacking off just because it is so cold outside and you really did try to get the live shot up on time."*

✓ **Heart.** This is where the understanding can, if the facts and judgments (EARS and MIND) are correct, turn to empathy for the speaker. You might say to the live truck operator, *"I know how frustrating you must have felt not to mention how cold it is out today and trying to yank on frigid metal must have been a real pain."*

Practice the delicate skill of not having all the answers yet still being in command of the operation. This requires active listening. An old corporate motto from the Bell System was "listening is the beginning to understanding." Listening opens the door to empathy. Hear what the team members are advising not just during critical live shot conditions but in more relaxed settings when you seek feedback on how to help the field team get back to the station early so they can make your deadlines. As you listen, repeat it back (active listening) in such a way so they know you have heard them. This will go a long way toward gaining respect for the tough juggling act you face bringing together all of the elements of the newscast into one coherent whole. Remember each of them, other than the assignment editor, is concerned with just one small aspect of the newscast. Unless they've sat in the producer's chair, they don't understand your juggling act. But you can help them understand it, and in the process many of these team members will not only respect you but in turn empathize as you fulfill the sometimes tough role that is yours alone, working one on one with what usually is the biggest ego in the newsroom—the anchor.

The Talent Team—The Fine Art of Ego Stroking

There is no more important relationship than the one between you and your anchors. Of course most producers will work in shops with two news co-anchors and weather and sports anchors, but this discussion will focus on the one-on-one relationship you need with a news anchor, and you can multiply that experience based on how many you have on your news team.

Veteran, award winning, Anchor Carl Day edits copy before the noon newscast on WDTN-TV (Dayton).

Before we talk about managing this relationship, we want to lay out some of the difficulties that can get in the way of a good producer/anchor relationship. There are differences between producers and anchors that you need to overcome and deal with:

- **Salary/workload.** Your anchors could make as much as five or six times your salary. You will work your butt off for eight to ten hours preparing your newscast, whereas your anchors may have less than an hour to prepare for their performance, especially for early evening newscasts. The perception in many newsrooms is that anchors don't work very hard, even though they make the highest salaries. Keep in mind, though, that on weekends when you're off, the anchors are sitting in festival booths and parade cars being the public face of the station. Also remember that if ratings are down, it's very unlikely a producer would ever be fired or demoted, but anchors are the first people on the chopping block. Yes, they get paid a lot more than you do, but they also have a lot more at stake!

- **Ego.** The best anchors have very healthy egos—fortunately most don't rule the newsroom with their egos, they lead as journalists. But night after night the anchors have to sit on the news set and put their own personalities and communication talent out there for viewers to accept or reject. Unlike other performers who play roles, anchors essentially play themselves. It takes quite a bit of confidence to put your own personality out there for people to react to every night. So there's a good reason for that ego.

- **Age/experience.** It's very likely that at least the first ten or so years of your producing career you will work with anchors who are older and more experienced journalists, often substantially older. Respect and use that experience, don't ignore it. Not only have your anchors probably been through many young producers who think they know it all, but they've also probably been burned by a few of them. Again, a little humility and respect goes a long way.

The individual one-on-one relationship you develop with each member of the talent team involves two main areas; on-air information communication and the off-air script writing process.

In chapter 9, "Life in the Booth," we talked about how to communicate with your anchors on the air. It's worth saying again, though. You are your anchors only lifeline during the newscast. You are the only person looking out for them, so keep the lines of communication open. It's easy for an experienced producer to watch a newscast and tell by the anchor's performance if he or she trusts the producer in the booth. Each anchor is different in how they want time cues and information fed to them. Find out their preferences and adapt to their style.

Michael Petchenik of WAGT-TV (Augusta) says this relationship takes nurturing. "For the most part I do trust my producer, though I have been burned once in a while. I think you build that trust over time through trial and error. In my shop, I'm also a producer, so I feel like I can appreciate what they're going through on a nightly basis."

Besides the critical on-air relationship the producer and the anchor interact through the news day in the script writing and rundown process. We asked several medium sized market anchors to offer insights about the writing partnership that develops between the producer and anchor. Michelle Frey, who now anchors in Nebraska but who has also worked as a morning producer in Phoenix, says the partnership requires balancing the anchor and the producer's egos.

> As a producer I hated it when anchors would change the scripts I wrote. I felt it was an unspoken disapproval of my writing style. Now as anchor, I

always try to tweak my scripts so they have my stamp on them. It has little to do with my producer's writing abilities and more to do with my own style. I want to read and present the newscast's stories and writing is critical to that function. However, communication is important here. As a producer, I would be very upset if an anchor changed a script so much that it was no longer accurate. I would have preferred they come to me and make sure the changes were okay. Now, I attempt to do that.

From the news director's vantage point this tug of war over the words can damage the anchor–producer relationship. Bruce Kirk, news director at WSET-TV (Lynchburg) advises to replay that oldie again!

Aretha Franklin had it right, R-E-S-P-E-C-T. Anchors must let the producers take some chances. Producers, let the anchor think it was their idea. Find the way you can share. Some producers like anchors writing the teases or leads. Find what works for you and polish it up. Communicate. Make sure you're talking about leads, teases, show flow, targeting viewers, etc. Producers in the end are hired to make anchors look good. No producer likes to hear that but it's true. And for goodness sake get over who has to be right. Too many producer–anchor teams are destroyed over "she changed my lead-in" or "I wouldn't have lead with that."

In script writing Anchor Shawn Patrick of KTAL (Shreveport) minces no words when the copy doesn't work.

I'm blunt when the writing isn't sharp and I need to take a chainsaw to the copy, but they know it's not personal, and it's to improve a product, making them and me look better. However, I've learned: think before you speak. An effective means of explaining a correction can have a much better impact than simply barking across the room, "What the hell kind of lead sentence is that? Who cares?" I know I wouldn't appreciate that sent in my direction. No reason for it. It enhances nothing in the newsroom. I know some anchors that just re-write everything and assume the producer will never get upset. (Yes, guilty as charged!) But I've learned you're only putting a band-aid on the problem. No one's learning here, including you. Take a few minutes after a newscast, or come in early and talk over those particular scripts, and watch what happens.

Former RTNDA Board Member and now media consultant, Paula Pendarvis-Milham spent 25 years in television news positions including news director and recalls the challenge it took sometimes to smooth out the producer and anchor relationship.

As a producer, I felt once I figured out an anchor's style, I got rid of my own "voice" in writing copy and truly wrote for that anchor. It made a huge difference in their delivery, and gives them confidence that you as a producer understand the anchor's role in selling that newscast you produced, to the viewers. It takes an energetic and talented producer with excellent news judgment, terrific communication skills, and creative writing power to assemble a great newscast. It takes an anchor who believes all those things about you to deliver the news just the way the producer envisions it.

Finally, Denise Eck an anchor/reporter from WSLS-TV (Roanoke) echoes the critical need for a strong producer–anchor relationship.

Chapter 11

It's got to be a partnership. An anchor won't roll her eyes or complain about story selection if she has a say in that story selection. It should not be a relationship of writer and reader. As an anchor, I always appreciated producers who didn't take any guff from big ego anchors. The best producers are the ones who take chances and believe in their work. They aren't afraid to stand up and defend their work to someone who may have the most famous face in town.

The anchor's face, and far more importantly the words that come from their mouths, create the image of credibility for your newscast. A heavy burden often rests on your shoulders to write words that sustain this image. Double checking facts as well as grammar and spelling go a long way toward making the anchor look good and your newscast credible.

WHIO-TV (Dayton) Anchor Jim Brown takes a quiet moment on the set before the noon newscast to go over scripts and mentally prepare for the half-hour ahead.

By far most anchors are not clones of *Saturday Night Live*'s "Weekend Update" or Will Farrell's "Ron Burgundy" of *Anchorman*—pretty faces racing back from a long dinner 20 minutes before air time shouting "Where's my script?" Credible anchors become your journalistic partner, often carrying the additional title of managing editor and helping you select the stories, coach young reporters, and shape the broadcast into a solid journalistic product. The journalistic partnership that should exist between you and the anchor can become one of your most rewarding and best learning experiences. Look to seasoned anchors to help fine-tune your journalistic habits from writing and story selection to ethical decision making. Shawn Patrick , a former anchor in Shreveport, now at KUSA (Denver), shared how this partnership unfolds into a relationship of trust in his shop at KTAL.

It takes awhile, day in and day out. Producers come and go quite often in small market news. The minute they get experience, and I do mean the minute, they're gone. So I've suddenly become quite skeptical of many before I can trust them. You develop the trust for each other when you experience those moments in news together. A breaking story minutes before the newscast when you land a live phone interview with the big "get," or the debate throughout the story meeting on why that story is so relevant for a newscast. Each day you bend and learn something about each other through those tough times that can really test you in the heat of the moment ... that's when you trust that person. They're with you through the hell, the gunfire.

Ironically the best examples of team players I've found have been my young understudies who produce my main newscasts. I'm so proud of them. My 10 p.m. and 6 p.m. producers, with no more than two years experience in this business, have so much understanding and compassion for getting a good newscast on the air. They can juggle their writing duties and stacking, with my neurotic needs as I'm putting together my

 package through the day and pestering them about the way they wrote their teases, as I re-write. No matter what, they don't take it personally and learn to ride the wave and find the good qualities in everyone and learn from them. It's amazing if you look deep enough, even into your least desirable coworker, you will find something you can learn from that person.

Shawn Patrick, KUSA-TV (Denver).

Shawn's attitude of professional humility—ever ready to learn from anyone—is exactly the one a producer should mirror. Nothing will humble you faster than working with the highly technical world of production and those who support the over-all on-air look of the newscast from the graphics artist to the director.

The Production Team: The Director, the Artist, and the Rest of the Techies

A successful local television newscast director, Chris Bade of WTVF-TV (Nashville), worked with hundreds of student producers in the 1990s taking courses at the Missouri School of Journalism. Instructing them in control booth etiquette Chris would explain that his job as newscast director was like a bus driver. "You're like the travel guide who arranges how everything should go," Bade would say. "But once the newscast starts up it is my job to keep it on the road and get us out on time."

Of course newscast directing is an elevated art form especially when multiple-incoming live shots and complex newscast segments using various studio elements are involved. But the bus driver analogy works in trying to understand how to manage your relationship with the director. As we noted in our chapter on "Life in the Booth," communication is key and knowing when to talk and when to stay quiet is critical.

WCPO-TV (Cincinnati) director, technical director, graphics operator, and producer in the control room during the newscast.

Other elements of this relationship include keeping the director informed as the news day unfolds. Any change you make could have multiple ripple effects ranging from how a complicated microwave shot is bounced back to the station to how many in-studio guests you want the anchor to interview, which impacts lighting and camera shots. Allow the director the authority he or she needs to keep the rest of the production team alert and ready for the instant changes live television news demands. Never undercut his authority in the booth. Recognize editorial preferences you may have sometimes fade at the mercy of production constraints. Spend time with the director away from the newsroom. Find time to take a dinner break off site. Your relationship is important and just as critical as fostering the one with the anchors. But unlike your anchors, or anyone else in the newsroom, most of the time you spend with the director is during the last minute rush to get everything done and in the stress of the on-air broadcast.

How to Manage Creative People

Former Broadcast General Manager Charles Warner lead the RTNDF/Missouri School of Journalism Management Seminar for a number of years. He summarized the best business thinking on do's and don'ts when working with truly creative people.

1. Do not interfere.

2. Do not criticize but give them specific feedback.

3. Do not compare them to others.

4. Do not threaten to fire them—either love and support them to the hilt or fire them—there's virtually no room in between.

Graphics

One additional key player in the on-air look of the newscast is the graphics artist. Managing this relationship can either be the most frustrating or the most fun. Graphics artists often live in a world of their own. They like it that way. It allows them the space and freedom to create. If you're seen as just someone who shouts an order for a map or complains about the video open for a special investigative series then your relationship with the artist will suffer. Talk to them about their favorite artists. More than that, talk with them about anything that interests them.

Beyond getting to know them, get to know their environment. Understand the capabilities of your graphics department, both the people and the equipment. Know how quickly they can turn around special graphics or animation, and how many different projects they can handle at a time. And just as you use the expertise of your director or anchors to make the newscast better, use your graphics artists, too. Don't just e-mail or message them that the graphic info is in a script, go down to the graphics department and talk through your ideas of how to illustrate a story or enhance a reporter package. They are artists, after all, and can often take a basic idea and really run with it. But most won't do that without a sense from you, the producer, that it's okay.

A graphic artist at WCNC-TV (Charlotte) develops graphics for the early newscasts.

When crunch time comes remember, just as it is difficult to write under deadline pressure and sometimes you just have to "let go" in the writing process, so too the graphic artist lives in a world of constant compromises. Artists have the desire for just five more minutes to "tweak it a little more." As with all your managing people relationships look for specific ways to compliment the artist.

Often someone from the graphics department also handles the character generator for titles and "supers," so make sure they have what is needed. Not all artists are great spellers! As the producer it is ultimately your responsibility to double check that names and locations are spelled properly and the numbers on full screen graphics are correct.

Each member of the newscast team, from anchors to directors to those supporting the look and feel of the broadcast, can provide you with the support you need to fulfill your responsibility to produce the day's news. Listening, remaining open and humble will teach you a great deal. The learning curve that can stir up the most fear for you is with those higher up on the "food chain"—your boss—the news director or in larger markets the trio of news director, assistant news director, and executive producer.

Managing Up: The News Director and the General Manager

Sometimes you might feel like you're being bent in the wind as you sway to follow policy and execute daily decisions. Maybe you even feel like you are second guessing what the boss wants. If that is the case the fault lays with their management skills not your follow-up ability. You'll understand that better as you climb the ranks of management yourself, someday perhaps becoming a news director. The first step on that career path is paying very close attention to managing your boss.

Managing your boss may sound odd, since the normal way of thinking is that they manage you. What we speak of here is the management of your relationship. It begins even before your first day at work by sending clear, written communica-

---

Managing Your Manager

The Poynter Institute's Jill Geisler listed these key points to manage up rather than "suck up" to the boss in a November 1999 article for RTNDA's *Communicator* magazine.

- Speak to your news director at least once a week.
- Remember: News directors worry about being out of touch.
- Consider: News directors hear bad news all day.
- Have all the facts before you complain.

- Never assume motive.
- Ask yourself: Is this a "Got a minute?" or a "Got a power hour?" Geisler counsels, "News directors are constantly struggling with time management. Help the cause by stating your needs clearly and every now and then, actually do so in a minute."

Geisler, J. (1999, November). "Managing Your Manager," *Communicator,* p. 69.

Jill Geisler, The Poynter Institute

tion either in the form of an acceptance letter for the position or a hand written thank you note accompanying the employment paperwork you turn in.

Buy yourself a set of professional note cards. Use them to communicate expressions of gratitude to your coworkers and your boss. But be careful about what you put in writing as you're leaving a paper trail. If you feel the need to complain to your boss about a fellow news team member, it is better to do it verbally and in person. E-mail has a seductive way of letting loose your self-expression and as a writer, when angry, the passion can flow in words you might later regret. Be wise about whatever you put in writing. A good rule of thumb is only say "good things" in written form and use verbal communication to convey complaints and frustrations.

Jennifer Rigby, news director of WSB-TV (Atlanta), offered a simple secret to managing your boss.

> As a producer you can manage up with the same approach you take to writing a news story. Present the story you want to tell clearly and concisely in a straightforward manner. Be ready to present solutions. Be the "go-to" member of the team. Become an expert in new technology or new processes and get involved in extra projects and assignments that expand your experience and knowledge while also helping your boss.

Managing your boss does not mean sucking up to her or him. People spot phony relationship building just as you spot and avoid over-eager sales staff in a store. Some focus on the personal approach first and try to find a connecting point, a mutually shared interest, to build the relationship. While this might work for some, gender, age, and other differences may make this uncomfortable or not practical for others. Find the style of your own but do not just ignore the fact that this relationship is critical and will impact your future. Bill Seitzler, news director of KJRH-TV (Tulsa), believes learning this skill was important in his career.

> Managing up is the most important thing I ever learned in the TV business. Most news directors and general managers hate suck ups. They do like people who keep them informed with the good and bad news. If you are not sure if your news director's detailed oriented ask one simple question: "I'm going to let you know when something really big happens with my show but do you also want me to keep you up-to-speed on the little stuff?" Nine times out of ten the news director will answer with only the big stuff. By asking the question you've put them on notice that you are willing to do either but they need to choose.

In an article for the *Harvard Business Review* titled, "Managing Your Boss" authors John Gabarro and John Kotter summarized five critical keys to this relationship.

> Develop and maintain a relationship that:
> 1. Fits both your needs and styles.
> 2. Is characterized by mutual expectations.
> 3. Keeps your boss informed.
> 4. Is based on dependability and honesty.
> 5. And selectively uses your boss's time and resources."
> (Gabarro & Kotter, 1980)

Chapter 11

Bruce Kirk, WSET-TV

News Director Bruce Kirk, at WSET-TV (Lynchburg), echoed the importance of point three, keeping the boss in the communication loop, but he also urged producers to be creative risk takers.

Check the landscape. In other words, know what your boss expects in shows, pacing, flow, content, design, etc. Once you get that, try to color within the lines. Take chances, assuming your boss backs that. Most will, they see producers as the real risk takers. Cover your backside with libel and ethics. When in doubt legally, always wake-up the boss, never just go with it. Keep them in the loop. We hate surprises. We hate that angry viewer call you knew about, but forgot to pass along from the night before because she's going to call back.

News Director Alan Hobbs, who worked for 20 years in TV news with stops from Greensboro, North Carolina (WGHP) to Monroe, Louisiana (KTVE), told us, "Know what your managers expect so you can answer the questions before they're asked. Be prepared to logically explain why you treated a story or coverage the way you did. Be open, but do not stray from the newscast's mission."

Managing up is about keeping managers informed about what's going on, making sure they don't get blindsided, and have as much opportunity to prevent problems as possible. Talk with your boss often. Stop in their office at least once a week. Do not come to them only when there is a problem. Pass out a sincere compliment. Talk about things outside of work.

Managing up is also about maintaining the chain of command. Anne Linaberger, executive producer of KDKA-TV (Pittsburgh), talks about working with your executive producer—often the person you directly report to.

TV bosses—in many cases your EPs—don't want to have to repeat themselves a million times, they don't want to have to beg you or fight with you to produce your show a certain way, they don't want to have to deal with every little detail or problem, and they want you to bring your ideas and creativity to the table instead of waiting for prompting.

For instance, your boss should only have to tell you once that the philosophy of the station is to lead with weather any time there's a watch or warning. If he or she has to remind you every single time to change your lead, that's a problem. Your boss should only have to explain once that your show is formatted a certain way. If you disagree, it's okay to express your opinion, but be respectful, and don't continually challenge your boss about it. I worked with one producer who continually violated formatting rules for a show, even though I kept reminding her not to. In one conversation about this, she implied that my ideas were small market because she had produced a different way in a larger market. Not a good way to impress your boss, especially since these rules may be station rules, not hers.

Depending on the hierarchy of your newsroom, don't send every whining reporter to your EP just because you don't want to deal with them. Your boss will appreciate it if you handle some of these situations, and you will demonstrate your ability to manage people, which you will need to learn to do if you have any aspirations to be a manager.

Finally, bring your ideas to the table and communicate your vision for your show—don't make your EP create one for you. I worked with one producer who wouldn't know how to produce or market the big story if it hit him over the head—or if he did he didn't show it. He would simply take what he was handed, stack it in the show, and figure his job was done. After awhile I got tired of continually prompting him to think creatively and basically wrote him off. Bottom line: don't make your boss' job any harder than it already is, and make it easier if you can. And let your boss know that you appreciate the things you are (I hope) learning from them.

That appreciation can come in many forms. A simple thank you delivered in person, a note of gratitude, or a more expressive letter about all that you learned when it comes time to move on to another market all work.

The same principles Anne suggests you use with your executive producer—be grateful for those who set the rules, use them and learn when they can be broken—can be applied to the other managers within the newsroom—such as an assistant news director, managing editor, or even the news director. Respect the chain of command. Learn it. It applies beyond the newsroom across the station from the sales director to the station's general manager. When it comes time for promotions, raises, or worse—when tough decisions have to be made about who to lay off in an economic slump—being known not only as a good team player, a solid, professional producer but an excellent station citizen who is respected and liked by others can be very important.

A Style of Your Own

The history of management in all professions has changed a lot in the last hundred years. In the 1920s, when the *Harvard Business Review* began publishing, it was all about polices, procedures, and command and control of an organization. Today management has evolved to a heavy emphasis on people, how they fit in the organization, meeting the mission, and quality of life. Our emphasis remains on people. But even people oriented managers execute their performance with different styles. Find a style of your own and develop it.

You might be comfortable looking for opportunities to build a relationship beyond the newsroom. Find ways to talk to your boss about non-news items. Look at their desk. Check out their wall. What pictures are prominently displayed? They give clues to your news director's or other managers' significant personal relationships and lifestyle choices. Learn the names of their family members. If they have children find out what sports or hobbies their children have. Tuck away this information—even write it down—so that later you can ask how their son's football team is doing or how the dance recital went.

People love to talk about themselves and their families. Be a good listener. Share something about your own life outside of the newsroom. Build the relationship by being interested in them as an individual not just as a manager. Find interests you have in common. An easy one is music. Another is film. No matter what the age difference might be, conversations about music and film interests can create mutual interests.

Finally, in all of your interpersonal relationships at work whether managing sideways with coworkers or managing up with your boss, remember the three basic "Bs" to build relationships of trust with those you interact with at work.

Be credible yet teachable.

Be confident yet caring.

Be smart but wise.

The key to wisdom in relationships with coworkers is to respect the individual nature of each relationship. Subtle nuances will exist as you manage people in critical relationships—reporters, the desk, the anchors, production crews, and your bosses. It is important to recognize those differences and not try to carbon copy a formula as you deal with each. Managing people you work with will be challenging but equally rewarding, often as creative as putting together a rundown.

Coupled together, producing and people skills enable you to serve the ultimate relationship that should matter most—with the viewer—in your commitment to be a true, professional journalist putting an excellent newscast on the air.

Sources

Gabarro, J., & Kotter, J. (1980, January-February). Managing your boss. *Harvard Business Review,* 99.

Geisler, J. (1999, November). Managing your manager. *Communicator,* 69.

Johnson, L., & Phillips, B. (2003). *Absolute honesty.* New York: AMACOM.

MANAGING SWEEPS: THE GOOD, THE BAD, AND THE UGLY

Her hands are clammy. She takes a deep breath for courage. It's day 15 and there are only five days left. As she approaches the room she listens for signs that it's going to be OK. There are only hushed whispers ... no morning laughter. That's not a good sign. Her stomach clenches. She walks into the room and stops. There they are. She closes her eyes and says a brief prayer. Then she can't put it off any longer. She opens one eye and peaks at the dreaded posting. Her heart sinks, and the quarter point panic digs its boney fingers into her gut.

No, that's not the opening to a thriller novel. It's the routine producers across the country go through daily for four weeks in February, May, July, and November. It's "Sweeps," "Ratings," "The Book"! It's the time of the year when local stations find out who and how many are watching the news and other programs. From that information advertising rates are set, so a change of even a quarter or half point can mean thousands of dollars, more or less, for the station in the following months. With that at stake, it's also the time of the year when relatively sane (no one who chooses television news for a career is completely sane, and we like it that way!) and intelligent news and station managers often lose their good judgment, ethics, and common sense in the "quarter point panic." It's the time of the year when we frighten with deadly tainted ice tea, shock with ultraviolet light on supposedly "clean" hotel sheets, titillate with undercover video of park bathrooms, go behind the scenes of favorite prime time programs, and even bribe with "watch and win" cash. All of that sweeps *stunting*, as some of the more outrageous stories, promotions, and contests are referred to, is done with the hope of getting viewers to do something they would probably do anyway if you just covered the news—watch more television.

But the news about news ratings isn't all bad. Sweeps periods are also the times when stations do their very best work. Investigative and longer enterprise stories, which often take months to complete, air during sweeps. As a producer, you get more resources and have a full staff to work with (no one takes vacation during sweeps and you better be on your death bed before you call in sick!). There's more promotion time devoted to your newscasts. Everyone's performance tends to be pushed up a notch, and all the live trucks are in good working order.

The problem with all this hype four months a year is it doesn't last and the viewers know it. Al Tompkins, head of broadcast journalism for The Poynter Institute, put it this way, "I don't think there's anything about four months out of the year—February, May, July, and November—that viewers mysteriously change viewing habits and change from one station to another. It's so difficult to get viewers to form a habit, let alone change a habit" (Owens, 2001, p. D1). In fact, a 2001 tracking study by the American Association of Advertising Agencies found that many stations that engaged in the worst sweeps stunting lost any ratings spikes after the sweeps period was over and they returned to routine news coverage.

Advertisers are critical of sweeps stunting because they think it leads to ad rates that are artificially high. They believe they are paying for viewers who aren't watching the other eight or nine months of the year when there aren't any special reports, flashy promotions, or contests. However, David Lippoff, a longtime news director and station general manager with Cox Broadcasting, notes that special sweeps reports and promotions are too expensive to be designed just for a short-term gain. "The goal is to create sampling with the hope that you'll get people who are not normally viewers into a particular daypart. If all you want to do is get your numbers up during sweeps, that's pretty shortsighted. It's really a long term goal to create sampling that you hope will turn into regular viewership" (Murphy, 2001).

The "R" Word

So just what are these ratings that can make the calmest anchors sweat, give news directors sleepless nights, and create month-long headaches for producers who have to deal with second-guessing managers and timing out overflowing newscasts? In the simplest definition, **ratings** are an estimate of the audience watching a given station or network at a given time.

Ratings data have been collected by Nielsen Media Research since the 1930s, starting in radio, to provide broadcasters and advertisers with some basis for buying and selling commercial time. When an advertiser buys commercial time on a station or network, it is really buying viewers' attention. The advertiser wants to know how many viewers are likely to see the ad and who those viewers are. Obviously Chevrolet is looking for a different viewer than Mercedes-Benz. How much a station or network can charge for its advertising time depends on how many of the clients' prime customers it can deliver. Different programs and different times of the day deliver different viewers. So both advertisers and broadcasters needed a way to count viewers and listeners. That's where Nielsen Media Research came in.

Nielsen is an independent company, not associated with any media or advertising companies. Media companies, networks, stations, and advertisers pay Nielsen hundreds of thousands to millions of dollars to collect ratings nationally and in local radio and television markets. Those ratings then form the basis for advertising sales rates.

Ratings Lingo

- **DMA (Designated Market Area) or Market:** The country is divided into 210 "markets" determined by population. New York City is #1. Glendive, Montana is #210. A market is not determined by geographic boundaries but by primary viewing. Viewers in areas that can receive signals from stations in more than one city belong to the market whose stations they watch the most.

- **TV Household:** Any residence in the DMA with at least one television

- **HUT (Households Using Television):** HUT levels are exactly what they sound like—the number of households in a market that have the television on during a given time period.

- **Rating:** Estimated percentage of *ALL TV Households* in a market watching your station.

- **Share:** Estimated percentage of *HUT* in a market watching your station.

Example: Market X

TV Households	500,000
HUT at 6 p.m.	200,000
Households watching Channel Z	50,000
Rating for Channel Z at 6 p.m.	10
Share for Channel Z at 6 p.m.	25

- **PUT (People Using Television):** To determine the demographics of who in the TV Household is watching, Nielsen also reports rating and share for people using television by age groups and gender. PUT levels are also reported for African American and Latino minority groups.

- **Diary:** Paper log in which viewers write down the programs they watch and mail in at the end of each week of the rating period.

- **Meter:** Electronic box attached to all TVs and VCRs in a TV household that continuously logs what channel the TV is tuned to or the VCR is recording while the TV or VCR is on. Meters record and download ratings data to Nielsen all year long, not just during sweeps months.

- **People Meter:** Device on top of the TV with a remote that allows each individual in the TV household to log in when he or she is watching. Viewers punch in their individual codes and their designated light on the device turns from red to green. The light flashes periodically to remind the viewer to push a button to indicate he or she is still watching. The viewer then logs out when done watching.

Chapter 12

- **Overnights:** In markets with meters the ratings data are downloaded overnight to Nielsen, compiled, and sent back to the stations first thing in the morning. These reports, called "overnights," only include total ratings, no demographic data, except in a very few markets that have local people meters.
- **Quarter Hour:** Viewing data is reported in 15 minute segments. In metered markets a viewer must watch a given station/program for at least 5 minutes in a 15 minute segment for the station to get credit for that viewer for that quarter hour.

How Does Nielsen Count Viewers?

Nielsen collects national and local ratings data. Both are done using random samples of TV households. National and local ratings data are collected separately, using different samples. These samples are random, scientific samples that are representative of the demographics of each market, as well as the nation as a whole. When a household is randomly selected, the people are contacted and invited to participate. If it's a meter market or the national sample, the meter equipment will be installed. If it's a diary household, viewers are sent log books to keep track of their viewing behavior and then the books are sent back weekly. "Nielsen Families" as they're called, receive a small payment for participating, but it doesn't amount to more than a few dollars a month, just enough to make people feel they should fill out the diaries, but not enough to make people wonder if they should lie and say they watched more TV than they really did because they were being paid.

National Ratings

National ratings are gathered from a sample of 9,000 households, with more than 18,000 viewers across the country. National ratings use the **people meter** system (see definition above), which not only measures when the TV is on and what it's tuned to, but also who is watching that program. People meters have been used in the national sample since 1987 and provide overnight data, including demographics, all year long. Currently each national rating point a program gets represents about a million viewers.

Local Ratings

Local ratings are collected in 210 local television markets (see definition above). Approximately the top 60 markets are now **metered markets,** which means that gross ratings data are collected electronically year round from a sample of TV households in each market that are wired with meter boxes. Stations in metered markets get overall ratings every morning for the previous 24 hour period. Then four times a year the meters are supplemented with **diaries** that provide demographic information about who makes up those gross ratings.

In the approximately 150 medium to smaller markets where meters have been cost prohibitive, diaries are the only source of ratings information. So these markets only get ratings during sweeps. And they don't get any data at all during the sweeps period. It takes about two weeks to tabulate the diaries, so diary market stations don't know how they did during the sweep period until about 10 to 14 days after the ratings period ends.

Diary data is collected for four weeks starting on a Thursday and ending on a Wednesday during the months of February, May, July, and November. Because summer viewing tends to be much lower than during the rest of the year—people on vacation, longer days, and so forth—the July sweeps is usually not considered that important. That means that the May book becomes the most important in diary markets because the sales department will sell those numbers right through the November and December Christmas retail.

Sample Overnight Ratings Data for Fictional Market-X

NielsenTV DMA Sample: 359 Reporting Households
Daily Grid

Time	HUT	NBC Affiliate	Rt	Sh	CBS Affiliate	Rt	Sh	ABC Affiliate	Rt	Sh	FOX Affiliate	Rt	Sh	Sh	OTHER	Sh
4:00p	39.9	ACCESS HOLLYWD	1.0	2	MONTEL WILLIAM	2.5	6	OPRAH WINFREY	6.7	17	MAURY POVICH	0.8	2	2		95
	42.5	_1.0__2_41.2	1.0	2		2.4	6		7.1	17		0.8	2	2		88
4:30p	44.0	CURRENT AFFAIR	1.5	3		2.0	4		6.5	15		1.6	4	2		88
	46.5	_1.9__4_45.3	2.3	5	_2.3__5_43.2	2.3	5	_6.7_16_43.2	6.7	14	_1.1__3_43.2	1.3	3	2		86
5:00p	49.8	NEWS AT 5PM	3.7	8	ACTION NEWS-500P	5.4.	11	EYEWIT NWS 5	9.9	20	SIMPSONS	1.8	4	2		75
	52.8	_4.5__9_51.3	5.0	9	_6.0_12_51.3	6.7	13	10.8_21_51.3	11.7	22	_2.0__4_51.3	2.2	4	2		70
5:30p	55.2	NEWS AT 530P	4.8	9	ACTION NEWS-530P	8.2	15	EYEWIT NWS5.30	11.5	21	KING OF HILL	2.3	4	3		66
	57.3	_4.0__7_56.2	3.3	6	_8.4_15_56.2	8.5	15	11.4_20_56.2	11.4	20	_3.0__5_56.2	3.7	7	2		64
6:00p	58.1	NEWS AT 6PM	4.5	8	ACTION NEWS-600P	8.5	15	EYEWIT NWS 6	13.6	23	FRIENDS	3.2	6	4		57
	60.0	_5.0__8_59.1	5.5	9	_8.0_14_59.1	7.5	12	14.3_24_59.1	14.9	25	_3.1__5_59.1	3.0	5	4		60
6:30p	60.6	NBC NITELY NWS	6.2	10	CBS EVE NWS	8.2	13	ABC-WORLD NWS	15.6	26	KING-QUEENS B	3.1	5	3		55
	60.6	_6.1_10_60.6	6.0	10	_7.4_12_60.6	6.6	11	15.1_25_60.6	14.6	24	_3.3__5_60.6	3.5	6	2		60
7:00p	59.1	JEOPARDY	5.6	9	EVRYBDY-RAY MF	4.3	7	INSIDE EDITION	13.8	23	KING OF QUEENS	4.3	7	1		69
	60.8	_6.0_10_59.9	6.4	10	_4.1__7_59.9	4.0	7	12.3_21_59.9	10.8	18	_4.3__7_59.9	4.2	7	2		73
7:30p	60.4	WHEEL-FORTNE	7.3	12	INSIDER	3.3	5	ENT TONIGHT 30	11.6	19	FRIENDS	5.1	8	1		73
	62.8	_7.4_12_61.6	7.6	12	_3.5__6_61.6	3.6	6	11.6_19_61.6	11.7	19	_5.1__8_61.6	5.0	8	2		69
8:00p	66.3	FEAR FACTR-NBC	4.4	7	KNG-QUEENS-CBS	4.6	7	NFL PRESN2-ABC	8.1	12	PRISON BRK-FOX	8.5	13			80
	68.0		2.9	4	_5.2__8_67.2	5.9	9		8.7	13		9.3	14	2		85
8:30p	68.2		2.5	4	EVRYBDY-RAY-CBS	6.3	9		8.5	12		8.8	13	1		89
	71.9	_3.0__4_68.6	2.4	3	_6.9_10_70.1	7.5	10		8.9	12		9.4	13	1		80
9:00p	73.2	LAS VEGAS-NBC	4.7	6	TWO&HLF MN-CBS	8.2	11		7.1	10		9.0	12			80
	70.3		3.4	5	_7.6_11_71.8	7.0	10		8.4	12		8.8	13			82
9:30p	70.9		3.2	5	TWO-MN 930-CBS	7.4	11		8.1	11		8.8	12			81
	67.2	_3.7__5_70.4	3.4	5	_7.4_11_69.0	7.3	11		6.0	9	_8.9_13_69.5	8.5	13			84
10:00p	67.7	MEDIUM-NBC	5.4	8	CSI:MIAMI-CBS	9.7	14		5.9	9	FOX NWS AT 10	7.9	12	1		78
	63.8		5.5	9		8.7	14		4.4	7	_6.1__9_65.8	4.3	7	1		83
10:30p	60.2		5.4	9		9.4	16		4.4	7	FOX NEWS EDGE	3.1	5			82
	57.2	_5.3__9_62.2	5.0	9	_9.3_15_62.2	9.3	16	_6.9_10_67.1	4.2	7	_2.7__5_58.7	2.4	4	1		81
11:00p	54.2	NIGHTCAST	9.0	17	ACTION NEWS AT 11	9.7	18	EYEWIT NWS 11	3.9	7	SIMPSONS	4.2	8			71
	49.2	_8.3_16_51.7	7.6	16	_9.1_18_51.7	8.5	17	_3.5__7_51.7	3.2	6	_4.2__8_51.7	4.3	9			66

(Numbers under the program title are average Rating (Rt), Share (Sh) and Households Using Television (HUT) for the entire program)

Chapter 12

Local People Meters—The End of Sweeps?

Right now there is a major change happening in local ratings that has set off a firestorm of controversy. Although people meters have been used in national ratings since 1987, they are just now being introduced in local ratings. Nielsen's first test market was Boston, starting in 2002. In 2004 New York, Los Angeles, Chicago, and San Francisco went to people meters for ratings. Nielsen is now using local people meters in all the top ten markets.

Local People Meter

Companies that own broadcast stations had fought the local people meters because the ratings produced usually show an audience drop for the local stations in favor of cable viewing. In Boston the local stations' ratings dropped 15 to 20% overall, and most of that went to cable. Since the ratings were no longer based on people remembering what they watched and then writing it down but on the simple push of a button, Nielsen and most advertisers believe people meters are more reliable measures of what people actually watched. So, for example, let's say you usually watch Channel X for the 11 p.m. news, but you see a promo for an interesting story on Channel Y on Monday night and watch it, will you remember that when you fill out the diary? Or will you simply fill in Channel X for every night at 11 p.m. because that's what you normally do?

The other larger controversy over local people meters has been concern about undercounting African American and Latino viewers. That prompted Fox and Univision, among others, to go to court and launch major public relations campaigns against the implementation of people meters. Nielsen's sample numbers show representation of these minorities matching the population distribution in the cities, but the problem is apparently that some groups of viewers, such as African American viewers, had a higher rate of unusable data and so their viewing was undercounted. Nielsen had to go in and retrain some groups of viewers in Boston to solve the problem and says it will do the same as needed in other local people meter markets.

If the Boston market is any indicator, local people meters could indeed mean the end of much sweeps stunting. With people meters, stations get demographic information with their ratings daily instead of just four times a year. Since demos are the information advertisers need, they don't have to wait and just set rates three or four times a year—the rates can be adjusted on a much more regular basis. Boston's WCVB-TV General Manager Paul La Camera says, "We no longer program and promote our TV stations to be successful in just three artificial sweeps months. We have to be sure to have a quality and compelling product on the air every day all year. It's far more rational" (McClellan, 2004, p. 12).

Boston stations are producing fewer sweeps-type special reports and ratings stunts and instead are investing their resources back into daily local news coverage. WCVB's Vice President for Programming Liz Cheng says, "We think one of the best things about people meters is that we are in the game 365 days a year. Our goal is to deliver a superior newscast day in and day out" (Potter, 2004, p. 64). Longtime network journalist and Newslab Director Deborah Potter notes, "How ironic that we might have Nielsen to thank for helping to bring TV news back to its senses" (Potter, 2004, p. 64).

And much more change is coming. In June 2006 Nielsen announced a major overhaul of its television rating system to "follow the video" and deal with viewers who now time-shift or download TV programs instead of watching live. Nielsen plans to link the web NetRatings system to its television ratings, expand local people meters to the top 25 markets and in mid-size markets install a more sophisticated meter system. The biggest change—Nielsen plans to shred paper diaries in all markets by 2011. It's not known what form of electronic ratings will replace the paper diary system in the smallest markets where meters are too expensive. However, whatever system Nielsen develops, we are stuck with sweeps months for a while.

Sweeps Survival 101

Chances are as a line producer you probably won't be included in early sweeps planning. That's usually done by a special projects producer or executive producer working with the news director, other news managers, and the promotion department. But that doesn't mean you should sit back and wait for sweeps to "happen" to you. Whatever is being planned will ultimately end up impacting your show. You know better than anyone what works best in your newscast. Don't be afraid to suggest story or project ideas for your show. There may be a way to do something special for a regular segment or put something special into coverage of a big story you know is coming up during sweeps. Sweeps projects also are a great way for line producers to get a break from newscast producing and do a little field work. If you have a good idea for a sweeps piece, pitch it to your managers, and ask if you can have time off your newscast to work on it. But remember that the planning process for the next book usually starts very soon after the last book.

At least a month before sweeps starts you should meet with your executive producer or assistant news director and find out exactly what is planned for your newscast during sweeps. Sweeps calendars are usually kept very confidential so word doesn't leak to the competition about what you're doing, but most managers will let producers into the process as it affects their newscasts. The worst kind of producing during sweeps is waiting until the day of and then just getting handed "today's special report," as if it's the lunch special at the diner! Just as you come in every day knowing what's making news that day, you should also come in every sweeps day knowing what specials you have and how they'll fit in your newscast.

Chapter 12

WCPO-TV (Cincinnati) Videographer and Editor Anthony Mirones works on a sweeps investigative story on road safety and speed limits.

The Sweeps Squeeze

One of the reasons it's so important to know the sweeps plan for your newscast is timing. During sweeps it becomes mandatory that you "hit your times." By hitting your times, we don't mean just getting the newscast out on time. In metered markets there typically will be a series of times you have to hit to exploit the way meters work to maximum effect.

You need a viewer to watch your newscast at least five minutes of every quarter hour to get credit for that viewer in that time slot, and the meters click to the next 15 minute segment exactly on the quarter hour. So one cardinal rule of meter market producing is you NEVER want to be in a commercial break when the meter clicks. That means at 15, 30, and 45 minutes after the hour, as well as on the hour straight up, you have to be in content. You should stay in content at least seven minutes after the meter clicks to give yourself a little cushion.

If you only have one commercial break to get in before the first quarter hour ends, you'll likely have a nice long first block, so you don't have to worry about giving the viewer the sense that the news is just a little filler to hold up the commercials. However if you have to get two breaks in before that quarter hour click, you'll have a tough time going a good solid seven minutes or more after the top of the hour, especially if your newscast starts at 59 or even 58:30 as many early newscasts do. And chances are your second block will be painfully short.

The second important rule in meter timing is you want weather to straddle the end of that seven minutes in the second quarter hour. Viewing often drops off in the second half of a newscast after people have seen their news, but the rating for the entire newscast will be an average of the quarter hours. So to keep viewers long enough to get credit for that second quarter hour, and thus maintain the rating for the whole half-hour, we put the one thing nearly everyone wants—the weather—in the 17:00/18:00 to 21:00/22:00 minute slot. That gives you five minutes plus a little pad. That's why when you flip around to different stations, you see weather hitting about the same time in most half-hour newscasts. That's also why—sorry sports folks—you put the sports after the 22 mark in a half-hour. At that point you already have credit for the viewer for that quarter hour locked down, so if a viewer is not interested in sports (and about two-thirds aren't), they can switch channels or turn off and you still got credit for them.

All this timing is a delicate dance under normal circumstances, now drop a hefty sweeps piece into the mix, and you're dancing with two concrete left feet. Those 3:00– 4:00+ minute extravaganzas take a chunk out of your news time, and you still have an executive producer breathing down your neck demanding that you stuff one more live shot and two more vosots into your news block.

The irony is probably the month before sweeps your dance card was empty and you had to go out on the floor by yourself because so many staff members were tied up doing

Newscast Timing in a People Metered Market.

sweeps specials. Now everyone's back working for your newscast, plus a big part of that newscast is already filled with a preproduced sweeps piece.

The question of how best to incorporate sweeps pieces into your newscast is one producers and EPs have wrestled with for years. It's rare that you're going to have a sweeps piece strong enough to lead the newscast unless it's an investigative story. However when you do get a powerful investigative piece, don't overlook it as a possible lead, especially if it's not a big news day. If you are a late news producer and your lead-in is a news magazine show such as *20/20* or *Dateline*, a strong investigative piece might be just the ticket to keep that audience watching into the newscast. But more typically your sweeps behemoth is going in the second or third blocks. One great strategy for sweeps pieces is to block them so they straddle the quarter hour click, starting about 13:30-14:00 minutes into your newscast. A good sweeps piece and then weather is a great second quarter hour one-two punch.

Since you typically can't control the length of sweeps pieces you have to exert tight time controls on writers and reporters in the rest of your newscast. You still want the viewer to have the feeling that they have seen the day's news—even though you probably only have about two-thirds of your normal news hole because of the sweeps specials. Shave five to ten seconds off every story, so you have the time to spread over a decent number of stories. When your viewer has come to expect a full plate of news from your newscast, you don't want to disappoint him during the most important viewing time!

You also might check into lightening your commercial load. Many stations do this automatically during sweeps. By taking just two spots out of the normal break load, you pick up an extra minute of news time. If you know ahead of time that you'll have a heavy sweeps story schedule, check with a news manager and see if your commercial breaks can be shortened—especially the first break. That will give you more upfront news time to bulk up your news blocks.

The bottom line is don't underestimate the difficulty of managing your time during sweeps. It's a big mistake to think your job is easier because you've got four minutes of your newscast already filled.

Sweeps Specials—The Good, The Bad, and The Ugly

Throughout this chapter we've referred to some of the strategies stations use during sweeps, now we're going to get specific. But it's not too far out to say expect anything! Most sweeps specials are one-hit wonders. In other words, they are stand alone stories. The days of multipart series drifted away with the audience's changing viewing habits. In the 1970s and 80s it was typical to run four or five part series during sweeps. But as viewers habits changed from daily news consumption to now maybe 3 days a week if you're lucky, programming changed as well. A viewer who missed parts 1 and 2 is unlikely to want to watch parts 3 and 4 of a series. So now we do longer stand alone stories.

As we've mentioned previously, unlike the westerns where the good, bad, and ugly guys were easy to distinguish, during sweeps, your station may well play all three roles.

"Good" Channel 5 duels "Bad" Channel 5 during sweeps.

The Good

Some of the best work done during sweeps is the investigative journalism that stations do. In markets such as Houston, Los Angeles, Minneapolis, Dallas, and Cincinnati stations have made the investment and committed the time and resources to investigative units, often called I-Teams. And that commitment isn't small. You may only get four or five pieces a year from a reporter–producer team, because a good I-Team story likely needs anywhere from two to six months to come together. You also need someone who's good at manipulating databases, you need a solid researcher, and photographers and editors who can commit to a project for weeks at a time. Then you need a strong manager and a good lawyer. But the stations that make that commitment produce outstanding work that uncovers local corruption, fraud, consumer rip-offs, flaws in government systems, and major health and safety issues. Often good investigative journalism leads to major changes in government policy at all levels.

Two Good Guys

WCPO-TV (Cincinnati): "WCPO-TV's I-Team stadium investigation is an extraordinary undertaking by a television news organization. WCPO-TV took the lead in serving as the watchdog for citizens of Cincinnati over the billion-dollar expenditure on new sports stadiums for the Reds and Bengals. The multi-year investigation uncovered broken promises, manipulation of numbers in official reports, political cronyism in contract awards, creation of "pass-through" companies and other questionable, possibly illegal activities. The I-Team's relentless and courageous pursuit of the truth resulted in a state investigation of stadium spending. In addition, the investigation found Hamilton County well short of its stated goal to award 15% of the work to companies owned by women and minorities. As a result, the county hired a minority business development director and committed to hiring a contract monitor for the second stadium. Reporter Laure Quinlivan, assistant news director Mark Shafer, news director Scott Diener and former news director Stuart Zanger, along with photographers and editors Jeff Keene and Kenneth Fulk, were tenacious in their commitment to the people of Cincinnati. For conscientious and reliable investigative efforts with significant local impact, a Peabody Award goes to WCPO-TV, Cincinnati." From *2001 Peabody Award for Investigative Efforts*. Available at http://www.peabody.uga.edu/archives.

KHOU-TV (Houston): "For years, motorists found themselves in deadly crashes when the tread on one of their Firestone ATX tires peeled off at high speed. Acting on viewer complaints and a tip from a local attorney in late November 1999, KHOU's Investigative Unit led by David Raziq, reporter Anna Werner, and editor/photographer Chris Henao began researching accidents connected with Firestone's ATX and ATXII tires, which were original manufacturer's equipment on Ford Explorer Sports Utility Vehicles. Beginning with local crashes and expanding to accidents nationwide, Raziq, Werner, and Henao accumulated boxes of court cases and accident reports and discovered over 30 deaths connected with the problem. The team also consulted tire-engineering experts and obtained sealed court documents, which confirmed crashes had been occurring because of tread separation on Firestone tires. After the Investigative Unit presented this evidence to the National Highway Transportation Safety Administration (NHTSA), the station ran an extensive initial report on the hidden danger in early February and then continued throughout the year with follow-up reports, including coverage of recalls in foreign countries. KHOU-TV's reports also led to national media coverage of the problem, and as a consequence of KHOU-TV's initial investigation, NHTSA officials collected numerous accident complaints and launched a federal investigation into the ATX, ATXII, and Wilderness AT tires. A congressional investigation followed and led to passage of the TREAD (Transportation, Recall Enhancement, Accountability, and Documentation) Act of 2000. For its groundbreaking, comprehensive reports that saved lives and had a decided impact upon national and international policy, a Peabody goes to KHOU-TV for 'Treading on Danger?'" From *2000 Peabody Award for Investigative Efforts*. Available at http://www.peabody.uga.edu/archives.

Award winning Investigative Reporter Stewart Watson logs video for a follow-up story to one of his special reports (WCNC-TV, Charlotte).

The important thing for you to keep in mind is don't mess with the lead in or tag or any other copy associated with an investigative story. Chances are every word has been approved by a lawyer. And as was mentioned in the promotion chapter, be very careful with any teases or headlines you write using the story. In fact, given that sweeps specials are typically heavily promoted outside your regular teases and promos, it's not a bad idea to focus on other stories in your preshow promos and headlines so viewers know they're also getting the news.

The Bad

Sadly for every one good investigative or enterprise story, there's probably 20 examples of bad sweeps pieces. Most of these stories have no redeeming news value, they are simply designed to create fear or titillate viewers. And thanks to consultants, many of the worst ideas spread from station to station if they show any kind of ratings spike. Here are a few examples of some of the stories stations have done and heavily promoted for sweeps—see if you can find the news value!

- **Hotel Horrors**—In the mid 1990s it seemed at least one station in every market was taking a black light, like you see on forensic shows such as *CSI,* and running it over hotel bed sheets to dutifully inform viewers about the body fluids of past guests that remained on the sheets even after laundering. You can just imagine the disgusting mix of fluids these stories "uncovered."
- **Germ Chasers**—There are a whole series of stories that have been done chasing germs. Two common ones are testing ice tea machines and kitchen dishcloths or sponges. And of course once all those nasty germs are found, we

can't wait to scare the common sense out of our viewers with promos touting "Cleaning up with Killer Germs—The story at 11."

• **Drug Money**—Testing dollar bills for cocaine residue was a popular sweeps piece in the early 1990s. Since a rolled up dollar bill is often used to snort cocaine, there are many bills floating around with cocaine residue. For this piece the reporter would ask prominent people such as the police chief or sheriff, the mayor, a drug counselor, and others to borrow the dollar bills in their wallet and then test them. You can just hear the tease for this story ... "We caught the police chief with cocaine in his pocket, and you could be next!"

• **Put It to the Test**—Consumer reporters everywhere love these stories. Not all testing stories are bad. True product testing to see if products do what they claim can be valuable to the viewer. One popular test that, if done correctly, can be very valuable is the Toy Test. Take the hot new toys for Christmas to a daycare center for four weeks and find out which toys last more than a week and keep the children's interest after they rip them out of the box. But taste tests or who delivers the fastest pizza are silly. Just because six random people thought the local coffee house latte was better than Starbuchs doesn't mean your viewers will. And who cares if Dominos gets my pizza to the house five minutes faster than Pizza Hut? Is delivery time really a factor in the decision of which pizza to order?

• And finally an all time favorite ... drum roll please ... **The Search for Sasquatch**—Yes, it's true. A station in Lexington, Kentucky sent a reporter up to the woods of southeast Ohio with a university professor to look for signs of Big Foot! Southeast Ohio?!? For three weeks before the series, the station ran promos that looked more like movie trailers with eerie music and dark pictures touting "The Search for Sasquatch" and making it sound very much as if the search was successful. Then it aired and for three nights viewers followed this reporter, ridiculously decked out in jungle camouflage gear, as he stalked through the woods in a "serious" hunt for the creature Big Foot. Sadly, we were all disappointed when at the end of three highly anticipated nights there were no footprints, no Big Foot droppings, no hair clumps or teeth marks, and no big hairy beast! But at least we knew it was safe to walk through the woods of Southeast Ohio—not that anyone in Lexington, Kentucky did that.

The Ugly

It would be nice to say it doesn't get any worse than the Search for Sasquatch, but that wouldn't be honest. There are two other sweeps stunts that unfortunately tend to work pretty well, but make a mockery of news ratings: watch and win contests and program tie-ins.

Contesting—We've already mentioned this technique a couple of times. The idea is that viewers watch the newscast and sometime during one of the commercial breaks a number or a word is flashed. If the viewer can match the number to a promotional card received in the mail and calls the station in 10 minutes or before the end of the newscast, he or she wins cash. In other contests the viewer just has to be the first caller after a word, such as an anchor's name, flashes during a commercial break. There's also typically a grand prize at the end of the sweeps, in which all callers are entered into the drawing. In the worse case scenarios, the winner of the grand prize is drawn live on the newscast!

Does Contesting Work?

The 4A's tracking study of ratings in and out of sweeps was triggered by some aggressive sweeps contesting in the Pittsburgh market. Pittsburgh is a highly competitive television market with the difference between first and third place in the news often less than a full rating point. It is a market that represents the best and worst of sweeps stunting, with the top three stations doing strong investigative and consumer reporting but also lots of germ testing, prime time tie-ins, and contesting. Two stations engage in heavy contesting (WTAE-TV and WPXI-TV), while the third station KDKA-TV bitterly criticizes the contests and in fact made national news by pulling out of the Nielsen ratings system in the mid-90s because the station thought the ratings were too highly tainted by the escalating money given away during sweeps contests. The Pittsburgh Post-Gazette newspaper compiled average ratings in sweeps versus nonsweeps months in 2003. The differences clearly show a spike during sweeps months (February, May, November) compared with the rest of the year.

	5 p.m.		6 p.m.		11 p.m.	
	Sweeps	Nonsweeps	Sweeps	Nonsweeps	Sweeps	Nonsweeps
KDKA	8.7	8.8	10.4	10.2	13.9	12.7
WTAE	9.9	8.3	10.2	8.6	9.7	8.6
WPXI	9.4	7.7	9.5	8.1	11.8	10.9

It should be noted that the "watch and win" contests ran in the early news on WTAE and WPXI and the strongest sweeps stories and investigative pieces typically ran on the 11 p.m. news for all three stations.

The competition for viewers can get so nasty that competing contests escalate to ridiculous amounts of money. In one market it got so bad stations were running each other's contest numbers so viewers wouldn't have to leave their newscast to see if their number came up on the competing station.

Watch and win contests are bad on so many levels, but the worst thing they do is degrade the news to a carnival atmosphere. It's disrespectful to assume viewers will only watch the news if they get a prize. Most viewers watch the news to get information. And those viewers who only watch to get a chance at winning cash aren't coming back to watch after the contest is over. Nielsen usually flags ratings numbers for stations that contest as a way to let advertisers know these numbers may be artificially high. It's a travesty when even 10 seconds of news time is used to add a watch and win huckstering spot.

Program Tie-ins—You can't ignore the fact that lead-in program ratings influence news ratings. Even in today's remote surfing and zapping world, one of the biggest factors for one show's rating is the rating of the lead-in program. If a lead-in program has a large audience, the station wants to do everything possible to keep those viewers for your newscast. For the early news your station decides what programming to buy as a news lead-in. In the mid 1990s during the ratings heyday for *Oprah*, there was no better lead-in for a 5 p.m. newscast. In market after market, the station with *Oprah* as a lead-in won the 5 p.m. newscast. They certainly won at least the key 25 to 54 women demo. For the late news most stations are at the mercy of their network. If you are an ABC affiliate you hold your breath until the *Monday Night Football* schedule comes out. If you have a game with your hometown team during the November book, you can almost guarantee to win the 11 p.m. ratings for that book just on the strength of the audience you'll get that one night. And it's no coincidence that big season and series finales are broadcast in May, during the May sweeps.

Taking advantage of lead-in programming in sweeps planning is not bad by itself. It makes sense to know who the audience is for a lead-in program and then target sweeps specials that will reach that audience and can be promoted to them. As mentioned in the chapter on promotion, your own air is your best promotion tool. Thus, stations that do investigative reporting usually save those pieces to run on nights when they have a news magazine audience watching.

The problem is entertainment audiences aren't always news viewers, so instead of looking for real stories that might appeal to the demographic who watches the entertainment program, stations take the easy way out and pander to that audience with program tie-ins. The worst of this trend has surrounded the blockbuster hit shows *Survivor* and *American Idol*. We've seen CBS affiliate reporters and anchors live at *Survivor* parties, even dressed in island garb, as well as doing stories of surviving under difficult conditions, and look out if one of the island castaways is from your market! Of course Fox affiliates, and often other stations, too, cover the tryouts when *American Idol* comes to town, and there are a plethora of stories about struggling artists trying to get their big break. It's all fun to watch, but it's NOT news!

Another way stations try to capture a non-news viewer is with "behind the scenes" stories. These stories take viewers to the scene where the show is being taped and let you see what goes on when the cameras aren't rolling. Viewers get to hear from the stars and get the inside scoop. They're great promotables inside the primetime show, but they're NOT news!

Finally in the program tie-in category there are the "could it happen here" or "it did happen here" stories. In these sweeps specials stations take the storyline from a program and find a "real life" story locally to tell. Big budget disaster movies are favorites for this kind of story. How would our town survive a killer tornado/earthquake/terrorist attack? Or they tie into the theme of the show, such as taking *CSI* viewers inside their local or state crime lab, doing a medical story that matches the storyline from *ER*, or looking into your local community's unsolved police cases following the show *Cold Case*. These stories may very well keep an entertainment viewer to watch your newscast, but they're NOT news!

Reality Check

The bottom line is sweeps is a reality in virtually every newsroom. The best thing you can do as a producer is keep your focus on producing good, quality newscasts while the craziness of ratings swirls around you. You will have to adapt your shows to accommodate special reports, but don't stop producing the news. If all the effort to get viewers to watch during sweeps is going to have any positive effect, it should be to keep some of those viewers after the glitz and flash of sweeps stunting goes away. That's where consistency in your news coverage, especially during sweeps, can make a difference. Former longtime news director and now The Poynter Institute faculty member Scott Libin put it this way,

> Concentrating all the "good stuff" during sweeps is a little like cramming for exams. You can increase your odds of passing, but [the] chances of retaining what you've learned are not good. Luring an audience for a few nights at a time rather than building loyalty can have similar results: viewers slip away like obscure facts memorized in an all-night study session. (Potter, 2001, AJR.org)

Sources

McClellan, S. (2004, May 31). Nielsen's Whiting stands firm. *Broadcasting and Cable*, 2–3.

McClellan, S. (2004, May 31). NYC braces for local ratings. *Broadcasting and Cable*, 12.

Murphy, J. (2001, September 10). *Study Slams Stations' Sweeps Stunting*. Mediaweek.com.

Nielsen Media Research. (2006). *What TV Ratings Really Mean ... And Other Frequently Asked Questions*. Available from http://www.nielsenmedia.com.

Owens, R. (2001, February 22). TV stations often promise more than they deliver when playing the promotional ratings game. *Pittsburgh Post-Gazette*, p. D1.

Potter, D. (2001, May). From Silly to Shameless. *American Journalism Review*, AJR.org.

Potter, D. (2004, April/May). The end of sweeps? *American Journalism Review*, 64.

Raymonda, J. (1997, March). Confessions of a Nielsen household. *American Demographics*, 24–32.

MANAGING
THE BUSINESS

*"Television stations are licenses to print money—I could put color bars on
TV between the commercials and still make money."*
Roy H. Park, Founder and former CEO Park Communications, 1979

When Roy H. Park made those comments to graduating seniors at Ithaca
College, his media company was the only one to own the maximum
number of AM, FM and TV stations the FCC allowed at the time, 12 of
each. And he was right. Television stations were licenses to print money because
they had little competition—there was no cable, no internet, no home video. At
that time, when the authors of this book were beginning their television news
careers, we didn't think much about who owned the station we worked for—it
wasn't relevant to what happened in the newsroom. Quite frankly, the owners
were just as likely to be in the elegant, carpeted offices upstairs, as to be head-
quartered in some other city.

The media ownership landscape has changed dramatically in the last 25
years, and the changes are having a direct impact on local television newsrooms.
It's now very important that you understand what's going on in the media industry at the big picture level and where the company that owns your station fits in
that big picture. It will affect the resources you have, the way your newscasts are
produced, and even how your job as a producer is defined. It will likely also impact you personally in terms of salary, benefits, and future mobility. In this chapter we're going to look at some of the major trends in the media industry overall
and their impact on journalism, with special emphasis on local television news.

Major Trends

In 2004 the Project for Excellence in Journalism brought together information
and research from dozens of different sources to create *The State of the News*

Media 2004 report. The Project now makes its *State of the News Media* an annual report on American Journalism. The comprehensive report covers eight media sectors including network television, cable television, and local television, and examines everything from content and technology to economics and ownership. It's worth looking at for anyone working in journalism, or about to enter the field. You can see the reports annually at www.journalism.org. The report suggests that all of journalism is undergoing "an epochal transformation, as momentous probably as the invention of the telegraph or television" (The Project for Excellence, 2004, p. 1). The 2004 report outlines eight major trends in journalism that define or shape this transformation. Some of them we've discussed elsewhere in this book, others we will go into more detail about here, focusing on how they might impact your local newsroom:

- **A growing number of news outlets are chasing relatively static or even shrinking audiences for news.** See chapter 2.
- **Much of the new investment in journalism today—much of the information revolution in general—is focused on disseminating the news, not collecting it.** This is often seen in budget cuts, staff positions not filled or eliminated, and demands to do more news with fewer people. Many local stations are doing an extra hour in the morning, an extra half-hour to hour in the early evening, producing a 9 or 10 p.m. newscast for a sister station and doing expanded weekend morning shows. But staff sizes haven't increased commensurate with the increased workload.
- **In many parts of the news media—primarily television—we are increasingly getting the raw elements of news as the end product.** This is seen most often in the 24 hour news media—especially cable news where the viewer is taken live to news conferences or news scenes with very little reporting to order the information, add context, and balance. But local television is increasingly going live as stories break and offering the same type of "raw" coverage or video without the benefit of journalistic editing and values.
- **Journalism standards now vary even inside a single news organization.** This seems especially true when it comes to the line between news and advertising. A live remote planned at a big advertiser's location might be acceptable for the morning news or weekend morning, but would never be allowed on the early evening or late news. The difference is even more stark when you compare the broadcast network morning shows with their evening news. This lack of consistency feeds viewers' perceptions that the media are unprofessional, driven by financial motives.
- **Without investing in building new audiences, the long-term outlook for many traditional news outlets seems problematic.** Right now many media outlets are trying to maintain profitability in the face of declining audiences by raising ad rates, increasing ad content, and cutting costs. The problem is more advertising and less news, as well as poorer quality news because of fewer resources, adds up to more audience loss.
- **Convergence seems more inevitable and potentially less threatening to journalists than it may have seemed a few years ago.** Convergence is crossing media boundaries to deliver news and information. It is television,

newspaper and radio partnerships, and online journalism outlets for all three. It is looking at a story and figuring out which medium best can tell that story, and then focusing resources on that medium first, while still preparing versions for the others. We will talk a lot more about convergence.

- **The biggest question may not be technological, but economic.** As the media consolidate into bigger companies, owning a wider variety of media and looking to the future online, there may be a need for a different economic model. If advertising and/or subscriber base won't work, what will? The gathering and providing of local news has been an economic boom for the media, but what if it doesn't work online or with the next new technology. If gathering and disseminating news can't provide a source of revenue, will it continue? (The Project for Excellence, 2004, p. 2)

These trends bring up many issues we will discuss further: Media consolidation, convergence, online journalism, and cost cutting measures that have lead to more automation and less local content.

Media Consolidation

Certainly the glory days for Roy H. Park as CEO of the only company owning the maximum number of television and radio stations allowed are long gone. The government no longer even limits the *number* of stations one company can own, only the total percentage of the national audience one company's stations can reach (now 39%). A company can own 50 stations in the bottom 50 markets or 10 stations in the top 10 markets, as long as the combined audience reach of those stations is not more than 39% of the country's total viewing households.

While in 1979 Park sat on top of the heap with 12 television stations, by 1995 the top 10 television station companies had nearly $6 billion in revenue and owned more than 100 stations—by 2002 those same top 10 companies doubled their revenue and owned more than 300 stations (The Project for Excellence, 2004, p. 14). Let's look at the even bigger picture of the media industry overall. The chart below shows the 2004 revenue for the top 100 media companies. Notice that just the top 5 companies account for more than 40% of the more

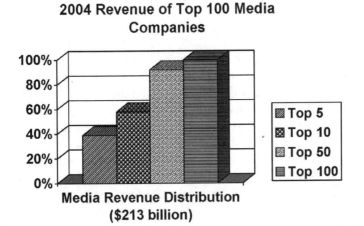

2004 Revenue of Top 100 Media Companies

Media Revenue Distribution ($213 billion)

- Top 5
- Top 10
- Top 50
- Top 100

than $200 billion, the top 10 companies, more than half. That's a huge chunk of revenue concentrated in just a very few companies.

You may be thinking that all this talk of billions of dollars doesn't really touch you personally. You're going to be a news producer in a single station making $30 to $50+ thousand and dealing with local viewers and local news. Those billions trading hands at the corporate level won't mean anything to your job. But consider this—five of the top broadcast TV companies are also in that top ten above, three in the top five! So there's a very good chance that you're going to be working for one of them. In fact in a 2004 survey of 400 television news and production employees belonging to unions, more than half said their station was involved in a corporate merger in the last few years and 20% said they had been laid off because of consolidation. But still the question is what does that mean for you as a news producer in the smallest television station owned by a multibillion dollar company? More than you might think. First let's look at some newsroom-wide issues, and then we'll look specifically at news content.

Ways Consolidation Impacts Newsrooms

Positives	Negatives
More and/or Better Resources—a larger organization has much more clout in buying and negotiating for resources.	Investment is often made in equipment and technology at the expense of people —the search for cost efficiencies may lead to detrimental automation or centralization of some news operations.
Small and medium market stations get same benefits as larger market stations— higher quality production value such as graphics packages, access to consulting and research, Washington bureau, additional video feeds, the best syndicated material.	Loss of local control in many decisions —what's right for a major market newsroom may not be for a smaller market, especially in areas such as the branding and look of the newscast, as well as choice of nonlocal content.
Typically, corporate benefits and compensation packages are better for employees, and there is much more room to grow within the company.	Media may be only a small part of the overall business of the corporation, and responsibility to stockholders (i.e., the bottom line) outweighs responsibility to viewers or the public at large.

Two examples of centralization and diminishing of local control are the concepts of "central casting" and "hubbing." **Central casting** involves producing content for two or more stations in a group from one location. For example, Bahakel Communications owns stations in Columbia, South Carolina and Charlotte, North Carolina. The news for the Columbia station is produced from Charlotte, 90 miles away. The most extensive use of central casting is in the Sinclair Broadcast Group, as detailed in the accompanying box, "Central Casting." When central casting is fully implemented at all Sinclair stations the company expects to cut its local news costs in half, while at the same time bringing local news to many of its stations that were not producing it before.

Central Casting

The Sinclair Broadcast group owns 62 television stations across the country, mostly WB, UPN, and Fox affiliates. In 2003 Sinclair started experimenting with central casting. Basically the stations' newsrooms produce local news stories and then toss to an anchor out of Baltimore who does a world and national news segment. Sports and weather casts also come out of the Baltimore studios, but are customized by market. Sinclair says central casting has allowed the company to start inexpensive news operations in stations that didn't do news before—as many as 30 Sinclair stations didn't have local news. The newsrooms that use central casting typically have a third to a half fewer staff than competing stations in the same market and all the staff covers is local news.

Sinclair's Vice President of Corporate Relations Mark Hyman described it this way in a PBS story, "The lifeblood of a local newscast is the local news, and that's what's really important, and that's really what makes our news work so that each of these markets where we build a news operation, literally from the ground up on occasion, and staff it with professionals, we're collecting and reporting local news" (Smith, 2003).

But critics rail against Sinclair's central casting as stealing the localism out of local news. One group fighting media consolidation and its results is the Center for Digital Democracy. CDD Executive Director Jeff Chester reacted to the idea of central casting in the *New York Times,* "The goal is homogenization in order to contain costs. But that homogenization creates a kind of cookie-cutter blandness" (Rutenberg & Maynard, 2003). And that blandness takes away the opportunity for local producers to decide which national and world stories are most relevant to their community. Not to mention trying to do local weather for Flint, Michigan from Baltimore, Maryland. In addition some critics say similar news sets and fake "tosses" attempt to deceive the viewer into thinking the central casting content is in fact local. Longtime news director and news corporate vice president, Marty Haag, pulled no punches when he talked about the idea. "I think that it's deceptive, period, simply, purely deceptive. The idea is that, I think, in order for journalists at a time where they're probably questioned more about why they did certain stories and how they arrived at a certain treatment, et cetera, et cetera, should be transparent and this broadcast certainly is not" (Smith, 2003).

Hubbing involves centralizing certain station operations, usually the master control system that feeds commercials, promotional segments, and the full-length programs into a station's broadcast signal, in one location where one set of engineers oversees the broadcast feeds for several stations simultaneously. Several station groups are trying various forms of hubbing. NBC has hubbed master control and graphics operations at its 29 affiliate and Telemundo stations into four regional hubs, saving the company $30 million. Emmis Communications completely programs its southeastern stations from an Orlando hub, leaving local news as the only locally produced programming.

More common than producing local programming and news from a remote location, or hubbing master control and engineering functions, is merging operations of two stations in the same market. Media companies now can own two or

Chapter 13

more television stations in the same market, known as a duopoly, as long as only one is an affiliate of one of the big four networks (ABC, NBC, CBS, Fox). One of the first things to merge is usually the news operations, often creating one newsroom out of former news competitors. KCAL-TV and KCBS-TV (Los Angeles), now both owned by Viacom, is one example; WNYW-TV and WWOR-TV (New York), now both owned by News Corp, is another. All four of these stations had independent newsrooms before they became duopolies. The two merged newsrooms have much smaller staffs than when they were independent.

However, in smaller markets, duopolies have allowed less profitable stations to continue to offer local news or create a news product. Nexstar Broadcast Group operates duopolies in three small to medium markets. Former Nexstar Vice President of News Susana Schuler says, "It's designed to allow a station that has been a poor performer ratings- and revenue-wise to keep news by combining behind-the-scenes people. We've come in and combined resources of photography, editing, and in some cases assignment management" (Huff, 2003, p. 36). But Tom Rosenstiel, head of The Project for Excellence in Journalism believes duopolies are bad for news quality and only about the bottom line, "You can either cut your cost or produce more product. These duopolies offer a further platform for doing that. When you've gotten to the point where you cannot produce more news at one station, you can produce more at another station. What we've seen is stations producing more with the same or fewer resources" (Huff, 2003, p. 37).

Local News Quality

To bring the impact on consolidation really down to the newscast level, we can look at some specific quality measures and see how newsrooms fare depending

WCNC-TV (Charlotte) is owned by a mid-sized media company, Belo Corp., which is known for its quality news production. WCNC is recognized annually for its quality journalism, regularly winning the top awards in broadcast journalism.

on the size of the company. The Project for Excellence in Journalism did a five year study on the quality of local newscasts across the country. Below you can see which stations did the best and which did the worst on some of those measures, based on the size of the company that owns the station. It doesn't speak well for the biggest companies. However, just because the biggest aren't the best, doesn't mean that the few remaining independent, locally owned stations are the answer. Clearly the greater resources available to a station group do impact news quality, as seen below.

Coverage	*Best*	*Worst*
More enterprise stories	Midsize companies	Top 10 companies
Local relevance	Midsize/small companies	Top 10 companies
Named sources	Small companies	Top 10 companies
Fewer short stories (>:20)	Small companies	Top 11–25 companies
Fewer syndicated feed stories	Midsize companies	Top 10 companies
Coverage	*Local Ownership (%)*	*Nonlocal Ownership (%)*
Local stories	78	80
National stories	22	20
News quality: Grade A	7	21
News quality: Grade F	6	0

The Project for Excellence in Journalism. (2004). *State of the News Media 2004.* journalism.org

When you talk to people working in television newsrooms at all levels, from anchor to the tech crews, there are some pretty strong responses to consolidation, especially among those belonging to one of the trade unions representing television employees. Here are their responses to a 2004 survey asking about the impact of future consolidation based on current experiences:

- 86% cited less diversity of viewpoints in local news coverage.
- 78% feared a general, continuing decline of news quality.
- 86% thought control of news and programming decisions will be concentrated in too few corporate hands.
- 79% predicted growing corporate bias in the news.
- 72% foresaw less local community coverage
  (Poll summary released July 20, 2004 by the AFL–CIO Department of Professional Employees).

The bottom line is media consolidation is a reality, and it does impact local news. That's why it's important for you as a producer to know about the company that owns any station you want to work for. Find out where all stations owned by the company rank in their markets. There typically will be a consistent pattern. If most of the local newscasts at the stations are among the lowest rated news programs in their markets, chances are local news is not a priority for the company. On the other hand if many or most of the company's stations have the top rated local news in their markets, that's not a coincidence—that company invests in local news, and likely leaves much of the control of the news product to the local station.

Media Convergence

Often hand-in-hand with consolidation we talk about media convergence. One doesn't necessarily always lead to the other, but many times they are closely related. It's very hard to get a firm definition of convergence, but most people in the business agree that convergence is about cross-platform delivery of information and/or entertainment. Instead of thinking about television news, newspapers, radio news, and online news separately, you just think about news and the various media become nothing more than distribution platforms for that news. It works something like this: A company might own a newspaper, a couple of radio stations, one of the television stations, and operate a city Web site all in one community. News generated by reporters from one medium would be used on the other media and some specialized reporters might regularly serve all the media. Often the sales and marketing functions are coordinated, too, allowing clients to buy an advertising package that includes print, broadcast, and online media.

The Ideal?

In a truly converged newsroom, when a story breaks one of the first coverage decisions would be which media platform can best tell the story and how can the other media platforms support that main coverage. For example, if the story was a county budget battle and possible income tax referendum, most coverage resources would probably go to the print or newspaper version of that story, with online coming close behind and providing an outlet for detailed financial statements, links to the county's complete budget, and/or salary impact tables. The broadcast platforms might do "real people" reaction stories, but the main story will be best told in print. If the story is a coming hurricane, clearly the broadcast platforms, television especially, are going to tell the story in real time. Again online is going to provide constant access to radar pictures, lists of road closings, power outages, and emergency help numbers. The newspaper stories are going to follow with aftermath, but a newspaper can't provide people with the immediate information they need in a severe weather situation.

Reality

In practical application we typically only see partial convergence—some form of working partnership between print, broadcast, and/or online journalism that involves sharing resources and information, but for the most part, producing independent stories. At the end of 2004 the "Convergence Tracker" produced by The Media Center for the American Press Institute had on record more than eighty major news convergence relationships among television, radio, newspaper, and online media within various markets. It noted partnerships in all but about 15 of the top 50 television markets, and several markets had more than one. (Check out the "Convergence Tracker" at americanpressinstitute.org then click on The Media Center.) In a 2003 convergence survey of media organizations researchers reported that about nine out of ten newspapers and eight out of ten television stations responding reported some sort of working partnership sharing content and/or staff with at least one other media platform (Criado & Kraeplin, 2003). A 2001 survey of television stations found that more than 90% have a Web site, ranging from 97% of the top 25 market stations to 83% of 151+ market stations (Papper & Gerhard, 2001). So even in your first producing job, you will likely have to deal with at least a Web partner. As the FCC relaxes rules about cross-media ownership, it's likely that convergence will grow with consolidation. Media companies will buy additional television and radio stations in markets in which they own newspapers and vice versa.

WHIO-TV (Dayton) and *The Dayton Daily News* newspaper are both owned by Cox Communications and work together on several projects.

Convergence Models

There are several different ways the various media might enter into a convergence partnership. The most obvious is cross-ownership as mentioned above—when one company owns more than one media outlet in the same market—for example a television station and newspaper, newspaper and radio, or television and radio. In this model we often find the most active partnerships, including a joint Web site, and joint advertising sales and marketing efforts as well as news. The company most often mentioned as a leader in this area is Media General, which emphasizes strong working relationships among its newspapers, television stations, and online site in several markets. In Tampa, the television station, WFLA-TV, *The Tampa Tribune* newspaper, and TBO.com (Tampa

Bay Online) are all located in the same building and share multiple resources including a centralized assignment desk.

There are partnerships among media with different owners in the same market. This is most typical between newspapers and television stations and usually is limited to news and information sharing or joint community projects.

Some newspapers have started their own broadcast outlets to further disseminate the news they gather. *The Chicago Tribune* has a television production area and multiple cameras right in the newsroom that repackage *Tribune* stories for a cable station, CLTV, and the cable superstation, WGN-TV (Chicago).

Converged Consumer

In a sense the media industry is catching up to consumers who are already converged in their media usage. The Media Center looked at simultaneous media consumption and found that about 75% of television viewers read the newspaper while they watch and about two-thirds of viewers surf the Web while they're watching (The Media Center, 2004). And what was the biggest selling area of consumer electronics for Christmas 2004? Gadgets and gizmos that multitask—cell phones that take pictures, surf the Web, play FM radio or MP3; handheld organizers with MP3 players and video games; MP3 players that store digital pictures, and so on (Reinhardt, 2004).

The point is more news consumers than ever want news on demand wherever they are, not where they have access to a TV and when a station schedules a newscast. That means the industry has to respond, and traditional media, such as local television, need to figure out how to be part of that 24/7 consumer demand.

One answer that is popping up in several local markets, regions, or even statewide is localized 24 hour cable news operations. Just as CNN, Fox News, and MSNBC run 24 hours of news, these local or regional operations do the same. In Florida, Texas, and Ohio there are statewide news networks operated by broadcast media companies. In Chicago and Tallahassee the *Tribune* newspapers started 24 hour local cable news operations to repurpose the material generated by their print staffs. Time-Warner Cable has started local cable news stations in 12 of the cities in which it has the cable franchise. In Pittsburgh, WPXI-TV also operates PCNC (Pittsburgh Cable News Channel), which reruns its local newscasts, as well as producing some original news programming including a news debrief/call-in show at 6:30 p.m. with the anchor and some of the reporters talking about the stories of the day just covered in WPXI-TV's early news block.

The amount of original news programming produced by these local or regional cable outlets varies widely, and the quality often doesn't come close to what the local broadcast stations produce. But the point is they are competition for you working at a local station. They are also opportunities to try a different kind of television news producing, usually with a lot more leeway to try new things, but also with many fewer resources to get out and cover news.

How Convergence Impacts Television News

Depending on the type of partnership and the level of convergence, there are many ways other media partners might be part of your newscast. Let's look at these relationships by individual medium.

Newspaper

Partnerships with newspapers have grown dramatically in the last 10 years, and many have nothing to do with cross-ownership. These relationships might be as simple as sharing information and pictures or video on breaking news or other jointly covered stories, to more complex sharing of assignment lists, reporters appearing in the alternate medium, and even working together on major investigative or civic journalism projects. In many newspaper newsrooms there is a camera position where a print reporter or editor can go live on the television newscast to debrief about a story. Likewise the broadcast meteorologist would produce the information for the newspaper weather section or a television consumer or health reporter might write a column.

When news budgets (the list of stories being covered that day) are shared, a late newscast might run headlines from the next day's paper—typically stories it is not already covering. This tends to serve the newspaper more than the television station and is really not much more than a promotional tool for the paper. But when television and newspaper investigative teams work together to tell a story, it can be incredibly powerful as in the example in the box, "Newspaper Investigation—Television Story."

The key for you as a producer is to find ways to make a newspaper partnership work for you and your newscast. Make it more than just a few headlines on TV. Talk about ways you can produce good televi-

WCNC-TV (Charlotte) Health Reporter Kara Linnstrom writes a weekly column for *The Charlotte Observer.*

Newspaper Investigation—Television Story

In this example a newspaper recognizes that its exclusive investigation into corruption among narcotics cops is best told as a television story, and working together the newspaper and its television station partner delivered the story with a strong one-two punch using each medium to its maximum advantage.

The *Dayton Daily News* newspaper managed to get an undercover video tape showing cops conducting a sting on a local drug dealer, but there was no report, no arrests, and the drugs were never logged in as evidence—the cops just kept the illegal drugs. The newspaper knew it could do the legwork to verify the tape's legitimacy, but the story would have its strongest impact if the tape was seen and heard. So the newspaper took the tape to WHIO-TV (Dayton), which is owned by the same company as the newspaper. The two longtime competitors had forged a working relationship through a strong civic journalism project, and there was a level of trust. Investigative teams from the paper and the television station worked for several weeks on the story and produced stories that lead to a major investigation in the local police department. The two together created the strongest possible presentation and understanding of what became a very complicated story that quite frankly neither alone could have accomplished.

---

sion, covering aspects of the story that print simply can't do well, such as the visual and emotional part of a story. Another example from the *Dayton Daily News*/WHIO-TV partnership—the newspaper used to produce daily Data Sheets that covered a wide range of facts on a different topic each day of the week. Monday might be education, Tuesday, crime, Wednesday, traffic, and so forth. These weren't stories, they were simply a full page of stats that the research department dug up. But many times there were good stories hidden in these stats, so WHIO's 6 p.m. producer would get an advance list of what the Data Sheet would cover and select interesting ones for full blown stories on the 6 p.m. news the day before, and then promote more details in the next day's Data Sheet. Some of the better stories were the worst intersection in Dayton for fatal accidents, the neighborhood with the highest burglary rate, and lead test results for drinking fountains in area parks.

Radio

Chances are as a producer you won't be affected much by a radio partnership. It's usually going to mean your news, weather, and sports anchors will record or do live reports and newscasts for the radio station. You may have to write a radio promo for your newscast, or your newscast might even be simulcast on the radio. But even if it is simulcast, it is unlikely you'll be asked to make any accommodations for radio.

The one thing to keep in mind about a radio partnership is in the case of a spot news story, that local radio station might be first on the scene and can provide information or even live phone reports. So don't forget those partnerships in the chaos of breaking news.

Online

As mentioned previously most television stations have some sort of online presence. It may be a Web site just for the station, or as many stations are doing, it may be a city portal site in which the station provides news and information, weather, sports, and special reports. If more than one media outlet in a market contributes to the site, it's likely to take this form, such as TBO.com mentioned above.

Television station Web sites offer a variety of content from news stories in text and often video form to entire streaming newscasts, from live cams to live weather radar, from community calendars to traffic information and school closings. Beyond the material generated from the television news and other station content, the Web site might offer job listings, news talent bios, local government information, and a wide variety of other material that is more often associated with a newspaper such as personals, travel info, home and garden sections, entertainment listings and reviews, and so forth. There are also typically lots of community links as well as links to the network the station is affiliated with.

Many station Web sites also offer people breaking news and severe weather e-mail alerts that will automatically send a message to viewers when there's a major news story developing or severe weather watches and warnings are issued. They might also offer e-mail promos of what's coming up on an early evening or late newscast.

Amy Lehtonen is the Web manager for WCNC-TV (Charlotte) and leads a staff of three to maintain and update wcnc.com.

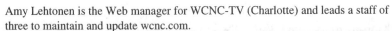

As a news producer you may have very little to do with the Web site or you may be involved with contributing content and reformatting items from your newscast. In a 2001 survey of television station Web sites just over 15% required newsroom staff to help with content, and the smaller the market, the more likely TV staff was involved—up to more than 20% in markets 150+ (Papper & Gerhard, 2001).

There are several different ways that television station Web sites operate, and that can also have a big impact on whether you as a producer will have any Web responsibilities. There are companies that will design and operate your Web site—one of the largest is IBS—Internet Broadcast Systems. IBS uses station content, but manages the site and hires all Web workers. Usually at least one is located in the station newsroom, but the rest might work out of the company headquarters. A station may hire an outside company to set up the site and all the templates, but then manage the site itself, or it might do all the work and be completely responsible for the site. Stations might also use a network or station group template for their Web sites and then provide the local content. Here are some examples of good television station Web sites, multimedia Web sites, and city-based Web sites:

- **Murrow Award/Online News Association Award Winners**
  news14charlotte.com (Time-Warner cable station, Charlotte, North Carolina)
  WQAD.com (WQAD-TV, Moline, Illinois)
  News12.com (Rainbox Media cable station, Woodbury, New York)
  katv.com (KATV, Little Rock, Arkansas)
  NBC4i.com (WCMH-TV, Columbus, Ohio)
- **Multimedia Web Sites**
  Newsday.com/news/specials (Online special reports for *Newsday*)
- **City Web Sites**
  TBO.com (Tampa Bay Online, WFLA-TV, *Tampa Tribune*)
  GoCarolinas.com (WSOC-TV, Charlotte, NC)
  PittsburghLive.com (*Tribune-Review* newspapers, KQV Radio)

Remember, as a producer there are many ways you can make use of your Web site to serve your viewers better and provide them with more customized information. Let's say your lead story is state test scores are released and a local school is put on probation. You do the story about the one school, but then on the Web site you list all area schools' test scores and show parents how to link to the state education Web site to compare with state averages. Maybe you have a story on a property tax levy and you show one example of how the levy would affect a homeowner of a $100,000 home. On the Web site you could put an interactive calculator that helps people figure out what the levy will cost each of them. Any time you do a story that comes from some type of database, you can put the entire database or links to it on your Web site so people can make that story their own—this is a great tool for in-depth investigative stories that often require gathering a mountain of information that never makes it into the final television story. As some police departments, district attorney offices, and courts put more documents online, you could provide links to actual reports, warrants, or transcripts for viewers. Many viewers would find it fascinating to see the actual documents that your reporters use all the time. If you give phone numbers, addresses, or other Web sites, you can put a contact page for your newscast that repeats all that information.

Matt Miller, news director at WGXA-TV (Macon), also uses his station's Web site as an in-house research tool to gage interest in various stories the newsroom covers.

> I had my IT (information technology) person set up an administration page that shows which stories posted on our Web site were the most accessed in a 24 hour period. I then make sure that the top stories shown are the ones we make sure to do follow-up stories on. I also get a sense of what stories people are most interested in seeing, not only on our Web site, but most likely also in our newscast. It helps drive people in a circle between our Web site and our newscast.

One important point about making your Web site really work for you is to be specific. Don't just send a viewer to your Web site "for more information." Tell them specifically what's there that they might want to access. That gives the viewer a sense that they're getting something more instead of making them feel as if they didn't get the whole story from watching your newscast.

What's Next?

Convergence and consolidation are realities of the media industry right now, and, to be honest, no one is willing to predict what local news may look like in 10 years, but it certainly will be nothing like what we produce now. However, there will always be an appetite for information—people want to know what's going on in their world. Learning the skills to use other media platforms and integrate content delivery will only help you be part of this changing media landscape. One consistency in this upheaval that we hear from current managers of multimedia operations is they want people who know how and where to gather information, how to critically analyze that information, and then how to write and communicate it. Those are all skills a good producer needs. If you are working with other media partners in some type of convergence relationship, learn as much as you can about what that partner has to offer and how it operates. That will allow you to maximize use of your partner's resources in your newscast, and prepare you for what's next.

Sources

Criado, C., & Kraeplin, C., (2003, April 4). *Convergence Journalism*. Available from http://www.convergencejournalism.com.

Huff, R. (2003, April). Duopoly 101. *Communicator*, 34–37.

The Media Center. (2004, March 24). *Seventy percent of Media Consumers use Multiple Forms of the Media at the Same Time*. Available from the American Press Institute at http://www.americanpressinstitute.org.

The Media Center. (n.d.). *Convergence Tracker*. Available from the American Press Institute at http://www.americanpressinstitute.org.

Papper, B., & Gerhard, M., (2001, May). What do consumers want from a station Web site? It's the question everyone's asking. *Communicator*, RTNDA.org.

The Project for Excellence in Journalism. (2004). *State of the News Media 2004*. Available from The Project for Excellence in Journalism at http://www.journalism.org.

Reinhardt, A. (2004, December 20). Merry "Convergence Christmas." *BusinessWeek Online*.

Rutenberg, J., & Maynard, M. (2003, June 2). TV news that looks local, even if it's not. *New York Times*, NYT.com.

Smith, T. (2003, December). The controversy over central casting. *The newshour with Jim Lehrer.* Available from http://www.pbs.org/newshour.

Special report: 100 leading media companies. (2003, August 15). *Ad Age*, Adage.com.

Chapter Fourteen

MANAGING LIFE

> *"Work is difficulty and drama, a high-stakes game in which our identity, our esteem, and our ability to provide are mixed inside of us in volatile, sometimes explosive ways."*
>
> David Whyte, Poet and Business Consultant

> *"We are all looking for ideas large enough to be afraid of again."*
>
> Ken Burns, Documentary Film Maker

*I*t is a fact. Many producers excel at managing the complexities of a television newscast but fail miserably in their personal lives. As a producer, stress is the high octane that fuels your workday. You thrive on pressure. Rest and relaxation seem to be foreign concepts. However, without balance in your life, a producer's job can create anxieties that, if unheeded, can have a serious impact on your personal happiness. These anxieties stem from being "burned out" because of a loss of job satisfaction and/or stress overload and from "encore anxiety" when you feel you have "been there, done that, now what?"

We'll address these issues, offer tips to help you chart a smooth course for your career, and show you how the creation of a personal mission statement might help you navigate exactly the kind of life you want to lead. Our goal is to help you see the bridge between the world of work and the landscape of your personal life and provide ideas for mapping out your career so it complements other important aspects of your life. David Whyte, a Fortune 500 consultant and an English-born poet, articulated why such a link is needed.

> We may do the same work and do it well, but we may do it well in a way that does not engage our deeper powers in any real conversation, so that we lose any sense of personal edge ... We may be admired in our work, but the admiration blinds and insulates us from the loss of something robust and lifelike inside us. (Whyte, 2001)

To recover from a sense of loss about your career requires that you face two critical questions: What business am I in and why am I in this business? Producers can struggle trying to answer the first question. Is my business the telling of current events? Or is it the advertising delivery business? You might be surprised to learn if you travel overseas and watch TV news, commercials only appear in certain legally designated time slots. When the ads are broadcast they must be clearly identified with a billboard stating an advertisement is about to appear. The line between news and sales in many other countries remains sharp, distinct, and unblurred.

In America the line between advertising and news is less defined creating difficult choices and potential problems for concern. Pressure can easily build on you the producer to tear down the traditional firewall between news and sales. The gimmicks mentioned in the Sweeps chapter, like giving away prizes in the newscast or choosing stories only because they cross-promote a prime time network movie, can leave you conflicted about your career. Such experiences can erode the journalism passion you once felt when you first got into the news business. It makes you confront the second question.

Why am I in this business? Am I a journalist producing a newscast or a ringmaster producing a show? When you feel conflict between your duty as a journalist and the pressure to "sell the news" tough questions linger at the end of the workday. Am I a producer because I want to inform the public about news that gives currency to their lives? Or, am I a producer because I'm a stress and adrenaline junkie or because I thrive on creativity and want to create shows utilizing the best "whiz bang graphics" and latest tricks of the trade? The answer is probably yes to each of these questions, but it should be yes with some important qualifications. First, you recognize, respect, and feel a sense of reward in a profession that deals in such a vital product as news, but you also enjoy tapping into your creative energy. And second, you do your best work under pressure.

But at some point you may feel out of balance, overwhelmed, angry, or even apathetic toward your job of producing. When that happens it is time for a self check-up. An important part of managing life is a frequent self check-up with your mind, soul, and body.

A Producer's "Life Check-Up"

It is a good idea to conduct a self check-up once a month to make sure your professional and personal needs are being met. Consider doing this in a journal so you can set goals related to health or spending time away from work. A goal not written down is only a wishful dream. A journal is also a way to do some "soul tracking"—keeping a record of your private feelings about the issues you face in both your professional and personal life.

Conduct a regular self-check up in these categories:

✓ Physical health.

✓ Emotional (spiritual) health.

✓ Financial health.

Self Check-Up—Physical Health

Do not kid yourself about how much a producer's job can drain your physical health. Alison Woo, who spent a decade producing in five different news shops including CNN Headline News in Atlanta, knows the physical toll producing can have on your health. "I worked for more than two years as a Morning EP," Woo told us. "The physical stress of sleeping only four to five hours a night while putting in a 10 to 12 hour day, five days a week took its toll." Pay close attention to how much sleep you get. Watch your exercise and eating habits. Each of these can take their different tolls on producers working odd shift hours.

Play it smart. Once you get home after work, learn to let go of the day's stress. "You need a detox period each day. Whether it's at the end of your shift or the end of your week you need a healthy way to let off steam," Woo says. Conditioning yourself to not take the day's work pressure home with you is tough in any business. For producers, whose television news lifeblood is available 24/7, it is especially hard. News confronts you the moment you walk in your home after work, and again before going to bed when you wonder if you should check the cable news headlines. News Director Bruce Kirk, WSET-TV (Lynchburg) advises, "Leave work at work. Burn off the energy after work and do not drink it off, there is a big difference."

Physical exercise can help burn off the excess energy, which often comes as a rush right at the end of the workday when your newscast actually hits the air. Anchors too feel this end-of-the-day adrenalin rush and find it hard to come down from the pressure high. Anchor Shawn Patrick, like many producers, finds jogging a perfect way to unwind, keep in tune physically and mentally, and let go of the day's newsroom hassles.

> I love to run ... my escape. I'm running for health, and running away from my stress or problems, where no one can find me or catch me. I'm going at my own pace, and finding my own discoveries along a new route, and like life, the journey is the most exciting part. Find a hobby, an exercise, one as important to you as your job, imagine that. You'll find yourself talking about it and consuming yourself with it. Then you'll forget about the audio guy clipping your mic, or the prompter operator falling asleep at the wheel.

An important but tough lesson to learn in a deadline driven business is that sometimes things can be put off until tomorrow. Chris Hayes, an investigative reporter at KPHO (Phoenix) shared with us an important lesson he had to learn when he moved to a big market. It's very applicable to producers. "When I first arrived in the Phoenix, Arizona market I was putting in 60 hour weeks. The job was nearly taking over my life. It's always been hard for me to put work away at the end of the day. But I soon found I was more efficient when I drew a line and decided certain things could wait until the morning." Prioritizing, balancing work while maintaining vital aspects of your physical health, like getting enough sleep, is important to managing your professional life.

It is odd but producers who live by the clock at work are often lousy managers when it comes to controlling time in their personal lives. Producers are among the hardest workers in the newsroom, but, in truth, many may work too hard putting at risk their physical and mental well being. Sean McGarvy, a field producer for WTTG (Washington, DC) advised, "Work your eight hours and do your best to walk away from all of it at the end of the day."

Learn to let go of the news day pressure. In Shreveport, Louisiana Anchor Shawn Patrick lets go by adopting the following healthy attitude, "When I'm gone, I'm gone. They have my cell phone number, but they don't have my soul." A quality news director will not deliberately set you up to become overworked and overtired at the expense of other aspects of your life. Patti McGettigan, news director of WOOD-TV (Grand Rapids) urges, "Get out of work on time when possible."

Going home means letting go of the fear that if you leave the newsroom after putting in a full day's work you might miss something like a major breaking story. This "giving up" by going home is a healthy attitude that applies not only to the daily work schedule but also to taking vacation. "Don't be afraid to go a day or two without watching a newscast or reading a newspaper," says Alan Hobbs who produced at six different stations before becoming a news director at KTVE (Monroe). A former Washington, DC bureau chief for the Sinclair Broadcast Group, Jon Leiberman, echoed these feelings:

> In order to avoid burnout ... use your vacation days! I went three or four years in this business never taking a vacation day. Why? I didn't want to miss a big story. I didn't want to slow down because I felt that if I slowed down, I would never get ahead. This is a prescription for burn out. Take some days off—treat yourself. There will be plenty of stories when you return!

> Sean McGarvy, WTTG-TV
> (Washington, DC)

News veterans know there always will be another big story. Sean McGarvy admonished,

> When you're on vacation (and don't forget to take your vacation) turn off the pager, turn off the cell phone, don't read the paper or watch the news. Resist the temptation to get involved in the one thing that drove you to needing a vacation in the first place. If you need a map to find some cool byways and back roads off the beat track while on holiday isn't just such a guiding document important to keep your career on a straight path to success?

Mapping Your Career— Personal Mission Statements

If work is a journey then you need a map to get there. How do you know when you have reached the destination? Where exactly are you going anyway? A career map, which we call a personal mission statement, is a good place to start.

The business world has used corporate mission statements for a number of years. Many media organizations, perhaps even your station, might have such a team vision hung on the wall of your station's conference room. If you remember the opening scene of the Tom Cruise movie *Jerry McGuire* you know exactly what a personal mission statement is. Cruise, frustrated with work as a sports agent, wakes up one morning and begins to write a set of principles that he wants to use to guide his life. He heads out the door to the photocopy shop, makes several copies, and then distributes them to his associates.

Time management guru Stephen R. Covey whose company, Franklin Covey, is noted for advising individuals and corporations on how to create successful work habits has a Web site called "mission builder" (http:// www.franklincovey.com/ missionbuilder/) that walks you through (for free) creating a personal mission statement. In this section we will also share a simple way for you to create one. The President of another personal management company Nella Barkley, of Crystal-Barkley, defines a personal mission statement as a "broad and specific statement of direction that has the capacity to frame activities for the rest of your life."

As a news producer, when should you write a personal mission statement and why? If you have experienced burnout or encore anxiety certainly a personal mission statement can help you refocus or realign your career. Writing one before you experience either anxiety can even help avoid them.

Personal mission statements are for people who want to build an arch between their career and private life. They serve as the bridge that brings balance between the personal and the professional, and provide clear thinking when ethical issues or tests of your fundamental values, such as honesty, confront you. A personal statement can help you sort out career options. For family oriented producers, as well as others, it can help keep important personal relationships ahead of professional aspirations, assuring that no professional success outweighs failure in home life.

The process to create a personal mission statement involves three steps:

1. Take a block of time (an hour or a day) to be self reflective.
2. Find a location that contributes to some deep thinking (rarely possible in the newsroom environment).
3. Answer in writing several key questions.

Two such questions that management experts use are "What tribute will your loved ones and friends pay to you on your 80th birthday"? (Stephen R. Covey) or "Given a paid, two-year sabbatical what would you do?" (Crystal-Barkley clients). The answers lead you to discover what things are most important to you. By identifying these pillars of your personal life you then can create a structure, turn your answers into affirmation statements, and later formulate specific goals to the bridge to your professional life.

We asked a wide variety of people in news management positions about personal mission statements and found very few who actually had taken the time to create one. Career goals are not the best tool, we believe, to resolve problems such as burnout or encore anxiety. A personal mission statement can be far better. News Director Bruce Kirk explained: "Life in the news business often doesn't go as you expect. You have a goal for the next station and position but sure enough that's not the door which opens. I believe goal success is directly connected to networking with colleagues as you come through the ranks. They'll help you realize your goals as you climb the ladder."

Anchor Shawn Patrick adopted his personal mission statement from an experience in high school.

I found my personal mission statement in high school, Carl Jung, BALANCE. That's my life. I try not to get carried away, and remember there's a flip side to everything. You can never get enough viewpoints, or angles or opinions. Sometimes we put on that tunnel vision under the rapid deadline fishing out what we want to hear for the sound bite, doesn't always work that way. Surprise yourself and listen for what you didn't expect. You won't just balance the issue, but find a deeper one.

Shawn Patrick, KUSA (Denver).

Career goals are so important but don't let them sit on your shoulders as an overbearing weight. Yes, you want to write down goals, but a law professor once told me, write them down in pencil, because as life changes, you change, and you'll need that eraser to update your list. Want to give God a good laugh, try making plans in life. You never know what's in store. Have that compass handy, pointing you in the right direction, but don't kill yourself trying to get there, remember the journey, not the destination, or you'll miss everything you passed by.

Career maps come in all sizes and shapes. They may be articulated as a personal mission statement or lodged deep in your heart's core as an inner calling to what you want to be. The career map can keep you on course, but it cannot prevent you from traveling too far, too fast so that all of your creative energy begins to mass into a glob of frustration over work.

Burnout Factor—
Why It Happens and How to Smother It

Burnout is not a matter of just being over worked or in need of a vacation. Burnout occurs when work loses its zip, dulls and rolls into feelings of frustration and even anger. Burnout occurs when the workload becomes out of balance with the rewards you get from your job. "I used to think 'burnout' meant that I needed a vacation. I tried that, it didn't work" Sean McGarvy told us. "Finding a project, something fresh to work on that I really enjoyed and looked forward to completing was the key. Motivation and excitement at work isn't work."

The Duty to Delegate

Smart producers know they can accomplish more if they spread the workload.

1. Before you delegate—eliminate anything that you can. Why make more work for someone else if it isn't necessary?

2. As you delegate—communicate. Set up a system for those you delegate to, to "return and report back" to you.

3. Do delegate anything routine.

4. Don't delegate anything that's your core responsibility. But do give authority along with responsibility.

5. Praise and reward then delegate some more.

Adapted from www.getmoredone.com

We talked with a variety of producers and news managers from across the country about the motivational factors that can contribute to producers burning out on their jobs and asked them what can be done to prevent it. We found that many producers lack a critical skill—delegation. "Good producers," Bruce Kirk of WSET-TV told us, "know how to get others to help carry the weight." Bill Seitzler, news director of KJRH-TV, told us, "People who get burned out aren't usually delegating enough, or they are not allowing other people to do their jobs. My favorite Will Rogers' quote comes into play. 'If you find yourself at the bottom of a deep hole the first thing you should do is quit digging.'"

Delegation is an important step to digging out from the feelings of burnout. Delegation opens up the door to freedom and creativity, which often becomes a very powerful reward for producers. Many producers take on too many tasks without prioritizing and delegating. Your executive producer or news director can help you complete a self-check of your work routines including setting up priorities and delegating tasks. They understand what drains and energizes you because often they've been a producer before. Former producer and now news director at WSB-TV (Atlanta), Jennifer Rigby, shared with us how delegation can dig you out of burn out and re-open the door to creativity.

> If you can, delegate the tasks that drain you and focus on those things that excite you and prompt your creativity. If you're feeling "burned out" or low on energy, take a look at what you've been doing and make a change. If it's a special project that energizes you, ask for the assignment. If it's simply getting more hands on involvement in breaking news or creating new graphics or writing a special report on your favorite topic, do it. Determine your priorities and work a plan that balances your life in such a way you are able to control stress, re-energize when needed and generally have fun. Only you can experiment, try new things, assess what works and make it happen.

> We don't work in a factory and there are plenty of outlets for creativity, growth, and imagine this ... fun. You need to understand what those things are and make them happen for yourself. As Aida says in the Broadway musical, "If you don't like your fate, change it. I don't see any shackles on you."

Unchaining yourself from binding routines is important for producers. Find new ways to think about your work. Look for opportunities to expand your duties to include something that motivates you or that is a change of pace. Patti McGettigan, news director at WOOD-TV (Grand Rapids) suggested producers feeling burned out should "Ask for another assignment, volunteer for field work or a long form project." A sharp news director puts in place feedback loops to help him recognize and see warning signs if producers are burning out.

The burnout factor can have serious implications in terms of managing relationships with your boss. And sometimes this condition can even happen to news directors. "No general manager wants a 'burned out' news director leading a 'burnt out' staff," Gary Darnell, whose spent 14 years in television news, 10 of those in management, told us. Part of the problem is producers, like news managers, often live too much in a TV world. Producers tend to "think of the world around them as a news story" and constantly ask themselves, "How should this be covered?" Darnell noted. Being a TV junkie contributes to the condition. "I don't think you can avoid burnout if 'TV' is your hobby."

Anchor Shawn Patrick recognizes the importance of watching programs other than news. "If that means turning on MTV when you get home instead of CNN, do so. Your life is news all day, you're not compelled to watch it 24/7. Don't get me wrong, I almost do, it's in your blood, but don't crucify yourself if for one day, you just don't want to hear about another roadside bombing. You're human, enjoy this life, you only have one. Take time to catch a silly movie or Nick At Night."

The overwhelming response, when we asked how to avoid burnout, was to focus on building a life outside the newsroom and find activities and friends away from the station. "You have to have outside interests," Allison Woo shared with us. "You have to find a way to create balance in your life or else you will burn out. It's a very high-stress and sometimes toxic profession. People in this business see everyone else's high and low points every day."

A sure way to avoid the over exposure you might feel with your colleagues and the toxicity of too much work is to focus on strengthening your family relationships and widen your circle of relationships. "Make friends outside of work, join a club, take a class," Patti McGettingan told us. "Have at least one thing you're passionate about that has nothing to do with work," Alan Hobbs urged.

The beauty and the benefit of widening your relationship circles and following passions not connected with work is, ironically, it puts you right back in touch with "real people" just like your news viewers. Meeting nonjournalists at the gym, karaoke bar, or church helps you harmonize with those outside the walls of your newsroom and lets you bring fresh ideas about stories and angles to coverage back into the newsroom.

Burnout is a condition that, if recognized early, can be curbed before it leads to a potentially bad attitude that could impact your job performance. But what if the feeling of frustration over work stems from a nagging fear that producing offers no real, long-term personal satisfaction? This is a different condition than burnout, something deeper than a feeling of exhaustion or frustration. Oddly the condition may be caused by too much success.

Encore Anxiety

Hard as it may seem for some people, success can actually decrease their self-esteem. It happens when people feel past accomplishments will not be repeated. Producers can be particularly prone to this condition, especially if you jump market sizes quickly so that by the time you reach age 25 you find yourself producing in a top market. Eventually, riding the high wave of a fast track career without taking enough time to mature in other important aspects of your life can create a condition called **encore anxiety.** It happens to intense, career oriented people who rise meteorically to responsible positions, enjoy significant financial rewards, and then one day stop to catch a breath and begin to worry that the next step in the career ladder is missing.

Writing about encore anxiety for *Sky* magazine in 1992, Rob Phillips said, "It applies to people who fear their own success the way most of us fear failure ... when people get the feeling they won't be able to repeat a past triumph or when they think they won't be able to maintain the success they've already attained" (Phillips, 1992, p. 20). Phillips noted the "encore anxiety" condition was first identified by Boston psychologist Dr. Steven Berglas (1986) in his book *The Success Syndrome: Hitting Bottom When You Reach The Top.* The condition can have physical affects. Dr. Douglas Labier (1986) in his book *Modern Madness: The Emotional Fallout of Success* found the people he studied enjoyed the perks of success but for some it spelled physical trouble including stomach problems, sleep disorders, headaches, and high blood pressure.

Encore anxiety can occur for producers and their reporters after working on a major story like a disaster or war. Jon Leiberman shared his experience after coming back from the Iraq War.

> I was overseas in Iraq—reporting for three weeks during the war. When I got back, I began to think that every other story pales in comparison to what was happening there. The best advice is to sit back, and evaluate everything. Everything is relative. Not every assignment is going to be "the big story." The key is to never forget why you got into this business. As long as you remember that, the passion won't go away. And if the passion ever does go away, find another career!

Anchor Shawn Patrick in Shreveport shared an antidote for producers and other news managers when the passion seems to evaporate.

> When I feel like the passion is leaving, I don't fight it and fill myself with doubts on whether I'm cut out for this. Let life run its course, ride the wave, and you'll float right back. I've seen people leave the business for different reasons. Circumstances may force you to adapt, financially, or romantically. But it's a long life. There's so much to do, and this isn't the only answer. When you've walked away mentally for a while, you tend to find yourself craving it right back after a few days or maybe even weeks. I've realized that it's okay to walk away and come back. Sure I love doing what I'm doing, but I used to feel guilty when I thought about quitting or became frustrated, and wondered if I still had the fire or the passion. I don't have the guilt any more.

Chapter 14

The realization that your passion for journalism may ebb and flow through-out your career can help you cope if you experience encore anxiety. It helps to realize coworkers from your anchor to your news director might be experiencing the same thing as News Director Bruce Kirk shared with us.

> I believe everyone in news gets to this point of encore anxiety at least once, sometimes more often. Often we react incorrectly, by acting on it. We escape and leave news, go into farming or make a 180 degree turn. Others fight through it. It may be driven by frustrations within. Talk with your boss. See what problems you've been dragging around which they might be able to help with. See if you can look at new duties within the newsroom, to re-ignite the passion.

A renewed focus on our passion for news and finding ways to rekindle it is one way to handle encore anxiety. Freelance writer Rob Phillips, in his article "Beyond Success," discovered another. Phillips writes:

> A person copes with the stresses of success as well as failure through indi-vidual adjustment of his or her perception of the world by developing a sense of humor, by balancing play and work, and by getting involved so-cially. ... Be an Indian, not a chief. Lose your identity in-group. The healthiest people have that commitment. (Phillips, 1992, p. 22)

Alan Hobbs advises when you experience the feeling that you have done it all, "Remember while the hardest part is knowing your best is behind you, you can still take solace in the fact that 75% of your best is better than someone else's 100% and that you are not defined by your job."

If you choose to not define your life as merely a news producer, who are you really then? Management consultant David Whyte believes, "We need, at every stage in our journey through work, to be in conversation with our desire for something suited to us and our individual natures" (Whyte, 2001, p. 23).

As part of this on-going conversation with yourself, as you seek to build a bridge between your work as a producer and your life as a private individual, take time to go back to that personal mission statement. Revise it. It becomes a written blueprint for this bridge of life between the professional and the per-sonal. The key to any revision is listening.

A Still, Small Voice

Learning how to enjoy the journey is not easy. Success exacts a price. It takes practice, gathering advice from others, and courageously trying a few career paths until something just feels right. There are so many voices, and far too many self-help books, promising answers about finding happiness in your ca-reer. Ultimately answers about your career as a producer and how to build the bridge between your professional and personal life have to come by doing a lot of listening. This truth was shared by many producers and broadcast journalists we spoke to in writing this book. Perhaps Producer Allison Woo articulated it the best.

Allison Woo, Producer

There's nothing worse than getting up each morning and dreading going to work. You have to listen to your own inner voice. Don't let someone else tell you, for example, that working for a network is the only path to happiness. I worked for one of the largest networks right out of graduate school and was miserable. I really missed the impact that local news had on communities. I promptly left and became very happy. Happiness is truly an individual thing. The goal should always be to challenge yourself. I think creative people are basically thrill seekers. But the thrill really is in the newness. I think the key is finding out how to keep it new for you. Is your job allowing you to tap into new areas? There's a real need to balance work stability with challenging yourself. Before you leave a job, I think you should ask yourself if you've learned everything you possibly could learn in your area.

Learning to listen to the still, small voice inside you—your inner soul, a conscience telling you what to do—is not easy. But it's worth mastering the skill. The newsroom is a noisy, bustling place. If you can recognize this inner voice it will help you decide what is news, how to understand your audience, and ratings. Master the art and science of producing including the nuances of tease writing and live shots. The voice will guide you through the tough terrain of ethical decision making and managing the business, managing people, and managing your life. The quietest voice in the newsroom is your own, inner voice. But it is the most vital. It is the voice great writers and great producers listen for. It is the voice of the creative muse, the factual hound, the balanced soul. Write down what you hear. Read and edit what you write. Then, listen again and again. That's the key to managing the news for the ethical and effective producer.

Sources

Berglas, S. (1986). *The success syndrome: Hitting bottom when you reach the top.* New York: Plenum.

Labier, D. (1986). *Modern madness: The emotional fallout of success.* Reading, MA: Addison-Wesley.

Phillips, R. (1992, November). Beyond success. *Sky,* pp. 20–22.

Whyte, D. (2001). *Crossing the unknown sea: Work as a pilgrimage of identity.* New York: Riverhead Books.

Chapter 14

Index

A

ABC
  audience research, 16
  disaster coverage, 66–67
  duopoly, 227–228
  lead story determination, 83
  News One, 80
  news ratings, 221
Action News format, 93, 140
Active listening, 183, 194–195,
    202, 205–206
Active voice, 117–118
Advertising
  audience research, 4–5, 24
  sales rates, 207–209, 212–213
African Americans
  news coverage, 25
  news ratings, 209, 212
  newsroom representation, 25
Age groups
  advertising demographics, 24
  audience availability, 23
  news-content preference, 21
  news source, 15
Agence France Presse (AFP), 82
Aidinian, Dawn (KPRC-TV/
    Houston), 2, 29, 31
Air Words (Hewitt), 72, 95, 96
American Association of Adver-
    tising Agencies, 208
American Idol, 221
American Society of Newspaper
    Editors (ASNE), 50
Anchor
  broadcast writing, 126
  command anchor function,
    104
  newscast format input,
    105–108
  producer relationship, 42–43,
    150, 156–157, 158,
    185, 195–199
Anchor blocking
  newscast format, 91, 105–107
  ping ponging, 106

stair-step technique, 107
two-shots, 106–107
Anchor tags, 104
Animated graphic open, 102–103
Asian Americans, 25
Assignment editor, 184, 188–189
Assignment manager defined,
    39
Assistant news director, 185,
    202–205
Associated Press (AP), 50, 82,
    174
Audience loyalty, 208, 222
Audience management, 185–188
Audience-oriented ethics, 57–59
Audience research, *see also* Age
    groups; Racial/ethnic
    research; Target audi-
    ence; Women
  civic mapping, 7, 22
  community demographics,
    6–7, 20, 22–26
  intimate medium perception,
    13–14
  media multitasking, 11–12
  news-content preference
    content analysis, 20, 21
    interest inventories,
      19–20, 24
    local news, 18–20, 21
    national news, 18, 19–20,
      21
    network news, 18
    research limitations, 18–19
    world news, 18–19, 20, 21'
  news source
    cable television, 15, 16
    Internet, 1, 15
    local news, 14–18
    network news, 15, 16
    newspapers, 15
    radio, 15
  news-viewing reasons, 15–18
  personal research, 26–27
  research assumptions, 23,
    24

target audience, 4–5, 20,
    22–26
  advertising demographics,
    4–5, 24
  audience availability, 22–23
  population diversity, 4, 5,
    24–26
  targeted content, 22–23
  visual attention, 11, 13
Audience Research and Develop-
    ment (AR&D), 61–62
Audience warning, 61, 104
Audio technician, 148

B

Backtiming
  defined, 74
  media diet, 77–81
  newsroom software system,
    74–76
  time management, 74–81
Bade, Chris (WTVF-TV/Nash-
    ville), 199
Bahakel Communications, 226
Barkley, Nella, 243
Barlett, David, 63
BBC, 78
Belo Corporation, 175, 228
Bennett, Reed (WCNC-TV/Char-
    lotte), 64 (photo), 192
    (photo)
Berglas, Stephen, 247
*Best Practices in Broadcast Jour-
    nalism* (Westin), 83, 88
Bewely, Ed, 61–62
BIGresearch Inc., 12
Blogs, 79, 175
Bonhart, Marsha (WDTN-TV/
    Dayton), 158 (photo)
Booth the newscast, *see* Control
    room
Brand image
  defined, 129, 140
  ethical journalism, 142–143
  examples, 141

251

newscast format, 93, 139–140
newscast promotion, 139–143
versus slogan, 140–141
Breaking news, *see* Live news
    coverage
Break out elements, 87–88, 89–90
Brewer, Joyce (WAPT-TV/
    Jackson, Alabama), 87
Brinkley, David, 1
Broadcast News, 91, 92 (photo),
    95
Broadcast writing, *see also*
    Newscast promotion
    anchor-specific, 126
    clichés, 120–121
    conversational writing, 114,
        116–118
    copy editing, 125
    good writer guidelines, 127–128
    good writing guidelines, 119,
        127
    intimate medium perception,
        113–114
    producer role
        huckster, 29, 37
        nitpicker, 29, 37–38
        poet, 29, 36–37
    story form
        short, 115
        simple, 115–116
    story structure
        end, 121, 124–125
        lead, 121, 122
        middle, 121, 122–124
    story transition, 126–127
    video referencing, 122–124
Brown, Gar (WHIO-TV/Dayton),
    33 (photo), 80 (photo)
Brown, Jim (WHIO-TV/Dayton),
    157 (photo), 198
    (photo)
Brown, Katie (KCCI-TV/Des
    Moines), 86 (photo)
    lineup meeting, 85–86
    newscast format, 93, 95, 96
    pace-flow balance, 98–99,
        104
    time management, 76, 77
Burnout, 244–246
Busiek, Dave (KCCI-TV/Des
    Moines), 86–87
Business management
    future directions, 237
    journalism trends, 223–225
    media consolidation, 223,
        225–230
        broadcast news impact,
            226–230
        central casting, 226–227

hubbing, 226, 227–228
local news impact,
    228–230
media convergence
    broadcast news impact,
        223, 232–237
    consumer utilization, 232
    convergence models,
        231–232
    cross-media ownership,
        231–232
    defined, 224–225
    ideal convergence, 230
    investigative journalism,
        233, 234
    practical application,
        230–231
    television-Internet,
        224–225,
        230–232,
        235–237
    television-newspaper,
        224–225,
        230–232,
        233–234
    television-radio, 224–225,
        230–231, 234

C

Cable television, 15, 16, 78, 80,
    232
Camera operator, 148
Career map, 239–240, 242–244
Cartoon Network, 1
CBS
    audience research, 16
    duopoly, 227–228
    Newspath, 80 (photo)
    news ratings, 221
Center for Digital Democracy
    (CDD), 227
Center for Media and Public
    Affairs, 77
Center for Media Research, 12
Central casting, 226–227
Central Florida University, 75
Character generator operator,
    148, 202
Charlotte Observer, The, 233
    (photo)
Cheerleader role, 29, 31, 183
Cheng, Liz (WCVB-TV/Boston),
    213
Chester, Jeff, 227
Chicago Tribune, The, 232
Chromakey wall graphic, 101
    (photo)
Chyron graphic, 100–101

Cihock, Haley (KXAN/Austin),
    8–9
Civic mapping, 7, 22
Clichés, 120–121
CLTV (Chicago), 232
Cluster stories, *see* Story clusters
CNN
    Headline News, 241
    media diet, 78, 79, 232
    Newsource, 80
    24-hour news, 232
Code of ethics, *see* Ethical jour-
    nalism; *specific orga-
    nization*
Cold Case, 221
Cold open, 103
Comedy Central, 1
Command anchor function, 104
Commercial breaks
    newscast format, 93
    newscast operations, 154, 158
    news ratings, 216
Commission on Freedom of the
    Press, 3–4
Communication skills, *see also*
    Managerial skills
    control room operations, 151,
        152, 156–157, 158,
        159, 167, 169,
        199–202
    live news coverage, 167, 168,
        169, 179
    newscast promotion, 139
    time management, 73, 88–90
Communicator (RTNDA), 47,
    94, 96, 174, 202
Community research, 6–7, 20,
    22–26
Computer database, 72, 146
Contesting, 219–220
Contortionist role, 29, 35–36
Contractions, 116
Control room
    director role, 145, 146–147,
        148–149, 150–152
    equipment orientation, 145–149
    newscast operations, 152–155
    producer relationships
        anchor, 150, 156–157,
            158, 195–199
        director, 146–147, 149,
            150–152,
            199–200
        technical crew, 146–147,
            148, 149–150,
            201–202
    producer role, 145, 146–147
        communication skills,
            151, 152,

156–157, 158, 159, 167, 169, 199–202
constructive criticism, 159
crises management, 157–159
early arrival, 149–150
live news, 149–150, 157–159
newscast operations, 152–155
professionalism, 155–159, 167, 169
stress management, 156
time management, 153–155
troubleshooting, 153
technical crew
audio technician, 148
camera operator, 148
character generator operator, 148, 202
floor director, 146–147, 148
graphics artist, 201–202
tape operator, 148
technical director, 148
teleprompter operator, 148
video engineer, 148
Conversational writing
active voice, 117–118
contractions, 116
defined, 114
passive voice, 118
past perfect tense, 117
past tense, 116–117
phone mom theory, 118
present tense, 116–117
Copy editing, 125
Counts, Glenn (WCNC-TV/Charlotte), 31 (photo), 190 (photo)
Covey, Stephen R., 243
Cox Communications, 141, 168, 208, 231
Creative-people management, 200, 201–202
Creativity
news block, 94–98
newscast format, 91–100, 104, 111, 112
Credibility, 92, 93, 95–96
Crime coverage, 61–65
Crises management, 157–159
Cronkite, Walter, 59 (photo), 82
Cruise, Tom, 243
Crystal-Barkley, 243
CSI, 221

D

Darnell, Gary, 246
DART Center for Journalism and Trauma, 67
Datelines, *see* Time management
Day, Carl (WDTN-TV/Dayton), 195 (photo)
Dayton Daily News, 231, 234
Deadlines, *see* Time management
Deep teasing, 134
Diary household, 209, 210, 211
Diener, Scott (WCPO-TV/Cincinnati), 217
Diercks, Ardith (WUSA-TV), 174
Direct lead, 122
Director
defined, 39
producer relationship, 146–147, 149, 150–152, 199–200
Disaster coverage, 66–67, 174
Dolan, Tom, 34–35
Dolan Media Management, 34–35
Double box graphics, 101 (photo)
Dove, Jim, 59 (photo)
Drill sargeant role, 29, 31, 32, 183
Drudge Report, 79

E

Ebony, 78
Eck, Denise (WSLS-TV/Roanoke), 98 (photo)
pace-flow balance, 98
producer-anchor relationship, 197–198
story management, 89–90
Economist, The, 79
Edward R. Murrow Award for Overall Excellence, 47, 48, 49, 77, 86, 98, 236
Edwards, John (KTVX/Salt Lake City), 190
Election night coverage, 180
Electronic Media, 63
Electronic news gathering (ENG), 93, 150, 162–164
Emmis Communications, 227
Empathy, 190–191, 194–195
Encore anxiety, 247–248
ER, 221
Espinoza, Mike (San Antonio News Channel), 2

ESPN, 110
Ethical journalism
audience-oriented ethics, 57–59
ethics triangle, 58
brand image, 142–143
broadcast journalists, 45, 48–49, 59, 60, 65, 67–68
code of ethics
magazines, 49
newspapers, 49–50
organizational comparison, 54–55
photographers, 50
Radio-Television News Director's Association (RTNDA), 3, 47–48, 49, 50, 51–53, 54–55, 56, 57, 58, 64, 65, 67–68, 69
Society of Professional Journalists (SPJ), 3, 49–50, 53–55, 56, 57
videographers, 50
wire service, 50
crime coverage, 61–65
guidelines, 63–65
disaster coverage, 66–67
family sensitive news, 61–65
Internet Web sites, 47, 50, 65
live news coverage, 177–178
newscast promotion, 135–136, 142–143
newsroom policy, 46, 50, 51 (photo)
organizational involvement, 68–69
producer decisions, 45–47
audience-oriented ethics, 57–59
humility, 65
objectivity myth, 59–60
personal ethics code, 55–57, 58–59
professionalism, 65, 67–68
public ethical dialogue, 57, 63–64
viewer warning, 61
Exclusivity, 132
Executive producer
defined, 39
managing up, 185, 202–205
Experts list, 171
Exploitation, 173–176
Eyewitness News format, 93, 140

F

Family sensitive news, 61–65
Fang, Irving, 93
Fear-mongering, 142–143
Felling, Matthew, 77
Field producer defined, 39
Firestone Tires, 217
Firm persuasion, 183
Fischer, Ken, 75
Flexibility
  newscast format, 93, 96, 109
  producer skills, 35–36,
    154–155
Floor director, 146–147, 148
Font graphic, 100–101
Foreign Policy, 80
Format, *see* Newscast format
Foss, Karen (KSDK-TV/St.
    Louis), 42–43
Fox
  duopoly, 227–228
  News Channel, 24, 80, 232
  news ratings, 212
France, 82
Franklin Covey, 243
Freeman, Melody (WCNC-TV/
    Charlotte), 94 (photo),
    184 (photo), 190
    (photo)
Frey, Michelle (NTV-Nebraska
    Television), 194
    (photo)
  lead story, 83–84
  managerial guidelines,
    193–194
  pace-flow balance, 105
  producer-anchor relationship,
    196–197
  time management, 77
Fry, Don, 122
Fulk, Kenneth (WCPO-TV/
    Cincinnati), 217
Full screen graphic, 102 (photo)

G

Gannett, 50
Garza, Leslie (KOAT-TV/Albu-
    querque), 6, 36, 153
Geisler, Jill, 32 (photo), 202
    (photo)
  Influence Inventory, 32–33
  managing up, 202
General manager
  defined, 39
  managing up, 185, 202–205
Grandy, Byron, 171

Graphics
  animated graphic open,
    102–103
  chromakey wall graphic, 101
    (photo)
  double box graphic, 101
    (photo)
  full screen graphic, 102
    (photo)
  live news coverage, 165–166,
    170, 179–180
  lower third graphic, 100–101
  map graphic, 102 (photo),
    170
  monitor graphic, 101 (photo)
  over-the-shoulder (OTS)
    graphic, 101
    (photo)
  production capabilities, 72,
    99–100
  production techniques, 99–100
  production tools, 99, 103–104
  ticker graphic, 103
Graphics artist, 201–202
Graphics equipment, 72
Great Britain, 76–77, 78, 79, 83
Green, Katherine (WTTG-TV/
    Washington, D.C.), 174
Grider, Erin (WCNC-TV/Char-
    lotte), 31 (photo)
Günter, Marc, 62–63

H

Haag, Marty, 227
Happy talk format, 93
Harig, Ron (KOTV/Tulsa), 92
Harris Poll, 14–15
Harvard Business Review, 203,
    205
Hayes, Chris, 241
Heartland Emmy, 152
Heaton, Terry (WRIC-TV/
    Richmond), 63
Heider, Don, 25
Helberg, Tiffani (WCNC-TV/
    Charlotte), 64 (photo),
    192 (photo)
Helicopter lease, 162, 163–164
Henao, Chris (KHOU-TV/
    Houston), 217
Hendrix, Phil (WLNS-TV 6/
    Lansing), 30–31
Hewitt, John, 72, 95, 96
Hispanics, *see* Latin Americans
Hobbs, Alan
  burnout, 246
  encore anxiety, 248

  KTVE (Monroe), 204, 242
  managing up, 204
  physical health, 242
  WGHP (Greensboro), 204
Hood, Lee, 123–124
Hubbing, 226, 227–228
Huckster role, 29, 37
Humility, 65, 194–195, 196, 199,
    202
Hunter, Holly, 91, 92 (photo), 95
Hurricane Katrina, 172, 175
Huston, Ethan (WOUB-TV/
    Athens), 109 (photo)
Hutchins, Robert, 3
Hyman, Mark, 227
Hyman, Valerie
  family sensitive news, 63
  newscast format, 96
  newscast mission statement,
    111
  technical skills, 72

I

Image promotion, *see* Brand
    image
Inner voice, 248–249
Insite Media Research, 18
Interest inventories, 19–20, 24
Internet Broadcast System (IBS),
    236
Internet Web site
  audience research, 1, 15
  broadcast writing, 127–128
  ethical journalism, 47, 50, 65
  journalism trends, 224
  media convergence, 224–225,
    230–232, 235–237
  news clichés, 121
  newsroom software, 75
  news source, 1, 15, 80
  stress management, 67
  wire service, 82
Interrupted Feedback (IFB) sys-
    tem, 146, 147 (photo),
    157 (photo)
Investigative journalism
  media convergence, 233, 234
  sweeps specials, 216–218
Iraq War, 68
ITN (Great Britain), 76–77, 83

J

Jerry McGuire, 243
Jones, Don (WDTN-TV/
    Dayton), 73 (photo)
Journalist role, 29

K

Katsuyama, Jana (WDTN-TV/
    Dayton), 5 (photo)
KATV (Little Rock), 236
KCAL-TV (Los Angeles), 228
KCBS-TV (Los Angeles), 228
KCCI-TV (Des Moines)
    journalism award, 77, 86, 98
    news director, 86 (photo), 87
        (photo)
    producer, 76, 77, 86 (photo),
        93, 95, 96, 98–99,
        104
    rundown meeting, 85–86
KDKA-TV (Pittsburgh),
    204–205, 220
Keene, Jeff (WCPO-TV/
    Cincinnati), 217
KHOU-TV (Houston), 217
Kicker, 35
Kirk, Bruce (WSET-TV/Lynch-
    burg), 204 (photo)
    burnout, 245
    encore anxiety, 248
    managing up, 204
    personal mission statement,
        244
    physical health, 241
    producer-anchor relationship,
        197
Kirkland, David (WCNC-TV/
    Charlotte), 85 (photo)
Kirsch, Libby (WDTN-TV/
    Dayton), 89 (photo),
    169 (photo)
KJRH-TV (Tulsa), 203.245
KOAT-TV (Albuquerque), 6, 36,
    153
KOMU-TV (Columbia)
    newscast mission statement,
        111–112
    rundown meeting, 84–85
KOTV (Tulsa), 92
KPHO (Phoenix), 241
KPRC-TV (Houston), 2, 29, 31
KQV Radio, 236
KSDK-TV (St. Louis), 42
    (photo)
KTAL-TV (Shreveport)
    life management, 242, 243,
        244, 246, 247
    managerial skills, 186, 187,
        197, 198–199
KTLA-TV (Los Angeles),
    176–177
KTTV (Los Angeles), 120–121
KTVE (Monroe), 204, 242
KTVX (Salt Lake City), 190

Kuralt, Charles, 88, 127–128, 193
KUSA-TV (Denver), 152,
    198–199
KVUE (Austin), 63–64
KXAN (Austin), 8–9
KXAS-TV (Dallas), 6

L

Labier, Douglas, 247
La Camera, Paul (WCVB-TV/
    Boston), 212–213
Lansing, John (WCCO-TV/Min-
    neapolis), 61–63
Latin Americans
    news coverage, 5, 25
    news ratings, 209, 212
    newsroom representation, 25
Lead story determination
    breaking news, 83, 88
    break out elements, 87–88,
        89–90
    influencing factors, 81, 83–84
    live news, 83, 88
    local news, 81, 83–84
    national news, 83–84
    rundown meeting, 84–87
    sidebars, 87–88
    target audience, 81, 83, 84
    three-eyed test, 83
    time management, 81, 83–88
    unbundling the lead, 87–88,
        95
    world news, 83–84
Lehtonen, Amy (WCNC-TV/
    Charlotte), 235 (photo)
Leiberman, Jon, 242, 247
Libin, Scott, 222
Life management
    burnout, 244–246
    career map, 239–240, 242–244
    encore anxiety, 247–248
    inner voice, 248–249
    personal mission statement,
        242–244
    physical health, 240, 241–242
    workload delegation, 245
Linaberger, Anne
    (KDKA-TV/Pitts-
    burgh), 204–205
Lineup, *see* Rundown
Linnstrom, Kara
    Charlotte Observer, The, 233
        (photo)
    WCNC-TV (Charlotte), 19
        (photo)
Lippoff, David, 208
Live news coverage
    audience response, 164–165

breaking news, 167, 169–178
    disasters, 174
    exploitation, 173–176
    newsroom disaster plan,
        172–173, 175
    producer preparation,
        169–171, 178
    production tools, 170–171
    unexpected events, 176–178
    weather, 171–173, 175
communication skills, 167,
    168, 169, 179
control room operations,
    149–150, 157–159
coverage guidelines, 35,
    165–167, 168–169,
    177–178, 179–180
election night, 180
ethical journalism, 177–178
journalistic justification,
    161–165
lead story determination, 83,
    88
newscast format, 93
professionalism, 167, 169
special events, 178–180
technology
    electronic news gathering
        (ENG), 93, 150,
        162–164
    financial investment,
        162–164
    graphics, 165–166, 170,
        179–180
    helicopter lease, 162,
        163–164
    production operations, 161,
        162–163, 166,
        169–170, 172,
        173, 175, 177,
        179–181
    rain fade, 163
    satellite news gathering
        (SNG), 93,
        162–164
    video delay, 177
Local news
    audience research, 14–20, 21
    lead story determination, 81,
        83–84
    media consolidation, 228–230
    news-content preference,
        18–20, 21
    news source, 14–18, 78
    viewing reasons, 15–16
Los Angeles Times, 62
Louisiana State University, 175
Lower third graphic, 100–101
Luce, Henry, 3

M

Maestro role, 29, 30–31, 32
Magazines, 49, 78–80
Magid Associates, 93
Managerial skills
　audience management, 185–188
　communication
　　active listening, 183,
　　　194–195, 202,
　　　205–206
　　assignment editor,
　　　188–189
　　audience, 185–188
　　control room operations,
　　　151, 152,
　　　156–157, 158,
　　　159, 167, 169,
　　　199–202
　　feedback, 186–188, 191
　　gatekeeper illustration,
　　　186*f*
　　reporter, 190–191
　　video tape editor, 193
　　written, 202–203
　creative people, 200, 201–202
　empathy, 190–191, 194–195
　firm persuasion, 183
　humility, 65, 194–195, 196,
　　199, 202
　Influence Inventory, 32–33
　personal style, 203, 205–206
　producer relationships
　　anchor, 42–43, 150,
　　　156–157, 158,
　　　185, 195–199
　　assignment editor, 184,
　　　188–189
　　assistant news director,
　　　185
　　director, 146–147, 149,
　　　150–152,
　　　199–200
　　executive producer, 185
　　general manager, 185,
　　　202–205
　　graphics artist, 201–202
　　managing up, 185,
　　　202–205
　　news director, 185,
　　　202–205
　　photographer, 185, 191–195
　　reporter, 185, 190–191,
　　　192–195
　　technical crew, 146–147,
　　　148, 149–150,
　　　201–202
　　video tape editor, 185,
　　　192–195

respect, 184, 190, 193–195,
　　196, 197, 204–205,
　　206
role title
　cheerleader, 29, 31, 183
　contortionist, 29, 35–36
　drill sargeant, 29, 31, 32,
　　183
　maestro, 29, 30–31, 32
　peacemaker, 29, 31, 32,
　　183
　stress management, 184–185
　teamwork, 183, 188–189,
　　196–199, 205
　trust, 183–184, 190, 206
　workload delegation, 245
Map graphic, 102 (photo), 170
Mason, Janet (WZZM-TV),
　　97–98, 111
Master chef role, 71–73, 76,
　　77–81, 85, 90
Matthews, Cindy (WCPO-TV/
　　Cincinnati), 140
　　(photo)
McGarvy, Sean (WTTG-TV/
　　Washington, D.C.), 242
　　(photo), 244
McGettigan, Patti, 242, 246
McHenry, Cheryl
　　(WHIO-TV/Dayton),
　　130 (photo)
Media Center for the American
　　Press Institute,
　　230–231, 232
Media consolidation, 223,
　　225–230
Media convergence, 223,
　　224–225, 230–237
Media diet, 77–81
Media ethics, *see* Ethical journal-
　　ism
Media Ethics (Patterson &
　　Wilkins), 57
Media General, 231–232
Metered market, *see* Sweeps
　　management
Miller, Matt, 237
Minorities, *see* Racial/ethnic
　　research; *specific race/
　　ethnicity*
Mirones, Anthony (WCPO-TV/
　　Cincinnati), 214
　　(photo)
Mission statement
　newscast, 91, 111–112
　personal, 242–244
Missouri School of Journalism,
　　45, 68, 84–85, 87,
　　111–112, 199, 200

Modern Madness (Labier), 247
Monday Night Football, 221
Monitor graphic, 101 (photo)
Morris, Mackie, 119
MSNBC, 78, 232
Munley, Katie, 66–67
Murrow, Edward R., 48 (photo)
　broadcast writing, 127–128
　ethical journalism, 45, 48–49,
　　59, 60, 65, 67–68
　fast facts, 49
　humility, 65
　journalism award, 47, 48, 49,
　　77, 86, 98, 236
　professionalism, 67–68

N

National Association of Radio
　　News Directors, 47–48
National Highway Transportation
　　Safety Administration
　　(NHTSA), 217
National news
　audience research, 18, 19–20,
　　21
　lead story determination,
　　83–84
National Press Photographer
　　Association (NPPA),
　　50, 69
National Public Radio (NPR), 80
National Weather Service, 172
Native Americans, 25
Natural sound (nat/sot), 137–138
NBC
　audience research, 16
　duopoly, 227–228
　family sensitive news, 62–63
　hubbing, 227
News Channel, 80
Network news, *see also specific
　　broadcast station*
　audience research, 15, 16, 18
　news source, 15, 16, 78–79,
　　80
Newell, Graeme, 132
News block
　anchor tags, 104
　command anchor function, 104
　creativity, 94–98
　credibility, 95–96
　first block, 34, 95–96
　flexibility, 96
　lead story, 95
　pace-flow balance, 96–99, 104
　second block, 34, 95–96
　story clusters, 94–95, 96–98,
　　105–106

story content, 96–97
story form, 96, 99, 106
story packing, 95
story stacking, 94–95
visualization, 104
Newscast booth, *see* Control room
Newscast format
   Action News format, 93, 140
   anchor blocking, 91, 105–107
   anchor input, 105–108
   brand image, 93
   commercial breaks, 93
   creativity, 91–100, 104, 111,
      112
   Eyewitness News format, 93,
      140
   flexibility, 93, 96, 109
   graphics, 99–103
   happy talk format, 93
   historical development, 93
   kicker, 35
   live news, 93
   news block, 94–98, 104
   newscast mission statement,
      91, 111–112
   news-driven format, 94
   newsroom software system,
      93
   pace-flow balance, 91,
      96–108
   producer skills, 34–35
   production tools, 99, 103–104
   show business analogy, 92
   sound, 99
   sports segment, 35, 91, 93,
      107–108, 109–111
   story clusters, 91, 94–95,
      96–98, 105–106
   story content, 96–97, 98–99
   story form, 96, 99, 106
   target audience, 93
   technology, 93
   two-shots, 106–107
   weather segment, 35, 91, 93,
      107–109, 111
Newscast mission statement, 91,
   111–112
Newscast promotion
   brand image, 93, 139–143
   fear-mongering, 142–143
   image promotion, 129
   promotional categories,
      129–130
   promotional costs, 131
   promotional writing
      communication skills, 139
      details, 138–139
      ethical journalism, 135–136,
         142–143

legal standards, 135–136
   red flag words, 139
   reporter tease, 139
   sense of immediacy,
      138–139
   story context, 136
   video referencing, 138
   viewing motivation,
      129–130,
      137–139
   sales rule of 150, 142
   sensationalism, 142–143
   story coverage, 135
   story oversell, 142
   story placement
      cross-show promotion,
         134, 135
      deep teasing, 134
      lead-in program, 133
      repetition, 134–135
      target audience, 130–131,
         133
      transitional flow, 133–134
   story selection
      exclusivity, 132
      video availability,
         131–132
      viewer relevance, 130–131
   teases
      deep teasing, 134
      defined, 37, 129–130
      promotional writing,
         135–139
      story placement, 133–135
      story selection, 130–132
   topical promotion
      defined, 129
      headlines, 129–130
      promos, 129–130
      teases, 129–130
News Corp, 228
Newsday, 236
News defined, 1–2
News director
   defined, 39
   managing up, 185, 202–205
Newslab, 125, 213
Newspapers
   audience research, 15
   code of ethics, 49–50
   inverted pyramid writing, 121
   media convergence, 224–225,
      230–232, 233–234
   news source, 15, 77–80
News ratings, *see* Sweeps management
Newsroom disaster plan,
   172–173, 175
Newsroom software system

backtiming, 74–76
computer database, 72, 146
control room, 146, 148–149
graphics equipment, 72
newscast format, 93
news source, 81
program capabilities, 75
quick links, 75
rundown, 73–76
time management, 72, 73–76,
   81, 90
News source
   audience research, 14–18
   blogs, 79, 175
   cable television, 15, 16, 78,
      80
   Internet, 1, 15, 80
   local news, 14–18, 78
   magazines, 78–80
   media diet, 77–81
   network news, 15, 16, 78–79,
      80
   newspapers, 15, 77–80
   newsroom software system,
      81
   radio, 15, 78
   time management, 77–81, 82
   wire service, 80, 81, 82
Newsweek, 79
News World Communications,
   82
New Yorker, The, 79, 80
New York Times, 62, 78, 79,
   227
Nexstar Broadcast Group, 228
Nielsen Families, 210–211
Nielsen Media Research,
   208–213
Nitpicker role, 29, 37–38
NTV-Nebraska Television
   anchor, 83–84, 105, 193–194,
      196–197
   producer, 77, 196–197
NYPD Blue, 133

O

Odegaard, Colleen (WCNC-TV/
   Charlotte), 107 (photo)
Ogle, Jim, 2, 155
Ohio University, 25, 75
Online News Association Award,
   236
Oprah, 23, 133, 221
O'Rourke, Tanya (WCPO-TV/
   Cincinnati), 14 (photo)
Outing, Steve, 79
Over-the-shoulder (OTS)
   graphic, 101 (photo)

P

Pace-flow balance
  anchor blocking, 105–107
  flow defined, 98–99
  graphics, 99–103
  news block, 96–99, 104
  newscast format, 91, 96–108
  pace defined, 99
  party analogy, 98
  production techniques,
      99–100
  production tools, 99, 103–104
  sound, 99
  story clusters, 96–98
  story content, 98–99
  story form, 99, 106
  two-shots, 106–107
Packing, 95
Park, Roy H., 223, 225
Park Communications, 223, 225
Passive voice, 118
Past perfect tense, 117
Past tense, 116–117
Patrick, Shawn
  burnout, 246
  encore anxiety, 247
  KTAL-TV (Shreveport), 186,
      187, 197, 198–199,
      241, 242, 244, 246,
      247
  KUSA-TV (Denver), 199
      (photo), 244 (photo)
  managerial guidelines, 186,
      187
  personal mission statement,
      244
  physical health, 241, 242
  producer-anchor relationship,
      197, 198–199
Patterson, Phillip, 57
Payne Awards, 45
PBS, 79
PCNC (Pittsburgh Cable News
      Channel), 232
Peabody Award, 217
Peacemaker role, 29, 31, 32, 183
Pendarvis-Milham, Paula, 197
People meter, *see* Sweeps man-
      agement
Personal mission statement,
      242–244
Petchenik, Michael (WAGT-TV/
      Augusta), 196
Phillips, Rob, 247, 248
Phillips, Tom, 94, 97
Phone mom theory, 118
Phoners, 170
Photographer, 50, 185, 191–195

Physical health, 240, 241–242
Pilotta, Joe, 12
Ping ponging, 106
Poet role, 29, 36–37
Portland Oregonian, 77
Potter, Deborah, 125 (photo)
  copy editing guidelines, 125
  news ratings, 213
Poynter Institute for Media
      Studies
  blogs, 70
  broadcast writing, 122
  family sensitive news, 63
  fast facts, 69
  Influence Inventory, 32–33
  live news, 177–178
  managing up, 202
  newscast mission statement,
      111
  news ratings, 208, 222
  technical skills, 72
  Web site, 69
Present tense, 116–117
Price, Dave (WHO-TV/Des
      Moines)
  managerial guidelines, 183
  pace-flow balance, 105
  rundown meeting, 85, 87
Producer defined, 39
Producer relationships, *see* Man-
      agerial skills
Producer skills, *see also* Live
      news coverage; Mana-
      gerial skills; Newscast
      promotion; Sweeps
      management
  daily responsibilities, 38–41
    internal schedule, 40–41
  Influence Inventory, 32–33
  newscast format guidelines,
      34–35
  producer-anchor relationship,
      42–43
  role title
    cheerleader, 29, 31, 183
    contortionist, 29, 35–36
    drill sargeant, 29, 31, 32,
      183
    huckster, 29, 37
    journalist, 29
    maestro, 29, 30–31, 32
    master chef, 71–73, 76,
      77–81, 85, 90
    nitpicker, 29, 37–38
    peacemaker, 29, 31, 32, 183
    poet, 29, 36–37
    strategic planner, 29, 33–34
Production capabilities, 72,
      99–100

Production techniques, 99–100
Production tools, *see also*
      Graphics
  cold open, 103
  live news coverage, 170–171
  pace-flow balance, 99,
      103–104
  video box, 104
  video off top, 103
  warm open, 103–104
  wipes, 103
Professionalism
  control room operations,
      155–159, 167, 169
  ethical journalism, 65, 67–68
  live news coverage, 167, 169
Program tie-ins, 219, 221
Project for Excellence in Journal-
      ism, 61, 223–225,
      228–229
Promotion, *see* Newscast promo-
      tion
Public service
  civic mapping, 7
  community research, 6–7
  media provision, 3–4
  news defined, 1–2
  producer role
    decision making, 1, 7–9
    news judgment, 8–9
  public defined, 4–7
  racial/ethnic research, 4–6
  service defined, 3–4
Pusatory, Bob (KUSA-TV/Den-
      ver), 152

Q

Question lead, 122
Quill (SPJ), 50
Quinlivan, Laure
      (WCPO-TV/Cincinnati
      ), 217

R

Racial/ethnic research, *see also*
      specific race/ethnicity
  audience diversity, 4, 5, 24–26
  news coverage, 4–6, 24–26
  news ratings, 209, 212
  newsroom representation, 4,
      5–6
Radio
  audience research, 15
  media convergence, 224–225,
      230–231, 234
  media diet, 78
Radio Act (1927), 3

Radio-Television News Director's Association (RTNDA)
  audience research, 14–15
  code of ethics, 3, 47–48, 49, 50, 51–53, 54–55, 56, 57, 58, 64, 65, 67–68, 69
  Communicator, 47, 94, 96, 174, 202
  crime coverage guidelines, 64, 65
  disaster coverage, 174
  Edward R. Murrow Award for Overall Excellence, 47, 48, 49, 77, 86, 98, 236
  family sensitive news, 63, 64, 65
  fast facts, 47
  journalism defined, 48, 65
  live news, 164
  national convention, 67–68, 69
  Web site, 47
Radio-Television News Director's Foundation (RTNDF), 19–20, 21*f*, 64, 65
Rainbox Media, 236
Rain fade, 163
Rantala, Lisa (WCNC-TV/Charlotte), 123 (photo), 166 (photo)
Ratings, *see* Sweeps management
Raziq, David (KHOU-TV/Houston), 217
Reed, Sharon (WOIO-TV/Cleveland), 58
Reporter, 185, 190–191, 192–195
Respect, 184, 190, 193–195, 196, 197, 204–205, 206
Reuters, 82
Riesen, Phil, 88
Rigby, Jennifer (WSB-TV/Atlanta), 168 (photo)
  burnout, 245
  live news, 168–169
  managing up, 203
Roberts, David (WUSA-TV), 174
Rolodex, 72
Rosenberg, Abe (KTTV/Los Angeles), 120–121
Rosenstiel, Tom, 228
Rubel, Steve, 79
Rundown, *see also* News block; Newscast format
  alternative terms, 72
  communication skills, 73
  defined, 72
  lead story determination, 84–87
  newsroom software system, 73–76
  time management, 72–76, 84–87
Rundown meeting, 84–87

S

Sales rule of 150, 142
San Antonio News Channel, 2
Satellite news gathering (SNG), 93, 162–164
Schaffer, Jan, 7 (photo)
Schlemon, Chris (ITN/Great Britain), 76 (photo)
  lead story, 83
  time management, 76–77
Schuler, Susana, 228
Scientific production, 71–72, 76, 90
Scripps-Howard Broadcasting, 45, 55
Seitzler, Bill (KJRH-TV/Tulsa), 203, 245
Sensationalism, 142–143
Shafer, Mark (WCPO-TV/Cincinnati), 217
Sidebars, 87–88
Simpson, O. J., 64
Simultaneous Media Usage Survey (SIMM V) (BIGresearch Inc.), 12
Sinclair Broadcast Group, 226–227, 242
Sisk, Bobby (WCNC-TV/Charlotte), 107 (photo)
Sky, 247
Society of Professional Journalists (SPJ)
  code of ethics, 3, 49–50, 53–55, 56, 57
  fast facts, 50
  Quill, 50
  Web site, 50
Soete, Jana (WCPO-TV/Cincinnati), 188 (photo)
Sound, 9, 137–138
Southern Illinois Carbondale, 75
Special event coverage, 178–180
Sports segment, 35, 91, 93, 107–108, 109–111
Sprinkle, Larry (WCNC-TV/Charlotte), 108 (photo), 172 (photo)
Stacking, 94–95
Stair-step technique, 107
Station manager
  defined, 39
  managing up, 185, 202–205
Stirsman, Bryon (WHIO-TV/Dayton), 193 (photo)
Story clusters
  anchor blocking, 105–106
  defined, 96
  newscast format, 91, 94–95, 96–98, 105–106
  pace-flow balance, 96–98
  story content, 96–97
  topical story, 96–97
  visual attention, 96–97
Story content, 96–97, 98–99
Story form
  broadcast writing
    short, 115
    simple, 115–116
  newscast format
    live package, 99, 106
    package, 96, 99, 106
    reader, 96, 99, 106
    time guidelines, 99, 106
    voice over (VO), 96, 99
    VO/SOT, 99
Story management, 88–90
Story oversell, 142, 192–193
Story packing, 95
Story stacking, 94–95
Story structure
  blind lead, 122
  broadcast writing, 121–125
  direct lead, 122
  end, 121, 124–125
  lead, 121, 122
  middle, 121, 122–124
  question lead, 122
  video referencing, 122–124
Story transition
  broadcast writing, 126–127
  newscast promotion, 133–134
Strategic planner role, 29, 33–34
Stress management, 67, 156, 184–185
Success Syndrome, The (Berglas), 247
Super graphic, 100–101
Survivor, 221
Sweeps management
  advertising rates, 207–209, 212–213
  audience loyalty, 208, 222
  commercial breaks, 216
  contesting, 219–220
  Designated Market Area (DMA), 216

diary household
    defined, 209
    local ratings, 210, 211
metered market
    defined, 209
    demographics, 209, 211
    diary household, 211
    local ratings, 210–211
    market defined, 209
    market share, 209
    quarter hour, 210,
        214–215
    time management, 210,
        214–216
Nielsen Families, 210–211
Nielsen Media Research,
    208–213
people meter
    defined, 209
    demographics, 209, 210,
        212–213
    local ratings, 212–213
    minority representation,
        209, 212
    national ratings, 210
    newscast timing, 214–216
    overnight data, 210, 211
producer strategies, 213–216
program tie-ins, 219, 221
ratings
    defined, 208, 209
    local ratings, 209,
        210–213
    national ratings, 209, 210
    terminology, 209–210
sweeps calendars, 213
sweeps specials
    bad journalism, 218–219
    good journalism, 216–218
    investigative journalism,
        216–218
    ugly journalism, 219–221
sweeps stunts, 207–208,
    212–213, 218–221
time management, 214–216

T

Tampa Bay Online, 231–232,
    235, 236
Tampa Tribune, The, 231–232,
    236
Tape operator, 148
Target audience
    audience research
        advertising demographics,
            4–5, 24
        audience availability,
            22–23

population diversity, 4, 5,
        24–26
targeted content, 22–23
lead story determination, 81,
    83, 84
newscast format, 93
newscast promotion,
    129–131, 133
Teamwork, 183, 188–189,
    196–199, 205
Teases, *see* Newscast promotion
Technical director, 148
Technology, *see* Graphics; Live
    news coverage; Pro-
    duction tools
Teleprompter operator, 148
Television News, Radio News
    (Fang), 93
Terrorism
    disaster coverage, 174
    family sensitive news, 64
Texas Cable News, 29, 158
Thomas, Helen, 82
Three-eyed test, 83
Ticker graphic, 103
Time, 3, 79
Time management
    backtiming, 74–81
    blogs, 79
    communication skills, 73,
        88–90
    control room operations,
        153–155
    cooking analogy, 71–73, 76,
        77–81, 85, 90
    datelines, 76–81
    deadlines, 76–81
    lead story determination, 81,
        83–88
    media diet, 77–81
        news source, 77–80
        timelines, 80–81
    newsroom software system,
        72, 73–76, 81, 90
    news source, 77–81, 82
    production science, 71–72,
        76, 90
    rundown, 72–76
    rundown meeting, 84–87
    story management, 88–90
    sweeps, 214–216
Time-Warner Cable, 232, 236
Tobias, Ed, 174
Today Show, The, 103
Tompkins, Al, 177 (photo)
    live news, 177–178
    news ratings, 208
Topical promotion, *see* Newscast
    promotion

Trainer, Heather (WCPO-TV/
    Cincinnati), 8 (photo)
Transportation, Recall Enhance-
    ment, Accountability,
    and Documentation
    (TREAD) Act (2000),
    217
Trust, 183–184, 190, 206
Tsunami Disaster (2004), 66–67
Two-shots, 106–107
    stair-step technique, 107

U

Unbundling the lead, 87–88, 95
United Press International (UPI),
    82
University of Colorado (Boulder),
    123
University of Florida, 75
Univision, 212
U.S. Census Bureau, 22
U.S. News & World Report, 79
USA Today, 78

V

Viacom, 228
Vibe, 78
Video delay, 177
Video engineer, 148
Videographer, 50
Video off top, 103
Video referencing
    broadcast writing, 122–124
    newscast promotion, 138
Video tape editor, 185, 192–195
Viewer Bill of Rights, 51 (photo)
Viewers, *see* Age groups; Audi-
    ence research; Racial/
    ethnic research; Target
    audience; Women
Visual attention
    audience research, 11, 13
    story clusters, 96–97
Visualization, news block, 104

W

WAGT-TV (Augusta), 196
Wald, Jeff (KTLA-TV/Los
    Angeles), 176–177
Wallace, Quincy
    (WHIO-TV/Dayton),
    97 (photo), 154 (photo)
Wall Street Journal, 79
WAPT-TV (Jackson, Alabama),
    87
Warm open, 103–104

Warner, Charles, 200
Washington Post, 78, 79
Washington Times, 82
Watson, Stewart (WCNC-TV/
        Charlotte), 218 (photo)
WCCO-TV (Minneapolis),
        61–63
WCMH-TV (Columbus), 236
WCNC-TV (Charlotte)
    anchor, 2 (photo), 107 (photo)
    assistant news director, 85
        (photo)
    crime reporter, 31 (photo)
    graphic artist, 201 (photo)
    health reporter, 19 (photo),
        233 (photo)
    Hurricane Katrina, 172
    Interrupted Feedback (IFB)
        system, 147 (photo)
    media ownership, 228
    meteorologist, 108 (photo),
        172 (photo)
    news director, 24 (photo), 62,
        105 (photo)
    news manager, 2 (photo), 46
        (photo)
    news meeting, 2 (photo), 46
        (photo), 184 (photo)
    producer, 2 (photo), 24
        (photo), 31 (photo),
        46 (photo), 85
        (photo), 94 (photo),
        105 (photo), 184
        (photo), 190 (photo)
    reporter, 2 (photo), 46
        (photo), 64 (photo),
        123 (photo), 166
        (photo), 190
        (photo), 192
        (photo), 218 (photo)
    satellite news gathering
        (SNG), 163 (photo)
    technical director, 24 (photo)
    videographer, 64 (photo), 192
        (photo)
    video journalist, 132 (photo)
    Viewer Bill of Rights, 51
        (photo)
    Web manager, 235 (photo)
    Web site, 235
WCPO-TV (Cincinnati)
    anchor, 14 (photo)
    assignment editor, 188
        (photo)
    assistant news director, 217
    control room, 8 (photo), 200
        (photo)
    editor, 214 (photo), 217
    graphics operator, 200 (photo)

investigative journalism, 217
news director, 200 (photo),
        217
newsroom staff, 4 (photo)
Peabody Award, 217
photographer, 217
producer, 8 (photo), 200
        (photo)
reporter, 217
technical director, 200 (photo)
teleprompter operator, 12
        (photo)
traffic reporter, 140 (photo)
videographer, 214 (photo)
WCVB-TV (Boston), 212–213
WDTN-TV (Dayton)
    anchor, 17 (photo), 158
        (photo), 195 (photo)
    assistant producer, 126 (photo)
    brand image, 141
    copy editing, 126 (photo)
    electronic news gathering
        (ENG), 150
        (photo), 162 (photo)
    news director, 146 (photo)
    producer, 30 (photo), 68
        (photo), 146 (photo)
    producer pod, 185 (photo)
    reporter, 5 (photo), 89
        (photo), 169 (photo)
    video engineer, 73 (photo)
    videographer, 89 (photo), 150
        (photo), 169 (photo)
    video review, 30 (photo)
Weather
    breaking news coverage,
        171–173, 175
    Hurricane Katrina, 172, 175
    meteorologist, 108 (photo),
        109, 172 (photo)
    newscast format, 35, 91, 93,
        107–109, 111
    storm warning, 172
    storm watch, 172
    Tsunami Disaster (2004),
        66–67
Wendel, John (WCNC-TV/Char-
        lotte), 172 (photo)
Werner, Anna (KHOU-TV/
        Houston), 217
Westin, Av, 83, 85, 88
WFLA-TV (Tampa), 231–232,
        236
WGHP (Greensboro), 204
WGN-TV (Chicago), 232
WGXA-TV (Macon), 237
WHIO-TV (Dayton)
    anchor, 130 (photo), 157
        (photo), 198 (photo)

audio engineer, 148 (photo)
brand image, 141
control room, 60 (photo)
Interrupted Feedback (IFB)
        system, 157 (photo)
media convergence, 234
media ownership, 231
news director, 114 (photo),
        147 (photo), 151
        (photo)
producer, 97 (photo), 154
        (photo)
promotional techniques, 130
        (photo)
script, 38 (photo), 97 (photo),
        114 (photo), 151
        (photo)
special-projects videographer/
        editor, 193 (photo)
technical director, 114
        (photo), 147 (photo)
videographer, 33 (photo), 193
        (photo)
video journalist, 80 (photo)
White News (Heider), 25
WHO-TV (Des Moines)
    anchor, 183
    senior reporter, 85, 87, 105
Whyte, David, 239, 248
Wilkins, Lee, 57
Williams, Brian, 62–63
Wipes, 103
Wire service, *see also specific
        service*
    code of ethics, 50
    news source, 80, 81, 82
WKYT (Lexington), 2
WLKY-TV (Louisville), 244
        (photo)
WLNS-TV 6 (Lansing), 30–31
WNYW-TV (New York), 228
Woelfel, Stacey (KOMU-TV/
        Columbia), 84–85
WOIO-TV (Cleveland), 58
Women
    audience research
        advertising audience, 4–5,
            24
        assumptions, 23, 24
        news-content preference,
            20
        stereotypes, 24
        target audience, 4–5, 23
        viewing availability, 23
    journalistic credibility, 93
Woo, Allison, 249 (photo)
    burnout, 246
    inner voice, 248–249
    physical health, 241

WOOD-TV (Grand Rapids), 242, 246
World news
    audience research, 18–19, 20, 21
    lead story determination, 83–84
Wortham, Mike (KXAS-TV/ Dallas)
    community research, 6
    news judgment, 8
    producer-anchor relationship, 158
    producer skills, 29
WOUB-TV (Athens), 109 (photo), 110 (photo)
WPXI-TV (Pittsburgh), 220, 232
WQAD-TV (Moline), 236

WRIC-TV (Richmond), 63
Writing, see Broadcast writing; Newscast promotion
WSB-TV (Atlanta), 168 (photo), 203, 245
WSET-TV (Lynchburg), 197, 204 (photo), 241, 244, 245
WSLS-TV (Roanoke)
    anchor, 197–198
    investigative reporter, 89–90, 98, 197–198
WSOC-TV (Charlotte), 236
WTAE-TV (Pittsburgh), 220
WTTG-TV (Washington, D.C.), 174, 242 (photo)
WTVF-TV (Nashville), 199
WUSA-TV, 174

WWL-TV (New Orleans), 175
WWOR-TV (New York), 228
WZZM-TV, 97–98, 111

Y

Yohey, Dan (WDTN-TV/Dayton), 89 (photo), 150 (photo), 169 (photo)
Young, Bob (WCNC-TV/ Charlotte), 62

Z

Zanger, Stuart (WCPO-TV/ Cincinnati), 217